Journal of Semitic Studies Supplement 21

A CATALOGUE OF PREVIOUSLY UNCATALOGUED ETHIOPIC MANUSCRIPTS IN ENGLAND: TWENTY-THREE MANUSCRIPTS IN THE BODLEIAN, CAMBRIDGE UNIVERSITY AND JOHN RYLANDS UNIVERSITY LIBRARIES AND IN A PRIVATE COLLECTION

by

Steve Delamarter and Demeke Berhane

Published by Oxford University Press
on behalf of the University of Manchester
2007

OXFORD JOURNALS
OXFORD UNIVERSITY PRESS

Great Clarendon Street, Oxford OX2 6DP

Oxford University Press is a department of the University of Oxford.
It furthers the University's objective of excellence in research, scholarship,
and education by publishing worldwide in

Oxford New York

Athens Auckland Bangkok Bogotá Buenos Aires Cape Town
Chennai Dar es Salaam Delhi Florence Hong Kong Istanbul Karachi
Kolkata Kuala Lumpur Madrid Melbourne Mexico City Mumbai Nairobi
Paris São Paulo Shanghai Singapore Taipei Tokyo Toronto Warsaw

with associated companies in Berlin Ibadan

Oxford is a registered trade mark of Oxford University Press
in the UK and in certain other countries

Published in the United Kingdom
by Oxford University Press, Oxford

© The University of Manchester, 2007

The moral rights of the author have been asserted
Database right Oxford University Press (maker)

First published 2007

All rights reserved. No part of this publication may be reproduced,
stored in a retrieval system, or transmitted, in any form or by any means,
without the prior permission in writing of Oxford University Press,
or as expressly permitted by law, or under terms agreed with the appropriate
reprographics rights organization. Enquiries concerning reproduction
outside the scope of the above should be sent to the Rights Department, Journals
Division, Oxford University Press, at the address above

You must not circulate this book in any other binding or cover
and you must impose this same condition on any acquirer

A catalogue for this book is available from the British Library

Library of Congress Cataloguing in Publication Data
(Data available)

ISSN 0022-4480
ISBN 0-19-921909-5
ISBN 978-0-19-921909-4

Subscription information for the *Journal of Semitic Studies* is available at the journal website:
jss.oxfordjournals.org

Printed in Great Britain by Latimer Trend, Plymouth

To Professor Getatchew Haile, our mentor and friend

Table of Contents

Table of Contents iv
Introduction v
Bibliography and Abbreviations xiii
Table of Plates xv
Chapter One: Catalogue of the Manuscripts 1
Chapter Two: Quire Maps and Notes 37
Appendix One: Additional Information on the Bodleian Manuscripts 111
Appendix Two: A Study of Bodleian MS Aeth. b.2 121
List of the Manuscripts by Shelf Mark 127
List of the Manuscripts by Date 129
Index of Works 131
Index of Names 133
Description of Plates 135
Plates 139

Introduction

This catalogue presents information on twenty-three previously uncatalogued Ethiopian manuscripts held in three University Libraries and one private collection in England.

Two prior catalogues of the Ethiopian manuscripts in the Bodleian Library (Oxford) have been produced. In 1848, A. Dillmann described thirty-five manuscripts in his *Catalogus Codicum Manuscriptorum Bibliothecae Bodleianae Oxoniensis, Pars. VII. Codices Aethiopici* (Oxford). In 1951, Edward Ullendorff described another sixty-six manuscripts in his *Catalogue of Ethiopian Manuscripts in the Bodleian Library, Volume II* (Oxford). This catalogue describes another fourteen Ethiopian manuscripts at the Bodleian, bringing the total to one hundred fifteen.

Sixty-seven Ethiopian manuscripts in the Cambridge University Library have been set forth in 1961 by Edward Ullendorff, along with Stephen G. Wright and D.A. Hubbard, in their *Catalogue of Ethiopian Manuscripts in the Cambridge University Library* (Cambridge). This catalogue describes another two manuscripts bringing that total to sixty-nine.

In 1974, Stefan Strelcyn described forty-two manuscripts in the *Catalogue of Ethiopic Manuscripts in the John Rylands University Library of Manchester* (Manchester). This catalogue describes another three manuscripts bringing the total number of manuscripts in the Rylands collection to forty-five.

Along with the additions to the collections of the university libraries, we offer here the information on four other manuscripts held in the private collection of Dr Ian Mac Lennan of London, arriving at the grand total in this volume of twenty-three.

The largest collection of Ethiopian manuscripts in Britain, of course, is to be found at the British Library whose holdings have been set forth in three catalogues. The earliest eighty-two in this collection were catalogued by A. Dillmann in his *Catalogus Codicum Manuscriptorum Orientalium Qui in Museo Britannico Asservantur* (London, 1838). The largest number of this collection was catalogued by W. Wright in his *Catalogue of the Ethiopic Manuscripts in the British Museum Acquired since the Year 1847* (London, 1877). He provides information on four hundred and eight manuscripts, including some thirty-five which were acquired after 1838 and before the Magdala expedition of 1868. Thus, three hundred fifty were acquired through the Magdala expedition. The final catalogue is that of Stefan Strelcyn who, in 1978, published his *Catalogue of Ethiopian Manuscripts in the British Library Acquired Since the Year 1877* (London) which detailed another one hundred eight manuscripts (some twenty four of which he reckons to be from the Magdala expedition). This brings the total of the British Library collection to just under six hundred (598) manuscripts.

The other collections of note in the British Isles are to be found in the Royal Library, Windsor Castle and at the Chester Beatty Library in Dublin, Ireland at which Delamarter studied for a week in July of 2005. A description of the six sumptuous manuscripts at Windsor Castle is to be found in Edward Ullendorff's 'The Ethiopic Manuscripts in the Royal Library, Windsor Castle', *Rassegna di studi etiopici*, 12 (1954), 71-9. Beatty's fifty-three Ethiopian manuscripts have been catalogued by Enrico Cerulli in his *I manoscritti etiopici della Chester Beatty Library in Dublino*. (Rome, 1965). Mr Charles Horton, curator of Western manuscripts at the Chester Beatty, informs us that the library has acquired 'a few' more Ethiopian manuscripts since the time of Cerulli's catalogue, but that they are mainly Psalters and other well-known works.

The Ethiopian provenance of the twenty-three manuscripts described herein is known in only a few cases. For most, we know only the date they were acquired by the respective library and, perhaps, the person who donated it. However, in the case of the four manuscripts in the Mac Lennan collection, we know three of them to be from Magdala.

Steve Delamarter is Professor of Old Testament and Early Judaism at George Fox Evangelical Seminary in Portland, Oregon, USA. In the summer of 2004, assisted by a Theological Scholars Grant from the Association of Theological Schools (ATS), he traveled to Israel and Ethiopia to study the sociology of scribal communities. Delamarter arranged for an affiliation with the Institute of Ethiopian Studies (IES) of Addis Ababa University, the premiere research institution in Ethiopia. The IES was founded by Richard Pankhurst in the 1963 and occupies the Gännätä Lə'ul ('paradise of princes') palace given by Haile Sellasie to the University of Addis Ababa after the aborted coup in 1960. Delamarter and his translator, Mr Daniel Alemu of Jerusalem, studied manuscripts at the IES and took field trips into various regions of Ethiopia to interview some twenty-two scribes regarding their scribal practice and their social role, social location and the economic engines that affect the markets for their work.

The head of manuscripts and archives at the IES is Ato Demeke Berhane who gave a great deal of assistance to Delamarter and Alemu in their work in Ethiopia. Near the end of their time there, Demeke raised the issue of the need for a

Introduction

published catalogue of the holdings of the IES. Delamarter took Demeke's information and, at a conference on the Dead Sea scrolls at Trinity Western University in Langley, British Columbia, Canada, enquired about the idea with Professor George J. Brooke of the University of Manchester and one of the editors of the Journal of Semitic Studies. Brooke invited a proposal for the Journal's supplement series. Demeke produced the proposal in time for the meeting of the editorial committee in December of 2004. Reviews of the catalogue proposal were favorable and, in June of 2005, Demeke and Delamarter came to Manchester to work out the details for the publication of the catalogue. Professor George Brooke, whose gracious hospitality we wish to acknowledge, not only oriented us to the issues of the publication of that catalogue, but also gave us letters of reference to study Ethiopian manuscripts at other libraries in England.

Our plan was to visit the John Rylands Library, the Cambridge University Library, the British Library and the Bodleian Library in order to study an array of early, dated Ethiopian manuscripts for the purposes of paleographical analysis. With the exception of the British Library, we found uncatalogued manuscripts at each of the libraries we visited and made it one of the goals of our time in each place to provide descriptions of the manuscripts.

During our stay in London we were cared for by several members of the Anglo-Ethiopian Society at which Ato Demeke gave a presentation on the role of the IES in preserving Ethiopia's cultural heritage. Notable among these were John Mellors and Anne Parsons whose work on the scribes and scribal practices in Ethiopia had been a direct help to Delamarter in his work with scribes in Ethiopia. Mellors and Parsons have traveled to Ethiopia on several occasions and lived with scribes of South Gondar, commissioning works from them and studying their practices. They wrote the books *Ethiopian Bookmaking* (London: New Cross Books, 2002) and *Scribes of South Gondar* (London, 2002) and their work was featured in an exhibition at the museum at the Institute of Ethiopian Studies. In London, Dr Ian Mac Lennan graciously provided housing and hospitality for us. Dr Mac Lennan is a friend of Ethiopia and member of the Ethiopian Orthodox Church. He came to the attention of the popular media recently when he purchased an Ethiopian *tabot* (a sacred object which, in the thinking of the Ethiopian Orthodox Church, is connected with the Ark of the Covenant and sanctifies a place for worship) from a London antiquities dealer and returned it to the authorities of the Ethiopian Orthodox Church in Addis Ababa. Demeke and Mac Lennan met in Addis Ababa and Ian extended an invitation to stay at his home, should Demeke ever be in London. The offer was accepted and thus ensued many late-night discussions with tales of Ethiopia's history and culture. It was in this context that Dr Mac Lennan's manuscripts came up for discussion and he readily agreed to allow us both to study them and to produce high-resolution photographic images for deposit at the Institute of Ethiopian Studies and at the Hill Museum and Manuscripts Library in Collegeville, Minnesota, USA.

In each of the libraries we were blessed to receive the generous help of various persons.

Mr John R. Hodgson, Keeper of Manuscripts and Archives at the John Rylands University Library of Manchester, was of great help arranging for our arrival and in working with us to foliate the codices. Anne Young, Senior Special Collections Assistant, gave us every aid in our study of the manuscripts and in our work to publish the information about the three manuscripts from the John Rylands Library that appear in this catalogue. Likewise, Dorothy Clayton, editor of the *Bulletin of the John Rylands Library* worked closely with us to prepare an article for the *Bulletin* about their manuscripts. In addition, she worked with us in the process of getting the images for publication. We express our gratitude to the John Rylands Library of Manchester University for permission to publish photos of their manuscripts.

At the Cambridge University Library, Mr Richard Andrewes, Head of Cambridge University Library Music Department and Mr Godfrey Waller, Superintendent of the Manuscripts Reading Room, were of immense help to our general goal of inspecting nearly 20 manuscripts there, but also to our unanticipated work of cataloguing two undocumented manuscripts. We thank the Syndics of the Cambridge University Library for permission to publish images of their manuscripts.

At the Bodleian, Colin Wakefield, Deputy Keeper of the Department of Oriental Collections, and Doris Nicholson, Oriental picture researcher assisted us time and again during our initial visit in the month of June and in Delamarter's extended stay in July and August. As the notes below will show, Mr Wakefield provided many services for us, including research on manuscript provenance. He also proved invaluable in the decipherment of a hundred-year-old, hand-written note from a donor of one of the manuscripts. We extend our heartfelt thanks to these colleagues and to the Bodleian Library, University of Oxford for permission to publish images of the fourteen manuscripts in their collection.

In Oxford we also enjoyed the hospitality of John Roche, D.Phil., who tutors in the History of Science at Linacre College, Oxford University. Dr Roche assisted us with arrangements for transportation, housing and meals in Oxford and provided warm companionship as well.

These twenty-three codices can contribute to our knowledge of Ethiopian manuscripts in several ways. First, the social location represented by these

Introduction

manuscripts seems to be common, representing use by normal priests in everyday life. This is in contrast, for instance, to the sumptuous manuscripts one can see at the Windsor palace, the British Library, and the libraries at Oxford, Cambridge and Manchester, which represent social locations around royalty and in the upper echelons of the church. While, in previous generations and in popular circles, these latter drew much of the attention because of their exceptional size and quality and the richness of their illuminations, there is rising interest in our day about the common niche as the domain in which life was played out by the vast majority of people in Ethiopia's long and varied history.

There is much in these manuscripts that is of interest regarding matters scribal and codicological. Six of the items in this catalogue (4, 7, 13, 14, 15, and 17) contain at least one work with musical notation. Items 5, 12, 17, 20, and 22 have leather cases (a *mahdär*); item 13 has a cloth pouch and item 23 is in an amulet case. Items 2, 7, 12 and 16 are covered in tooled leather. Items 8, 13 and 15 employ a piece of parchment as a spine cover; item 22 has a strip that covers spine and fore edge in a different format than the other three. Items 2 and 14 have been rebound in the West. Several of these codices employ quire numbers on the first folio of some or all of the quires of the codex (the various forms and locations of the quire numbers providing another fascinating study).

Among all twenty-three codices, there are around 277 quires from which we can gain an idea of the various approaches to the construction of what we might call 'normal quires' in the body of a codex. We list here a few observations about the quires in this collection:

1. There is a grand total of 277 quires.
2. Of these, the front protection sheets constitute exceptions. They are generally one or two sheets because of their function. About 18 of the quires fall into this category.
3. Last and next-to-last quires constitute exceptions. Most of the one-, two-, and three-sheet, balanced quires (i.e. quires made up exclusively of full-sheets and, thus, the same number of folios in the front half as in the back half of the quire) fit this category. About 15 of the quires fall into this category.
4. Even among balanced, adjusted quires (i.e. quires that include the use of half sheets, with the same number of half sheets in the front half as in the back half of the quire), three were end quires and, as such, subject to 'special rules', i.e. finish the codex with as few sheets/folios as necessary. Three quires fit into this category.

5. This leaves a total 241 quires subject to what we might call 'normal rules', i.e. no particular constraints to make the quire short.
6. Of these 241, 104 or 43% are four-sheet, balanced quires.
7. Of these 241, 55 or 23% are five-sheet, balanced quires.
8. Of these 241, 10 or 4% are six-sheet, balanced quires.
9. Of these 241, 12 or 5% are three-sheet, balanced quires.
10. Of these 241, 16 are 5/4 adjusted balanced (a quire made up of three sheets and two half-sheets, one in the front and one in the back of the quire); five are 6/5 adjusted balanced; four are 6/4 adjusted balanced (two full sheets and four half-sheets) or 4/3 adjusted balanced or 5/3 adjusted balanced.
11. Thus, of the 241 quires, 25 (just over 10%) are adjusted balanced.
12. Of the 241 quires, 22 (just under 10%) are unbalanced quires (i.e. using usually only one half-sheet as part of a quire, rendering the total number of folios in the quire to be uneven).

It may be valuable at some point to try to correlate these quire construction statistics to the economic forces and practices at work among scribes. For instance, when it comes to common manuscripts (i.e. non-deluxe manuscripts made for persons of ordinary means), does the 4-sheet quire constitute the most ideal, preferable or manageable unit of micro-economic exchange? For what reasons: more frequent pay days (though smaller income per payday), i.e. operating on little overhead with little margins? Are the use of half-sheets with folio stubs—as seems to be not infrequent in common manuscripts—an attempt to press all available materials into service in a materials-scarce environment? These are just a few of the sorts of studies that the codicological information in these manuscripts can provide.

As the 'List of Manuscripts by Date' shows, these codices were produced across several centuries ranging from the 15th through the 20th centuries.

In June and July of 2006, we were privileged to spend four weeks together with Professor Getatchew Haile at the Hill Museum and Manuscripts Library at Saint John's University in Collegeville, Minnesota, USA. The focus of our work was on two other Ethiopian manuscript cataloguing projects. The first was a Catalogue of the Ethiopian Manuscripts in the Institute of Ethiopian Studies which will be published by the *Journal of Semitic Studies*, supplement series, and will contain entries for more than a thousand Gəʿəz manuscripts. The second project on which we worked was a Catalogue of Previously Uncatalogued Ethiopian Manuscripts in North America. This catalogue covers the contents of a digital collection known as the SGD Library of Ethiopian Manuscripts and will be published by Getatchew Haile and Steve Delamarter. The library is made up of 112 codices and 129 magic scrolls owned by

Introduction

three universities and 12 private owners in North America. High resolution images of all of the codices were produced as part of the project. The entire digital collection of these manuscripts (some 18 gigabytes of pdf files) is currently available at the Institute of Ethiopian Studies in Addis Ababa, Ethiopia, the Hill Museum and Manuscripts Library in Collegeville, Minnesota, USA, and the Septuagint Institute of Trinity Western University in Langley, British Columbia, Canada. In working on those catalogues we learned a great deal from Getatchew which we were able to bring to the final editing of this catalogue. We express our appreciation to Professor Getatchew and dedicate this work to him.

We should also say a word of thanks to Dr Jules Glanzer, dean of George Fox Evangelical Seminary and Delamarter's supervisor, for help in finding funds toward the cost of printing the colour images in this volume and to George Fox University for a load reduction in the fall of 2006 to be able to work on this and other catalogues of Ethiopian manuscripts.

Finally, we offer a word of appreciation to Bronwen Campbell, assistant editor at the *Journal of Semitic Studies*, for her help with various aspects of the publication process.

Bibliography and Abbreviations

AṢZ = አምስቱ፡ ጸዋትወ፡ ዜማዎች፡፡ እነርሱም፡ ፩ኛ-ጾመ፡ ድጓ፣ ፪ኛ-ምዕራፍ፣ ፫ኛ-ዚቅ፣መዝሙር፣ እስመ፡ ለዓለም፣ ፬ኛ-ዝማሬ፣ ፭ኛ-መዋሥዕት፡፡ Addis Ababa, 1965 EC.

Basset, *Apocryphes* = René Basset. *Les Apocryphes éthiopiens traduit en français I–XI*. Paris, 1903–9.

Budge, *Mary* = E A. Wallis Budge. *One Hundred and Ten Miracles of Our Lady Mary*. London, 1933.

Cerulli, *Maria* = Enrico Cerulli. *Il libro etiopico dei miracoli di Maria e le sue fonti nelle letterature del Medio Evo latino*. Rome, 1943.

Chaîne, *Répertoire* = M. Chaîne, 'Répertoire des salam et de malk'e contenus dans les manuscrits éthiopiens des bibliothèques d'Europe', *Revue de l'Orient Chrétien*, 2e série, 8 18 (1813), pp. 183–205 and 337–57.

EC = Ethiopian Calendar (=AD minus 7/8).

EMML = Ethiopian Microfilm Manuscript Library.

Hammerschmidt, *Texte* = Ernst Hammerschmidt. *Äthiopische Liturgische Texte der Bodleian Library in Oxford*. Deutsche Akademie der Wissenschaften zu Berlin. Institut für Orientforschung. Veröffentlichung, Nr 38. Berlin, 1960.

Lifchitz, *Textes* = Déborah Lifchitz. *Textes éthiopiens magico-religieux*. Paris, 1940.

MD 59 = መዝሙር፡ ዘዳዊት፡ [= *Mäzmurä Dawit*]. Addis Ababa, 1959 EC.

MG 59 = ሰባቱ፡ ኪዳናት፡፡ ቅዳሴ፡ ማርያም፡ መልክአ ጉባኤ፡፡ [= *Säbattu Kidanat. Qəddase Maryam Mälkə'a Guba'e*]. Addis Ababa, 1959 EC.

A Catalogue of Previously Uncatalogued Ethiopic Manuscripts in England

Strelcyn, *British Library* = S. Strelcyn. *Catalogue of Ethiopian Manuscripts in the British Library Acquired Since the Year 1877.* Oxford, 1978.

Strelcyn, *Lincei* = Stefan Strelcyn. *Catalogue des manuscrits éthiopiens de l'Accademia Nazionale dei Lincei: Fonds Conti Rossini et Fonds Caetani 209, 375, 376, 377, 378.* Rome, 1976.

Ullendorff, *Cambridge* = Ullendorff, Edward and Stephen G. Wright. *Catalogue of Ethiopian Manuscripts in the Cambridge University Library.* Cambridge, 1961.

Velat, *Me'erāf* I = Bernard Velat. *Me'erāf.Commun del'office divin éthiopien pour toute l'année. Partologia Orientalis*, vol. 34, 1–2 (1966), pp. I–XV and 1–413.

Velat, *Me'erāf* II = Bernard Velat. *Étude sur le Me'erāf. Commun del'office divin éthiopien: Introduction, traduction française, commentaire litugique et musica, Partologia Orientalis,* vol. 33 (1966).

Velat, *Ṣom Deggua* = Bernard Velat. *Ṣom Deggua. Antiphonaire du carême. Quatre premières semaines. Partologia Orientalis*, vol. 32, 1–2 (1966) and vol. 32, 3–4 (1969).

Wright, *British Museum* = W. Wright. *Catalogue of the Ethiopic Manuscripts in the British Museum Acquired since the Year 1847.* London, 1877.

Table of Plates

Plate 1: Bodleian MS. Aeth. b. 2, f. 3r. 140
Plate 2: Bodleian MS. Aeth. d. 9, f. 5r. 141
Plate 3: Bodleian MS. Aeth. d. 11, f. 8r. 142
Plate 4: Bodleian MS. Aeth. d. 14, f. 46r. 143
Plate 5: Bodleian MS. Aeth. e. 22, f. 130r. 144
Plate 6: Bodleian MS. Aeth. e. 23, f. 87v. 145
Plate 7: Bodleian MS. Aeth. e. 24, f. 13r. 146
Plate 8: Bodleian MS. Aeth. e. 25, f. 134r. 147
Plate 9: Bodleian MS. Aeth. e. 28, ff. 1v–2r. 148
Plate 10: Bodleian MS. Aeth. f. 19, ff. 21v–22r. 149
Plate 11: Bodleian MS. Aeth. f. 20, ff. 1v–2r. 150
Plate 12: Bodleian MS. Aeth. f. 21, f. 113r. 151
Plate 13: Bodleian MS. Aeth. g. 22, ff. 42v–43r. 152
Plate 14: Bodleian MS. Aeth. g. 23, f. 22r. 153
Plate 15: Cambridge University Library, Or. 2547, ff. 36v–37r. 154
Plate 16: Cambridge University Library, Or. 2548, ff. 36v–37r. 155
Plate 17: Rylands Ethiopic MS 43, front cover and f. 1r. 156
Plate 18: Rylands Ethiopic MS 43, ff. 1v–2r. 157
Plate 19: Rylands Ethiopic MS 43, ff. 32v–33r. 157
Plate 20: Rylands Ethiopic MS 43, in case. 158
Plate 21: Rylands Ethiopic MS 44, spine. 158
Plate 22: Rylands Ethiopic MS 44, ff. 7v–8r. 159
Plate 23: Rylands Ethiopic MS 27 (left) and Rylands Ethiopic MS 45 (right). 160
Plate 24: Rylands Ethiopic MS 45, f. 2r. 161
Plate 25: Mac Lennan Codex 1, with case. 162
Plate 26: Mac Lennan Codex 1, spine. 162
Plate 27: Mac Lennan Codex 1, ff. 152v–153r. 163
Plate 28: Anklets sharing the same provenance as Mac Lennan Codex 1. 164
Plate 29: Iron cross sharing the same provenance as Mac Lennan Codex 1. 164
Plate 30: Mac Lennan Codex 2, ff. 137v–138r. 165
Plate 31: Mac Lennan Codex 3, cover and protection flap. 166
Plate 32: Mac Lennan Codex 3, ff. 27v–28r. 166
Plate 33: Mac Lennan Codex 4, cover and amulet case. 167
Plate 34: Mac Lennan Codex 4, ff. 8v–9r. 167

Chapter One: Catalogue of the Manuscripts

1. Bodleian MS Aeth. b.2
Seven Loose Folios with Illustrations
taken from One or Two Codices on the Saints

Parchment, seven loose folios, 42 x 39 cm, Gəʻəz, 1–2 columns, mid-19th century.

F. 1r: Two illuminations. The upper scene depicts the birth of Ewosṭatewos. The lower scene depicts six men: Ewosṭatewos with two followers and Täklä Haymanot with two followers.

F. 1v: fragment of a text mentioning Täklä Haymanot and the owners of the manuscript: Gäbrä Krəstos and his wife, Säbänä Giyorgis.

F. 2r: Two illuminations. The upper scene is a depiction of the crucifixion of Jesus. The lower scene shows Däjazmach Hailu (centre) and his soldiers (right).

F. 2v: fragment (8 lines) from Hymns of Saint John.

F. 3r: Illumination of Gäbrä Mänfäs Qəddus praying. A bird hovers by the left side of his face. Six lions flank him on the left and six leopards flank him on the right. The painter's name is mentioned: Liqä Gubaʼe Wäldä Giyorgis, who is identified as the painter to King Tewodros (1855–68).

F. 3v: Two illuminations. The upper scene depicts Abunä Märqorewos (holding a large hand cross in right hand and a handkerchief in left hand) on the left and a dragon on the right. The lower scene depicts Wäyzäro Warka (a female) praying with her entourage (seven on left, thirteen on right).

F. 4r: Full-page illumination: From atop a church building, a saint is hanging upside down. The Devil has just cut rope holding the man.

F. 4v: There are two words scribbled in a later hand in large blue pen or crayon: Gädlä Tsadqan.

F. 5r: Illumination of the crucifixion of Jesus. Colours: Black, red, green, blue, brown. Sun and moon stand at the top of the scene with Jesus on the cross in the centre.

A soldier pierces Jesus' side with a spear. Jesus is flanked by two smaller figures showing the two thieves on crosses. A soldier (right) offers Jesus a drink on a sponge. Satan is bound (left). Blood flows freely from several places on Jesus' body. Mary (left) and John (right), weeping, are at the foot of the cross. Saints (below) await resurrection. The skull of Adam is directly at the foot of the cross.

F. 5v: Illumination of Jesus (centre) and Ewosṭatewos (right) in a boat. Ewosṭatewos is described as the divider of the sea (Ewosṭatewos käfale bahǝr).

F. 6r: Two illuminations. In the upper scene, Jesus (centre left) takes the hand of Abunä Amoṣ, well-known official of Armenia, and raises him up. In the lower scene are four saints holding rosary beads.

F. 6v: A full-page illumination. Abunä Ewosṭatewos praying. He is flanked by two followers.

F. 7r: A full-page illumination. An (unidentified) king and the queen sit in royal array (centre). Servants hold royal umbrellas over each with one hand and fly swatters in the other hands. A large crown is on the queen. The king holds a hand cross in his right hand. Both hold handkerchiefs in their hands.

F. 7v: A full-page illumination. Saint Täklä Haymanot. Lower portion of his right leg is separated from the rest of the leg. He is flanked by two followers. The layout is identical to the illumination in f. 6v.

Purchased by the Friends of the Bodleian, 1986. Unless otherwise noted, the information about provenance of the manuscripts in the Bodleian comes from the 'Manuscript Handlist of the Bodleian Library' provided for us by Mr Colin Wakefield.

2. Bodleian MS Aeth. d.9
Miracles of the Blessed Virgin Mary

Parchment, 255 x 205 x 47 mm, two boards covered in tooled leather, rebound in the West (employing a leather spine cover and front and end papers), protection sheet + twelve quires, quires 3–6 numbered, ii + 98 folios, 250 x 190 mm, two columns, top margin 15–25 mm, bottom margin 55–60 mm, fore-edge margin 30 mm, inter columnar margin 12 mm, Gǝ'ǝz, 20–1 lines, late-18th, early-19th century.

Ff. 1r – 4v: A fragment of *Miracles of the Blessed Virgin Mary*.

Ff. 5r–97v. The *Miracles of the Blessed Virgin Mary*, seventy-four in number, incomplete (written in a different hand than the former text).

The standard works on the miracles of Mary are Cerulli, *Maria*, and Budge, *Mary*.

Notes:
1. The name of the owner, added in a second hand, was Wäldä Iyäsus.

Purchased from H.A.B. Fowler of Hartland, Devon, 1948.

3. Bodleian MS. Aeth. d.11
Hymns (Zəmmare) and Anthems (Mäwas'ət) for the Whole Year
with musical notation

Parchment, 230 x 187 x 45 mm. Two rough-hewn boards serve as covers. The front board is broken 55 mm from the fore edge and is repaired with three leather stitches. There are three other holes in the front board resulting from knots in the wood. A small yellow note pasted on the front cover says: 'MS Aeth d.11'. There are four rows of stitches. Three of the four are broken at the attachment to the back cover board. Two of four are broken at the attachment to the front cover. Protection sheet + nine quires, ii + 71 folios, two columns, top margin 15–30 mm, bottom margin 30–35 mm, fore-edge margin 25–30 mm, gutter margin 20–2 mm, inter columnar margin 18–20 mm, Gə'əz. Ff. 1–56 has 26 lines per folio; ff. 57 through the end are 22–3 lines. 18th century.

Ff. 1r–69r: Hymns (Zəmmare) and Anthems (Mäwas'ət) for the whole year, with musical notation. Cf. AṢZ, pp. 401–527.

F. 70v: Two notes in Amharic regarding the sale of the manuscript.

Varia:
1. Ff. ir–iiv(erso): prepared for text (margins, two columns, prickings and 26 lines), but blank.
2. Ff. 69v–70r, 71rv: blank

Purchased from Thornton's Bookshop, Oxford, 1971.

4. Bodleian MS. Aeth. d.14
Antiphonary (*Dəgg^wa*) with musical notation

Parchment, two rough-hewn, wooden boards (front board is broken and stitched in three places with string; back board is broken in two places and repaired with three and four stitches respectively), four chain stitches (perhaps secondary; a long string extends from the last stitching), protection sheet + 9 quires, quires 2–4 (and perhaps 8) are numbered, 91 folios, three columns, top margin 25 mm, bottom margin 50–3 mm, fore-edge margin 25–32 mm, gutter margin 15–20 mm, inter columnar margin 10 mm, Gəʿəz, 25 lines, 18th century.

Ff. 3r – 91r: Antiphonary, *Dəgg^wa*, with musical notation. EMML 1135; Velat, *Som Deggua*; and አምስቱ፡ ጸዋትው፡ ዜማዎች፡ Addis Ababa, 1965 EC, pp. 1–101.

1. Ff. 3r – 43r: Hymns (Zəmmare) with musical notation. See, 3. Bodleian MS. Aeth. d.11, above.
2. Ff. 43v – 44v: A guide for singing in the various styles (Gəʿəz, Araray, əzl).
3. Ff. 45r – 45v: Fragment from work about King Herod and the Killing of the Innocents.
4. Ff. 46r – 62r: Harp of Mary, Arganonä Maryam.
5. Ff. 62v – 66v: From Life of Abunä Abrəham, with musical notation.
6. Ff. 68r – 80v: Məʾəraf, with musical notation.
7. Ff. 80v – 91r: Mäwädəs, with musical notation.

Varia:

1. Inside the front cover, written on the wood in modern ink pen is: 'MS Aeth. d.14'.
2. Reinforcement tabs or just masking tape has been put around the gutter of the front and back protection sheets.
3. F. 43r, column three, pen trials; Owner of the manuscript is mentioned: Tewosalos and his teacher's name, Arsəlus (incorrect form, see f. 66v), his father's name, Asahel, his mother's name, Ermin, and his sister's name, Yäʾabi Kəbra.
4. F. 66v: Following a small *haräg* at the end of the third column, the name of the owner is given, Tewosalos, and his teacher's name, Arkä Səlus (correct form), his father's name, Asahel, his mother's name, Ermin.

5. F. 67v: List of items and witnesses.
6. F. 91v: column one (ten lines) contains an excerpt from the Hymns of Mary; column two contains an excerpt from a work mentioning the crucifixion and the cross. Bottom: pen trials.

Purchased from Dr Thomas L. Kane, 1979.

5. Bodleian Ms. Aeth. e.22
Psalter

Parchment, 165 x 115 x 58 mm, four Coptic chain stitches attached with bridle attachments to two rough-hewn boards (front board broken in one place about 25 mm from the spine and repaired with two stitches; back board broken in one place about 55 mm from the spine and repaired with three stitches), protection sheet + sixteen quires, 150 folios, ff. 3r–130r one column, ff. 130r–149r two columns, top margin 12–15 mm, bottom margins 40 mm, fore-edge margins 15 mm, gutter margin 12 to 15 mm, inter columnar margin 8 mm, Gəʿəz, 23–4 lines, 19th century, double-slip carrying case (*mahdär*) with strap.

Ff. 3r–149v: Psalter. Printed several times in Ethiopia, e. g. MD 59.
1. Ff. 3r–112r: 151 Psalms of David.
2. Ff. 112r – 123r: Fifteen Canticles of the Prophets of the Old and New Testaments
    a. First Song of Moses (Exod. 15:1–19), f. 112r.
    b. Second Song of Moses (Deut. 32:1–21), f. 113r.
    c. Third Song of Moses (Deut. 32:22–43), f. 114r.
    d. Song of Hannah, mother of Samuel (1 Sam. 2:1–10), f. 115v.
    e. Prayer of Hezekiah (Isa. 38:10–20), f. 116v.
    f. Prayer of Manasseh, f. 117r.
    g. Song of Jonah (Jon. 2:3–10), f. 118r.
    h. First Song of the Three Children (Dan. 3:26–45), f. 118v.
    i. Second Song of the Three Children (Dan. 3:52–6), f. 119v.
    j. Third Song of the Three Children (Dan. 3:57–88), f. 119v.
    k. Song of Habakkuk (Hab. 3:1–19), f. 120v.
    l. Song of Isaiah (Isa. 26:9–20), f. 121v.
    m. Song of the Virgin Mary (*Magnificat*, Luke 1:46–55), f. 122r.

n. Song of Zachariah (*Benedictus*, Luke 1:68–79) , f. 122v.

o. Song of Simeon (*Nunc Dimittis*, Luke 2:29–32) , f. 123r.

3. Ff. 123r – 130r: Song of Songs, divided into five sections. ብሉይ፡ ኪዳን፡ መጽሐፍ፡ ሃሌሉ፡፡ Published by the Catholic Mission, Asmara 1917 EC, pp. 283–9; see also H.C. Gleave, *The Ethiopic Version of the Song of Songs* (London, 1951).

4. Ff. 130r – 144r: Praises of Mary, Wəddase Maryam, arranged for the days of the week: Monday, f. 130r; Tuesday, f. 131r; Wednesday, f. 133v; Thursday, f. 136r; Friday, f. 139r; Saturday, f. 141r; Sunday, f. 142v. Karl Fries, *Weddâsê Mârjâm. Ein äthiopischer Lobgesang an Maria* (Uppsala 1892); Velat, *Me'eräf* I, pp. 76–91; tr. by Velat, *Me'eräf* II, pp. 284–96; and E.A. Wallis Budge, *Legend of Our Lady Mary the Perpetual Virgin and Her Mother Ḥannâ* (Oxford, 1933), pp. 279–96.

5. Ff. 144r–149v: Gate of Light, Anqäṣä bərhan. Text, Velat, *Me'eräf* I, pp. 69–75; tr. *Me'eräf* II, pp. 279–83; and Christopher Lash, "Gate of Light': An Ethiopian Hymn to the Blessed Virgin', *Eastern Churches Review*, vol. 4 (1972), pp. 36–46, and vol. 5 (1973), pp. 143–56.

Ff. 149v – 150v: The Angels Praise Her, Yəwedəsəwa Mäla'ekt lä Maryam, incomplete, in a different hand.

Varia:

1. The inside of the front cover has a large circle of about 70 mm in diameter that has been scraped down a few mm into the board. There is no indication what may have been posted in this depression.

2. There is not currently any cloth wrapped around the boards nor is there any evidence that there ever was (*pace* remarks in the *reading room list*, see appendix two).

3. F. 149v, just above beginning of The Angels Praise Her, in a later hand in pencil, is written the name of the owner of the codex: Wäldä Ṣäga-Ab.

Purchased from H.A.B. Fowler of Hartland, Devon, 1948.

Catalogue of the Manuscripts

6. Bodleian MS. Aeth. e.23
Psalter

Parchment, 195 x 185 x 70 mm, rough-hewn boards (both boards are broken and repaired with three stitchings each), protection sheet + 23 quires, i + 175 folios, ff. 2r–161v one column, 162r–175r in two columns, Gəʽəz, 19 lines, 17th century.

Ff. 2r–175r: Psalter. See Bodleian Ms. Aeth. e.22 above.
1. Ff. 2r – 137v: 151 Psalms of David.
2. Ff 138r–153r: Fifteen Canticles of the Prophets of the Old and New Testaments,.
   a. First Song of Moses (Exod. 15:1–19), f. 138r.
   b. Second Song of Moses (Deut. 32:1–21), f. 139r.
   c. Third Song of Moses (Deut. 32:22–43), f. 141r.
   d. Song of Hannah, mother of Samuel (1 Sam. 2:1–10), f. 143r.
   e. Prayer of Hezekiah (Isa. 38:10–20), f. 144r.
   f. Prayer of Manasseh, f. 145r.
   g. Song of Jonah (Jon. 2:3–10), f. 146r.
   h. First Song of the Three Children (Dan. 3:26–45), f. 146v.
   i. Second Song of the Three Children (Dan. 3:52–6), f. 147v.
   j. Third Song of the Three Children (Dan. 3:57–88), f. 148r.
   k. Song of Habakkuk (Hab. 3:1–19), f. 149r.
   l. Song of Isaiah (Isa. 26:9–20), f. 150v.
   m. Song of the Virgin Mary (*Magnificat*, Luke 1:46–55), f. 151v.
   n. Song of Zachariah (*Benedictus*, Luke 1:68–79), f. 152r.
   o. Song of Simeon (*Nunc Dimittis*, Luke 2:29–32), f. 152v.
3. Ff. 154r–161v: Song of Songs divided into five sections.
4. Ff. 162r–171r: Praises of Mary, Wəddase Maryam, arranged for the days of the week: Sunday, f. 162; Monday, f. 163r; Tuesday, f. 163v; Wednesday, f. 165r; Thursday, f. 166v; Friday, f. 168v; Seventh day(əlätä Sänbät), f. 170r.
5. Ff. 171r–175r: Gate of Light, Anqäṣä bərhan.

Varia:
1. F. i r: Fragment of a lost text, mutilated; only 3–4 cm remain of the page.
2. F. iv(erso) / f. 1r: The small flap that constitutes f. i v is treated by the scribe as a part of f. 1r: the text is written across both folios in a running text. At the

top of the folio is the record of a transaction of land and grain. At the bottom of the folio is an extract from the Annunciation.
3. F. 1v. Top, illegible. Middle, a text about a person, Abib, mostly illegible (it is not clear if this is the Abunä Abib or someone else).
4. Ff. 153r–v: Hymns to Gäbrä Mänfäs Qəddus, incomplete, later hand.
5. F. 175r: mentions the name of the owner, Mäzgäbä Səllase.
6. F. 175r–v: includes a 'genealogy of forefathers'.
7. There is a set of marginal navigational/liturgical markers in the Psalms. They begin on f. 7v and end on f. 137v (the end of the Psalms). There are 100 of them in the first 37 ff. (r and v) alone. They take the form ▮ and stand no more than about 3 mm. From f. 7v – 130r they have this two-coloured pattern, but in the last seven folios of the psalms, the red lines disappear and there is only the black down stroke and occasionally the black horizontal strokes above and below.
8. There are at least three very different kinds of stitching in this codex. The first is the way in which loosed pages have been re-stitched onto a neighbouring folio. This was done with a narrow strip of leather. A second set of stitchings are of repairs to pages in which the stitching is very close and the vellum at the stitching edges translucent. The third program of stitching is seen in certain repairs to torn pages that employ an open, wide stitch that backs over on itself and employs modern (?) white string and no translucence at the seam. We suspect that the first two examples are early and that the third is relatively late in the life of this codex..
9. Quires 5, 7, 10, 17 and 17 are all formed in the same way. All are made up of five sheets, but all include the use of two half-sheets in them with stubs that extend onto the other side of the gutter. All of the half-sheets are located at the same place in the quire to be the 3rd and the 7th folio in the quire. All of the quires end up having an even number of folios, eight.

Purchased from the Warden of All Souls, Oxford, 1959. Previously purchased by Sir F.R. Wingate, 1897.

7. Bodleian MS. Aeth. e.24
Antiphonary for Lent, Ṣomä Dəgʷa, with musical notation

Parchment, 192 x 135 x 43 mm, two boards covered with tooled leather, linen visible inside covers (deep red floral pattern on front cover; blue, red, yellow and black pictures on the back cover), 8 quires, iii + 66 folios, top margin 12–15 mm, bottom margin 27–30 mm, fore-edge margin 17 mm, gutter margin 5–7 mm, inter columnar margin 7 mm, Gəʻəz, 19th century.

Ff. 1r – 61v: Antiphonary for Lent, Ṣomä Dəgʷa, with musical notation. See, 4. Bodleian MS. Aeth. d.14, above.

Ff. 62v – 64r: Hymns (Zəmmare) with musical notation. See, 4. Bodleian MS. Aeth. d.14, above.

Varia:
1. A small yellow piece of paper is affixed to the spine with the following text written in ink: 'MS. Aeth. e.24'. On the leather of the inside cover is written: MS Aeth. e.24.
2. F. ir: pen trial and shelf mark of the Bodleian Library, 'MS Aeth, e.24'.
3. F. iv(erso): written in English: 'TSOMEW DIGGWA, MS in Geez. £ 25 [18th century] with musical notations', plus pen trial, 'hallelujah'.
4. F. iir: pencil drawing of person with arm across chest, unfinished.
5. F. iiv(erso): blank.
6. F. iiir: drawing outlined in black pen (modern) and with red on face and garment. Priest with praying stick and musical instrument.
7. F. iiiv(erso), drawing of priest in black. Holding praying stick and musical instrument.
8. There is an inter columnar navigational/liturgical system of numbers and letters. The lines above and below the numbers and letters are usually in red ink.

Purchased from Thornton's Bookshop, Oxford, 1971.

A Catalogue of Previously Uncatalogued Ethiopic Manuscripts in England

8. Bodleian MS. Aeth. e.25
Psalter

Parchment, 187 x 170 x 65 mm, four Coptic chain stitches bind the quires together and are attached to two rough-hewn boards (back board broken about 95 mm from the spine and glued back together). A thick piece of parchment covers the spine of the book and extends a couple of centimeters around the first and last folios of the codex. The outside wood of the covers has been painted black. Protection sheet + 20 quires, 166 folios, ff. 3r–146r one column, ff. 146v–166v two columns, Gəʿəz, 18th century.

Ff. 3r–165v: Psalter. See Bodleian Ms. Aeth. e.22 above.
  1. Ff. 3r–134r: 151 Psalms of David.
  2. Ff. 134r–146r: Fifteen Canticles of the Prophets of the Old and New Testaments.
      a. First Song of Moses (Exod. 15:1–19), f. 134r.
      b. Second Song of Moses (Deut. 32:1–21), f. 135r.
      c. Third Song of Moses (Deut. 32:22–43), f.136v.
      d. Song of Hannah, mother of Samuel (1 Sam. 2:1–10), f. 138r.
      e. Prayer of Hezekiah (Isa. 38:10–20), f. 138v.
      f. Prayer of Manasseh, f. 139r.
      g. Song of Jonah (Jon. 2:3–10), f. 140r.
      h. First Song of the Three Children (Dan. 3:26–45), f. 140v.
      i. Second Song of the Three Children (Dan. 3:52–6), f. 141v.
      j. Third Song of the Three Children (Dan. 3:57–88), f. 142r.
      k. Song of Habakkuk (Hab. 3:1–19), f. 143r.
      l. Song of Isaiah (Isa. 26:9–20), f. 144r.
      m. Song of the Virgin Mary (*Magnificat*, Luke 1:46–55) , f. 145r.
      n. Song of Zachariah (*Benedictus*, Luke 1:68–79), f. 145v.
      o. Song of Simeon (*Nunc Dimittis*, Luke 2:29–32), f. 146r.
  3. Ff. 146v–151r: Song of Songs divided into five sections (written in two columns!).
  4. Ff. 151v–161v: Praises of Mary, Wəddase Maryam, arranged for the days of the week: Monday, f. 151v; Tuesday, f. 152r; Wednesday, f. 154r; Thursday, f. 155v; Friday, f. 158r; Saturday, f. 159r; Sunday, 160r.
  5. Ff. 161v–165v: Gate of Light, Anqäṣä bərhan, incomplete.

Varia:
1. Ff. 1r – 2v: Excerpts from the Psalms of David.
2. F. 166r: Fragment from an unidentified work, perhaps a psalm of David, written in a later, clear and different scribal hand.
3. F. 166v: note of ownership: La'əkä Maryam
4. The boards appear to have been partially covered with leather at one time though this is no longer the case. There is a discoloration and remains of glue that are visible on both front and back covers (from the spine out some 60 mm and on the back cover from the spine out some 65 mm).
5. On the outside of the spine a small yellow tab is affixed on which is written: 'MS. Aeth. e.25'.

Presented to the Bodleian Library from the estate of the 2nd Viscount Rennell of Rodd, 1978.

9. Bodleian MS. Aeth. e.28
Harp of Praise, Arganonä Wəddase

Parchment, 160 x 145 x 65 mm, three Coptic chain stitches attached to two rough-hewn boards (both are broken and repaired with three stitches), fifteen quires, quires 2–5 numbered, 145 folios, 155 x 140 mm, top margin 17 mm, bottom margin 40 mm, fore-edge margin 20 mm, gutter margin 10 mm, inter columnar margin 10 mm. Ff. 1v – 65v (quires 1–7) are written in 17 lines; ff. 66r – 99v (quires 8–10) are 16 lines; ff. 100r – 109v (quire 11) are 14 lines; ff. 110r – 117v (quire 12) are 16 lines; ff. 118r – 137v (quires 13 and 14) are 15 lines; ff. 138r – 145r (quire 15) are 17 lines. Gə'əz, 17th century (based on the identification of the illuminator).

Ff. 2r–143v: The Harp of Praise, Arganona Wəddase, arranged for the days of the week: Monday ff. 2r – 29r; Tuesday, ff. 29r – 39r; Wednesday, ff. 39r – 61v; Thursday, ff. 62r – 90v; Friday, ff. 91r – 116v; Saturday, ff. 117r – 130r; Sunday, ff. 131r – 143v.
See the edition by Pontus Leander, *Arganona Ueddase: nach Handschriften in Uppsala, Berlin, Tübingen und Frankfurt*, (Leipzig, 1922).

Ff. 144r–145v : *Asmat* prayer (in a different hand)

Illuminations and Decorations:
1. F. 1v: Three holy figures (halos) stand side by side. The centre figure, a bit larger than the other two, has both hands upraised. The two figures flanking the central figure each have a sword in their right hand, tip pointing straight down. All three wear robes of elaborate geometric designs in black and red and white.
2. F. 2r: an elaborate *haräg* encloses both columns of text with designs in red, brown and black.
3. F. 38v: carpet page with colourful geometric designs.
4. F. 39r: elaborate *haräg* encloses both columns of text with designs in red, black and white.
5. F. 62r: a new work begins with a colourful *haräg* of red, brown and black. Unlike the *harägs* at the head of the two previous works, this one does not continue around the bottom of the two columns of text.
6. F. 91r: begins a new work with a colourful *haräg* of red, brown and black. Like the *harägs* around the beginnings of the first two works, this one does continue around the bottom of the two columns of text.
7. F. 117r: begins a new work with a colourful *haräg* of red, brown and black. This *haräg* continues around the bottom of the two columns of text.
8. F. 130v: elaborate carpet page of geometric designs some 120 x 125 mm. There is no text on the page.
9. F. 131r: begins a new work with a colourful *harägs* of red, brown and black that continues around the bottom of the two columns of text.

Varia:
1. Strings sewn into corners of folios: In eight places there are threads sewn to the upper fore-edge corner of a folio (1, 38, 58, 61, 90, 116, 130, and 143). All but two correspond to the end or beginning of a work. The thread visible on f. 1 was probably to assist in holding a cloth between the art on the facing pages ff. 1v and 2r. The thread at f. 58 has no obvious function.
2. There are small ending *harägs* on ff. 38r, 61v, and 143v.

Purchased from Sam Fogg, London, 2002 by the Friends of the Bodleian, with a grant from the V & A Purchase Grant Fund. This codex is item number 17 in catalogue 24 (entitled *Ethiopian Art*) published in 2001 by Sam Fogg Rare Books and Manuscripts. It is described there as:

The Harp of Praise [Arganonä Weddasé]
Lasta, 17th Century
147 x 160 mm
145 leaves, parchment, written in a fine hand in two columns in red and black ink; the scribe has signed his name, 'Baselyos'. Six large geometric framed headings around the opening text of each section and three full-page paintings, two purely geometric, one of three Ethiopian saints (Abba Giyorgis, Gäbrä Mänfäs Qəddus, Täklä Haymanot). The 'Harp of Praise' is a Marian text divided into days of the week.

The miniatures in our manuscript are by the artist responsible for those in the great Gospel book in the British Library (BL Or.516). This artist, known as the Ground Hornbill painter because of the appearance of those birds in one of his paintings, has a highly distinctive style. He is the earliest known and most distinguished artist working around Lalibela in the province of Lasta, where an independent school of painting appeared in the 17th century. The style of this school originates in the geometric paintings of medieval Ethiopian books. Two works by the Ground Hornbill artist survive in churches in Lalibela. Our manuscript is signed by the scribe 'Baselyos'. The style is a very graphic one, executed in ink rather than paint, and it is possible that in Baselyos we have the name of the Ground Hornbill artist.

References
Africa: the Art of a Continent, Munich 1995, p. 124, cat.2.2
B. Juel-Jensen, "The Ground Hornbill Artist of the 17th Century Ethiopic Manuscript," *The Book Collector*, I, 1977, pp. 61–74.
S. Chojnacki, *Major Themes in Ethiopian Painting*, Wiesbaden, 1983, pp. 491–4 and 521–4.
J. Mercier, *L'Arche Éthiopienne*, Paris 2000, pp. 142–3.

The asking price from Sam Fogg was £40,000, though, reportedly, the library did not pay that much. An account of the acquisition of the manuscript was first given by Lesley Forbes, 'Notable Accessions, Oriental Collections' *The Bodleian Library Record*, 400th anniversary commemorative issue, 17/6 (October 2002), pp. 483–4. The only information of note beyond that in the Sam Fogg catalogue is that this codex and the one mentioned in the British Library (BL Or.516) are the only manuscripts from this school of Ethiopian painting in a British public collection. Forbes also notes, 'The Bodleian has a very fine collection of Byzantine paintings and smaller collections of artistic material from other Eastern Christian traditions, for example from the Armenian, Coptic, Georgian and Syriac Churches, and this manuscript is especially interesting in its links with these traditions of early Christian painting, which are well represented in the Bodleian's collections' (p. 474).

10. Bodleian MS. Aeth. f.19
Praises of Mary (Wəddase Maryam), Gate of Light (Anqäṣä bərhan), Hymns (Sälam) to Rufa'el

Parchment, 132 x 95 x 40 mm, four Coptic chain stitches attached to two rough-hewn boards, protection sheets + five quires, quires 1–4 numbered, iv + 48 + six unlined folios at the end, top margin 12 to 15 mm, bottom margin 22 mm, fore-edge margin 15–20 mm, gutter margin 7mm, quire 1 is written with 19 lines, quires 2–3 are written with 17 lines, quires 4–5 are written with 15 lines, Gə'əz, 20th century.

Ff. 1r–29r: Praises of Mary, Wəddase Maryam, arranged for the days of the week: Monday, 1r; Tuesday, 3r; Wednesday, 7r; Thursday, 11v; Friday, 17v; Saturday, 22r; Sunday, 25r.

Ff. 29r–43v: Gate of Light, Anqäṣä bərhan, The (last two lines are in later hand). For publication information on Praises of Mary and Gate of Light, see Bodleian Ms. Aeth. e.22 above.

Ff. 44r–48v: Hymns to Rufa'el, Sälam to Rufa'el.

Varia:
1. Additional hands are evident: 1) erasure and overwriting in another hand: e.g. f. 21v; interlinear additions/corrections: e.g. 20r, 22v, 23r, etc.
2. The codex comes in a cloth cover of distinctive design: the lower portion looks like a traditional book cover (some 160mm high) with a pouch on either side in which the covers of the book would sit. However, when issued to me, the codex was in the right hand pouch, the left was folded over. A cloth strip some 46 cm is attached to the cover at top centre, intending, apparently to wrap around the fore edge of the codex. At the other end of the

strap is a round cloth strap. On the outside right there is some illegible writing.

Given by Bernard Wigan, Crowborough, Sussex, 1966.

11. Bodleian MS Aeth. f.20
Fragment from Gospel of John

Parchment, single sheet from a codex, 187 x 126 mm, Gəʻəz, 15th century.

Ff 1r–2v: Fragment from Gospel of John
    F. 1r, John 1:22ff.
    F. 1v, John 1:27ff.
    F. 2r, John 2:3ff.
    F. 2v, John 2:8ff.

Notes:
1. Numbering: One side of the sheet has been marked with a number one inside a small circle in the upper left corner; the other marked with a number two in the same way. We shall refer to the folios in the following way: the right side of the sheet when viewing side 1 is f. 1r. The left side of the sheet when viewing side 2 is f. 1v. The right side of the sheet when viewing side 2 is f. 2r and the left side of the sheet when viewing side 1 is f. 2v.
2. Wear: The sheet side one is particularly badly stained and worn. Probably 90 per cent of the letters are legible. Sheet side two is less stained and the portions of the text block nearest the gutter are very clear. There is a strip of wear about 20 mm wide that runs horizontally across the sheet. If we are to take the library's statement of provenance seriously, this strip of wear corresponds to the spine of 'Col. Hale's' book. The sheet seems prepared to fold inward along creases at the outside of this strip of wear, making sheet side one toward the book and sheet side two away from the book. This would account for why the text is most difficult to read along this strip of wear.
3. Trim: When viewing the sheet on the side marked one, the left edge of the sheet is roughly cut (assumingly as part of the rebinding of Col. Hale's book) and seems to indicate that some portion of the margin has been cut off.

4. Preparation of the sheet: The sheet has been prepared for writing with column prickings and line prickings visible as well as the lines scored for columns and text lines.

5. Margins: If we assume that the text blocks were laid out in bi-lateral symmetry on the left side of the sheet as well as the right it would indicate that the outer margin on the left should be an average of 23 mm instead of what it is now. This would indicate that the original size of the sheet was approximately 126 mm high x 195 mm wide. The folio dimensions are 127 x 95 with a text block of 80 x 67 mm (all four text blocks are completely visible). There are 18 lines of text in all four text blocks. Bottom margin is 30–35 mm. Fore-edge margin is 35 mm. Top margin is 10–12 mm. Gutter margin is 6 mm.

6. Full stop symbol: The full stop symbol is ❖. Its colours are especially visible in ff. 1r and 2v.

7. Navigational systems: There are two marginal navigation systems. The first makes use of a symbol that look either like this ⁓∶⁓ or like this ⁓∎⁓. These appear 3 times in f. 1r; at least 6 times in f. 1v; 6 times in f. 2r and perhaps 4 times in f. 2v (though the margin is worn and the symbols are barely visible). The second navigational system is made up of numbers written in the margins at a size fully as big as the letters in the text. Examples of this are particularly visible on f. 1v where the numbers $\overline{IF}$ (13), $\overline{I\bar{o}}$ (14), and $\overline{I\check{z}}$ (15) appear in the margins, with the red ink lines above and below. Three or four more examples of this are visible on f. 1r. One more is faintly visible, though illegible on f. 2v.

8. Binding: In the gutter of the sheet two binding holes are visible. These are 23 and 83 mm from the top of the sheet. In addition, two smaller holes are visible near the top and bottom of the sheet, 4 mm from the edge in both cases, apparently for use with a head piece and tail piece.

A Bodleian handlist says that the sheet was removed from the binding of 'Col. Hale's' 1532 copy of Chaucer. The sheet has certainly been in the Library since 1951.

12. Bodleian MS Aeth. f.21
Psalter

Parchment, 147 x 102 x 58 mm, four chain stitches attached to two rough-hewn boards (visible between the turn-ins) which are covered with tooled leather, apparently rebound since the stitching strings still hang from the bottom centre of the spine, protection sheet + 16 quires, ii + 127 folios, top margin 15 mm, bottom margin 30 mm, fore-edge margin 15 mm, gutter margin 8 mm, inter columnar margins 6 mm, ff. 1r–112r one column, ff. 113r–126v two columns, Gə'əz, 22–6 lines, 19th century. The codex is accompanied by a leather carrying case, a *mahdär*, with a strap. There is also an additional linen cover through which the strap passes and which slides down over and covers the *mahdär*.

Ff. 1r–126v: Psalter. See Bodleian Ms. Aeth. e.22 above.
   1. Ff. 1r–95r: 151 Psalms of David
   2. Ff. 95v–106v: Fifteen Canticles of the Prophets of the Old and New Testaments
      a.   First Song of Moses (Exod. 15:1–19), f. 95v.
      b.   Second Song of Moses (Deut. 32:1–21), f. 96r.
      c.   Third Song of Moses (Deut. 32:22–43), f. 97v.
      d.   Song of Hannah, mother of Samuel (1 Sam. 2:1–10), f. 99r.
      e.   Prayer of Hezekiah (Isa. 38:10–20), f. 100r.
      f.   Prayer of Manasseh, f. 100v.
      g.   Song of Jonah (Jon. 2:3–10), f. 101v.
      h.   Second Song of the Three Children (Dan. 3:52–6), f. 101v
      i.   First Song of the Three Children (Dan. 3:26–45), f. 102v. [out of order from standard order.]
      j.   Third Song of the Three Children (Dan. 3:57–88), f. 103r.
      k.   Song of Habakkuk (Hab. 3:1–19), f. 103v.
      l.   Song of Isaiah (Isa. 26:9–20), f. 105r.
      m.   Song of the Virgin Mary (*Magnificat*, Luke 1:46–55), f. 105v
      n.   Song of Zachariah (*Benedictus*, Luke 1:68–79), f. 106r.
      o.   Song of Simeon (*Nunc Dimittis*, Luke 2:29–32), f. 106r.
   3. Ff. 106v–112r: Song of Songs, divided into five sections.
   4. Ff. 113r–122v: Praises of Mary, Wəddase Maryam, arranged for the days of the week: Monday, f. 113r; Tuesday, f. 113v; Wednesday, f. 115r; Thursday, f. 117r; Friday, f. 119r; Saturday, f. 120v; Sunday, f. 121v.

5. Ff. 122v–126v: Gate of Light, Anqāṣä bərhan.

Varia:
1. To the spine is affixed a small yellow tag that says: 'MS. Aeth. f.21.'
2. Threads (as navigational aids) have been sewn into the upper fore edges of 16 folios.
3. Many of the sheets that make up this codex have been pricked twice, i.e. they have two sets of prickings on the folio edge.
4. Ff. ir–iiv(erso): blank.
5. The codex is accompanied by a modern card (88 x 209 mm) with the following written in a modern hand: 'Ethiopic / MS. Aeth. f.21 / Psalms, Canticles or Biblical Hymns, Song of Songs and Weddase Maryam or Praises of the Virgin. / Date uncertain. [Donated to the Library 11 May 1902; rediscovered January 1991.]

Inside the *mahdär* is a card (88 x 114 mm) of heavy brown card stock with a black edge which Mr Wakefield helped us to decipher. On it is written in an early 20th century hand: [recto] 'Dinghurst & John's Road / Clevedon. / 11 May 1902 / Reverend & dear Sir / The Bible I am sending was brought from Abyssinia for my niece. She is dead & so is hr [*sic*], and I therefore think it well to ask you to accept it & would you care to have now. Henri [verso] Lasserre's [1828–1900] Translation of the Gospels with the Imprimatur of the Archbishop of Paris & Cardinal Jacobini's letter by order of Pope Leon XIII. I am an old woman and I do not know what home these books may have at my death --- / I am yours Reverend and dear Sir. / With loving respect / Mrs) Mary Annette Dennison'.

We assume that the work was donated to the Bodleian shortly after this exchange.

13. Bodleian MS. Aeth. g.22
Book of Chants, *Zema*, with musical notation

Parchment, 100 x 75 x 30 mm, three Coptic chain stitches attached to two, rough-hewn boards, spine is covered with a strip that goes around all the quires, eight quires, 55 folios, top margin 7–10 mm, bottom margin 15–20 mm, fore-edge margin 3–10 mm, gutter margin 3–5 mm, Gə'əz, 14 lines, 20th century. Cloth pouch with a woven string strap about 60 cm long.

Ff. 3r–44v: Book of Chants, *Zema*
 1. Ff. 3r–11v: Mästägabə' prayer
 2. Ff. 11v–17v: Arba'ət prayer
 3. Ff. 17v–44v: Aryam prayer
Ff. 44v–55r: Chant Kəstät zä-aryam

Varia:
 1. F. 1r: Ornamentation, *haräg* designs without colour, graffiti.
 2. F. 2r: Childish miniature of St. Michael. Above and to the right of the drawing is written: 'Saint Michael', but badly spelled.
 3. F. 2v: *Asmat* prayer with a note at the bottom of the folio: 'Do not take or steal [this book] or erase the names.'
 4. F. 55v: Beginning of the First Epistle of St. John.
 5. Ff. 56r, 57r: Graffiti and pen trials from the opening line of first epistle of St. John.
 6. F. 57v: *Asmat* prayer. Recipe for making an amulet.
 7. F. 58v: Graffiti, and rudimentary drawing.
 8. Every quire in the codex incorporates at least one set of half sheets and sometimes two.
 9. Several folios are pricked on both side and bottom, suggesting the re-use of materials prepared originally for another codex.

Notes:
 1. Originally there was a problem in the folio numbers of this codex. The person putting the numbers on the pages skipped from folio 31 to folio 34. We pointed out the error and Mr Wakefield corrected the folio numbers.

Given by Dr A. Minio-Paluello, Rome, 1959.

14. Bodleian MS. Aeth. g.23
Praises of Mary and Gate of Light, with musical notation

Parchment, 111 x 82 x 38 mm, rebound and covered with a modern box case binding with an end paper in front and back, eight quires, 46 folios, top margin 10–13 mm, bottom margin 15 mm, fore-edge margin 12 mm, one column, Gəʿəz, 19th century.

Ff. 1r–34r: Praises of Mary, Wəddase Maryam, with musical notation, arranged for the days of the week: Monday, f. 1r; Tuesday, f. 4r; Wednesday, f. 9r; Thursday, f. 14v; Friday, f. 22r; Saturday, f. 26v; Sunday, f. 30r.

Ff. 34r–46v: Gate of Light, Anqäṣä bərhan. On the publication of Praises of Mary and Gate of Light, see Bodleian Ms. Aeth. e.22 above.

Ff. 45r–46v: prayer (almost illegible; the end is missing.)

Varia:
1. On the inside back cover is a book plate that has printed 'EX LIBRIS P.M. BORRELLI.'
2. Several of the sheets have been pricked twice. There are two sets on the fore edge of several folios.

Given by P.M. Borrelli, 1965.

15. Cambridge University Library Or. 2547
Liturgical Chants, with musical notation

Parchment, 130 x 87 x 30 mm, four Coptic chain stitches attached to two, rough-hewn boards, a spine cover sheet extends around all of the quires and over the weavings of the spine, extending about 2 cms around the first and last folios, protection sheet + six quires, ii + 48 folios (currently unnumbered), one column, 11–12 lines, top margin 8–10 mm, bottom margin 25 mm, fore-edge margin 15 mm, gutter margin 8 mm, Gəʿəz, 20th century.

Ff. 1r–44r: Liturgical Chants, with musical notation
   Ff. 1r–19v: First Chants: Daily Prayers to God, Qeddase Zä-Zäwätər, with musical notation, incomplete.
   Ff. 21r–33r: Second Chants: Chants of John the Baptist, Anqäs Zä-Zəmmare, with musical notation.
   Ff. 33v–44r: Prayers of John the Baptist, Prophet of Prophets, with musical notation.

Catalogue of the Manuscripts

Varia:
1. Ff. 20rv: explanation of blessings (in Amharic).
2. F. 44r: Prayer of John the Baptist, fragment, (see note below).

Notes:
1. This manuscript has been previously known as MS Picken 185.
2. On almost every page, the text is annotated with musical and liturgical notations above the line of text and in the left-hand margin of the text. The only folios not so marked are 20r and v.
3. Marginal numbers: The number two appears very frequently in the left margin of this codex. Occasionally the number three appears. These indicate that the material in these lines is to be repeated twice or three times.
4. Supralinear musical symbols: Above almost every line are several musical symbols in the nature of ligatures. In the first work, these are almost evenly in red and in black ink. In the second and third works and in the work on f. 44v, these are uniformly in black.
5. Supralinear lines and dots: These supralinear lines and dots likewise adorn nearly every line of text. In the first work, these are almost evenly in red and in black ink. In the second and third works and in the work on f. 44v, these are uniformly in black.
6. The final piece on f. 44v is clearly written in a different, and less legible, hand, It is a copy of text from f. 33v. It represents, perhaps, a copying exercise by a less experienced scribe.
7. Based on the use of red ink in the musical and liturgical notations in work one, it is possible that this hand is different from the ones in works two and three and in the brief work on f. 44v.
8. Ff. ir–iiv(erso), : blank
9. Ff 45r–48v: blank except for two brief notes on f. 48r:
    a. 'Good hand writing, approved by Jesus Christ'
    b. 'Sent to Isitrfos'
10. The manuscript is kept in a box with the title 'Ethiopic Liturgical MS. with Music' on the spine.
11. Accompanying the codex are two folded pieces of paper on which is written by hand:

A Catalogue of Previously Uncatalogued Ethiopic Manuscripts in England

An Ethiopic ms.

This ms. is of a liturgical character. There are intercessory prayers, litany, Hallelujahs, hymns. Athanasius, Basil, Gregory, Epiphanius, Dioscorus, Jacob of Senug, Cyril, and others with whose names liturgies are associated, are mentioned (rubricated).

The ms. contains a large collection of hymns—

(i) associated with people mentioned by name—e.g. Abba Anbasâ, Abba Pantâlêwon, Abba Aragâwi, Abba Ganimâ, Abba Libânos, Elijah, James & John, Jubit (mother of Qirgos), Peter & Paul, Abraham, Andrew, St. Ephraim, St. Helena, St. Stephen, Michael (archangel), the Virgin Mary, John the Baptist, Mary Magdalene.

(ii) associated with classes of persons, e.g. the college of the apostles, priests, virgins, holy women.

(iii) associated with things & occasions, e.g. the festival of the Cross, the rainy season, Eastertide, the emergence of Jesus from Hell, the strewing of branches (Hosanna), the birth of Jesus, His baptism, ascension & resurrection, the vigil of the Nativity, the festival of the watching angels, Dabra-Quesquâm (the place where the Holy Family sojourned in Egypt), Dabra-Tabor (the mount of Transfiguration)

I have not much experience of the dating of Ethiopic mss. If I were to hazard a guess, I should say it might be 18th century.

I can say nothing about the profuse musical notation. The word <u>ézel</u> occurs rubricated several times in the ms. – it is one of the modes of chanting.

<u>The writing on the flysheet. 1st two lines.</u>

The upper line records pen trials (this is common in Eth. mss.). The lower line consists of two words, viz., 'Jesus Christ.'

2nd two lines. Whether this writing, which contains Amharic letters, means anything or is just a scribble, I am unable to say. The writing facing these 4 lines (i.e. the last folio verso of the ms.) is in a poor hand, repeats the top of folio 12 (verso) from the end [f. 35v].

D.W.T. [identity unknown]

Publication (brought to our attention by Mr Richard Andrewes): Laurence Picken, 'A Note on Ethiopic Church Music', *Acta Musicologica*, v. 29 (1957), 41–2.

Formerly known in the library as MS Picken 185, Laurence Picken was apparently the previous owner before the codex passed into the hands of the library.

Catalogue of the Manuscripts

16. Cambridge University Library Or. 2548
Prayers of the Blessed Virgin Mary at Golgotha,
The Mystagogia, and Hymn to Jesus

Parchment, 112 x 88 x 45 mm, two rough-hewn boards covered with tooled leather, coloured linen (red and yellow floral design) is visible between the turn-ins, ridges of three chain stitches are visible through the leather of the spine, headband and tailband, protection sheet + 10 quires, quires 2–6, 8 and 9 have quire numbers, ii + 86 folios (currently unnumbered), top margin 13 mm, bottom margin 22–3 mm, fore-edge margin 8–12 mm, gutter margin 7–8 mm, one column, 11 lines, Gəʿəz, late-19th early 20th century.

Ff. 1r–44v:, Prayers of the Blessed Virgin Mary on Golgotha, Golgota.
Copied and printed several times in its Gəʿəz and Amharic versions, e.g., ጸሎተ፡ እግዝእትነ፡ ማርያም፡ ዘሰኔ፡ ጎልጎታ፡፡ በመቃብረ፡ እግዚእነ፡ ኢየሱስ፡ ክርስቶስ፡፡ Täsfa Press, Addis Ababa 1949 EC.; ጸሎተ፡ እግዝእትነ፡ ማርያም፡ (ዘሰኔ፡ ጎልጎታ፡) በአማርኛ፡፡ Täsfa Press, Addis Ababa 1963 EC.; see also Sylvain Grébaut, 'La prière de Marie au Golgotha', *JA*, vol. 226 (1935), pp. 273–86; and Basset, *Apocryphes*, V, pp. 30–47; Strelcyn, *Lincei*, no. 47, f. 73r; EMML 1213, f. 1a. Cf. CUL, Add. 1863 and Or 979, Ullendorff, *Cambridge*, XXI and XXIII.

Ff. 45r–58v: The Mystagogia, (also known as Doctrine of Mysteries and in Wright's catalogue as *Doctrina Arcanorum*.) Hammerschmidt, *Texte*, pp. 48–72; Lifchitz, *Textes*, pp. 40–52; Velat, *Meʿerāf* I, pp. 215–7; MG 59, pp. 9ff.

Ff. 59r–84r: Hymn to Jesus, Mälkəʾa Iyäsus.

Varia:
1. Ff. 84r – 85v: Scribal Exhortation: 'O brother, listen to me. The one who reads this book or who causes it to be read or who carries it will go to heaven. O my God, Hell is not good. Let our Lady intercede with Jesus Christ to cause me to go to heaven. Amen. Peace.'
2. F. 85v: contains a notice of ownership: 'This book belongs to Abba Gäbrä-Mädhən'. On this folio are also contained crude drawings and pen trials.
3. F. 86r: contains: 1) a crude drawing; 2) beginning of a prayer, 'in the name of the Father and the Son. . . .'; 3) the beginning of a letter in Amharic; 4) pen trials.

A Catalogue of Previously Uncatalogued Ethiopic Manuscripts in England

Notes:
1. The folios are dirty and the gutter side of many are water stained.
2. Additional hands:
    a. A scribal correction hand (small, fine, interlinear hand): 9r, 29r, 31r, 53r, 69v, 75v, 77v, and 82r.
    b. A hand in light blue ink or pencil: 16v, 17v, 18r, 32v, 33v, 80v, 81v, 82r, 82v, 83r, 84v. This hand seldom writes anything intelligible.
    c. A hand in light black: 35r and 35v.
    d. A hand representing the latest owner in blue ink (from an ink pen): 36v, 42v, 44r, 44v, 52r, 57r, 57v, 58r, 58v, 59r, 84r, 84v. In several places this hand has removed the name of the original owner and written in its place the name of the new owner: 'Gäbrä Egziabher' (f. 36v, 42v, 44r, passim) or 'Gäbrä Egziabher and Wälätä Kidan' (presumably his wife).
3. A form for 'Deposited Manuscripts' accompanies the codex. It is marked No 148 and on it is written: 'Rev. Dr B.E. Beck / 26, Hurrell Road / Cambridge CBL 3RH / Ethiopic MS. / From 17 Nov to 18 Dec 1998. / J. Butterworth'. This is followed by a note in pencil in another hand that reads: 'Now donated to U. L.'
4. On f. 58r, in the bottom margin is a crude drawing accompanied by the text: 'this is a picture of Abba Mäzgäbu Jämärä'. Cp. mention of the same person on f. iiv.
5. On ff. 44r and v, the scribe's name is mentioned: Gäbrä Amlak.

Donated by Dr B.E. Beck.

17. Rylands Ethiopic MS 43
Praises of Mary, with musical notation

Parchment, 130 x 70 mm, four Coptic chain stitches attached to two rough-hewn boards, six quires, 50 folios, Gə'əz, 16 lines (except for f. 48v with 12), 18th century. Leather case with strap of woven cloth.

Ff. 1r–26r: Praises of Mary, Wəddase Maryam, with musical notation, arranged for the days of the week: Monday, f. 1r; Tuesday, f. 3v; Wednesday, f. 8r; Thursday, f. 13r; Friday, f. 19r; Saturday, f. 23r; Sunday, f. 26r.

Ff. 29r–32v: Angels Praise Her, Yewedsewa Mäla'ekt lä Maryam.

Ff. 33r–48v: Gate of Light, Anqäṣä bərhan, in a new hand.

For publication information on Praises of Mary and Gate of Light, see Bodleian Ms. Aeth. e.22 above.

Notes:
1. Accompanied by a tag on which is written: 'Eth MS temp # R143816 (Richard Booth).'
2. The first two works are written by the same hand (thought the first has musical notations and the second does not). The third work is in a different hand. All hands appear to be of the 18th century.
3. Ff. 49rv contain pen trials.
4. Ff. 50rv: blank.

The manuscript was purchased from Richard Booth in 1978. It was given the accession number R143816. The records do not indicate if Booth were a private individual or a bookseller.

18. Rylands Ethiopic MS 44
Daily Prayer book and Funeral Ritual

Parchment, 95 x 88 mm, two rough-hewn boards (the front board is broken and the right portion of 40mm is missing; the back board is broken and the left portion of 50 mm is missing), eighteen quires (the first two are protection quires; the first one is bound upside down in relation to the rest), quires 4 and 5 are numbered (2 and 3 respectively, see below), v + 107 folios, for columns and lines per folio see below, Gəʻəz, 17th,18th and 19th century hands.

Ff. 15r–30r: Daily Prayer Book, Mästäbäquʻə, arranged for the days of the week: Introduction, ff. 15r–21v; Monday, ff. 21v–22v; Tuesday, ff. 22v–24v; Wednesday, ff. 24v–25v; Thursday, ff. 25v–27v; Friday, ff. 27r–28v; Saturday, ff. 28v–29r; Sunday [lit., Saturday], ff. 29r–30r.
Cp. Wright, *British Museum*, pp. 88–9, ms CXXXII.

Ff. 30r–70r: Funeral Ritual, *Mäṣḥafä Gənzät*. Published more than once: መጽሐፈ፡ ግንዘት፡፡ ጸሎት፡ ላዕለ፡ ምውታን፡፡ Addis Ababa, 1944 EC; መጽሐፈ፡ ግንዘት፡፡ ጸሎት፡ ላዕለ፡ ምውታን፡፡ Addis Ababa 1962 EC. For the sources and detailed description, see the description of Hs.or.9645 SBPrK Berlin in Six,

Handschriften, no. 57, pp. 162–5; see also Friedrich Erich Dobberahn, 'Der äthiopische Ritus', in Hansjakob Becker-Herman Ühlein (eds) *Liturgie im Angesicht des Todes: Judentum und Ostkirchen*, St. Ottilien 1997, Pietas Liturgica nos. 9 and 10, pt. I, pp. 137–316; *idem.*, 'Der äthiopische Begräbnisritus', pp. 657–84 and pt. II, 1397–1432.

Varia:
1. Ff. ir–ivv(erso): Excerpts from various prayers.
2. Ff. v recto and verso: pen trials.
3. Ff. 1r–2v: fragment of The Orthodox Faith, Retu'a Haymanot, a collection of homilies for various occasions (cp. Wright, *British Museum*, pp. 231–2, ms CCCXLIII.
4. Ff. 3r–7v: Prayer to God, incomplete.
5. F. 70v: fragment of the Gospel of John.
6. F. 71rv: pen trials and practice writing from the Greetings of Mary.
7. Ff. 72r–79v: Prayer to God, incomplete at beginning and end.
8. Ff. 80r–87v: Fragment of a Prayer to Mary, Sälotä Maryam.
9. Ff. 88r–107v: Fragment of the Missal, Qəddase Maryam. See, MG 59.

Notes:
1. This codex is comprised of codex fragments from other sources which have been bound together:
   a. Codex fragment one: Ff. ir–ivv(erso)/protection quire: Excerpts of various prayers. The quire has been inserted upside down in relation to the rest of the codex. The hand is rough and appears to be from the 20th century. The text contains practice writing made up of excerpts of various prayers.
   b. Codex fragment two: Ff. vr(ecto)v(erso)/protection (single) folio: miscellaneous letters without meaning. It is written in a different hand from the first protection quire and from the other quires that follow.
   c. Codex fragment three: Ff. 1r–2v constitute a one-sheet quire and represent an incomplete fragment from Retu'a Haymanot. The text is written in a different hand and appears to come from the 18th century. The cut of the folio along the bottom of this quire is similar to that of the cut along the bottom of the following quire and may indicate a common provenance however, the hand in the following quire appears to be earlier.

d. Codex fragment four: Ff. 3r–7v constitute one quire, with a fragment of a Prayer to God. Folio 3 is cut off at the centre; folio 7 is loose. The text is in two columns per page. The beginning and end of the work are incomplete. There are fourteen lines per page. The text of this quire is written in a hand different than the others and appears to be of the 17th century.

e. Codex fragment five: Ff. 8r–71v constitute quires 3–9, containing the Daily Prayer book (ff. 15r–30r), the funeral ritual Gənzät (ff. 30r–70r), a fragment of the Gospel of John (f. 70v) and pen trials and practice writing from the Greetings of Mary (on f. 71rv). Folios 8–17 constitute the first quire of the work. The second and third quires (ff. 18–27 and 28–38, respectively) are each marked with folio numbers two and three on their first pages. It is written in one column by a late 18th century hand. Twelve lines per page is usual.

f. Codex fragment six: Ff. 80r–87v/quires 10–11 contain a fragment of a Prayer to Mary, Sälotä Maryam.

g. Codex fragment seven: Ff 88r–107v make up the final three quires of the current codex, containing a fragment of the Missal, Qəddase Maryam. The text is laid out in two columns with 14 lines per page. It is fragmentary at both beginning and end. The hand appears to be of the early 18th century.

2. The codex is wrapped in a paper and cellophane wrapper which has the following written on it: 'GEEZ SCRIPT written on / Parchment By DABTARAS / (Songs of Solomon) / 17th/18th Century'.

The library staff report that this codex was acquired through the University collection and was marked simply 'Mrs Cliffe purchase'

19. Rylands Ethiopic MS 45
Prayers of the Blessed Virgin Mary on Golgotha

Parchment (fine), 85 x 54 mm, two Coptic chain stitches attached to two rough-hewn boards, protection sheets front and back + four quires, ii + 44, one column, Gə'əz, 14 lines, 18th century.

Ff. 2r–42r: Prayers of the Blessed Virgin Mary on Golgotha.

The Prayers of the Blessed Virgin Mary on Golgotha is one of the most common of the devotional works of the Ethiopian Orthodox Church. See, for instance, ISAAC EP, p. 77 under the heading 'Sacerdotals' in which he lists twenty six manuscripts where this is the primary work; many other manuscripts include it as a secondary work. See, 16. Cambridge University Library Or. 2548 above and 22. Mac Lennan Codex 03 below.

Notes:
1. Ff. i recto and verso, ii recto and verso, 1rv and 42v–44v: blank.
2. The codex is kept in a cellophane bag which has the following written on it: 'Old Prayer Book / Written in GEEZ by / Dabtaras (? Priests). / 18th/19th century'.

Library staff report that this codex, like the former, was acquired through the University collection and was marked simply 'Mrs Cliffe purchase'

20. Mac Lennan Codex 1
Psalter

Parchment, 110 x 110 x 80 mm, four Coptic chain stitches (repaired) attached to two rough-hewn boards (the back board is broken and stitched in three places with string), protection quire (upside down and backwards) + 22 quires (all bound with a reinforcement strip), iv + 173 folios (currently unnumbered), ff. 1r–152v, 170rv, 171v–172r one column, ff. 153r–169v two columns, top margin 10 mm, bottom margin 22 mm, fore-edge margin 20 mm, gutter margin 10 mm, Gəʿəz, 20 lines, 17th century. Case with leather strap.

Ff. 1r–169v: Psalter. See Bodleian Ms. Aeth. e.22 above.
1. Ff. 1r–131v: 151 Psalms of David.
2. Ff. 132r–145r: The Canticles of the Prophets of the Old and New Testaments.
    a. First Song of Moses (Exod. 15:1–19), ff. 132r–133r.
    b. Second Song of Moses (Deut. 32:1–21), ff. 133r–134v.
    c. Third Song of Moses (Deut. 32:22–43), ff. 134v–136v.
    d. Song of Hannah, mother of Samuel (1 Sam. 2:1–10), ff. 136v–137r.
    e. Prayer of Hezekiah (Isa. 38:10–20), ff. 137v–138r.

f. Prayer of Manasseh, ff. 138r–139r.
   g. Song of Jonah (Jon. 2:3–10), f. 139r.
   h. First Song of the Three Children (Dan. 3:26–45), ff. 139v–140v.
   i. Second Song of the Three Children (Dan. 3:52–6), ff. 140v.
   j. Third Song of the Three Children (Dan. 3:57–88), ff. 140v–141v.
   k. Song of Habakkuk (Hab. 3:1–19), ff. 141v–143r.
   l. Song of Isaiah (Isa. 26:9–20), ff. 143r–144r.
   m. Song of the Virgin Mary (*Magnificat*, Luke 1:46–55), f. 144r.
   n. Song of Zachariah (*Benedictus*, Luke 1:68–79), ff. 144r–145r.
   o. Song of Simeon (*Nunc Dimittis*, Luke 2:29–32), f. 145r.
3. Ff. 145r–152v: Song of Songs divided into five sections.
4. Ff. 153r–164v: Praises of Mary, Wəddase Maryam, arranged for the days of the week: Monday, f. 153r; Tuesday, f. 154r; Wednesday, f. 156r; Thursday, f. 158r; Friday, 160v; Saturday, f. 162r; Sunday, f. 163r.
5. Ff. 164v–169v: Gate of Light, Anqäṣä bərhan.

Varia:
1. Ff. iiiv(erso)–ir: (the protection quire is upside down and backwards in relation to the rest of the codex): fragment of the Hymns to the Four Creatures.
2. F. ivr(ecto): Hymn to Mary, 'All hosts of heaven glorify you', ኢኩሎሙ፡ ሠራዊተ፡ ሰማያት፡. EMML 1593, f. 92a; EMML 2085, f. 144a.
3. F. ivv(erso): Hymn to Mary, probably Chaîne, Répertoire, no. 336, not clear.
4. Ff. 170rv, 171v, 172r: record of income of the church in grain paid by a number of people.
5. Ff. 171r, 172v, 173r: pen trials.

Notes:
1. The sheets are of vellum of medium-to-poor quality.
2. Because of the presence of the reinforcement strips, the thickness of the codex varies from 88mm near the spine to around 70mm at the outer edge.
3. Navigation system: a series of strings sewn into the fore-edge, upper corner of ff. 1, 61, 88, 115, 118, 124, 131, and 145 (white string), ff. 16, 36, 73, and 151 (red string), and ff. 35, 44, and 51 (green string). In a couple of cases, the remnants are substantial.
4. F. 152v: In a later, bold, clear hand, owner of manuscript, is mentioned: Abuna Wäldä Libanos.

5. F. 173v: blank.
6. The codex is designated SGD S1 (supplement one) in the SGD Library of Ethiopian Manuscripts. Dr Ian Mac Lennan granted permission for us to digitize all of his manuscripts and to deposit them in research libraries for access by scholars. This was done and the manuscript is entered as a supplement to the SGD Library of Ethiopian Manuscripts.
7. The codex is currently unfoliated. However, the digital copy of the codex has been foliated digitally. The numbers assigned above to the content correspond to the foliation in the digital codex.

Dr Ian Mac Lennan bought the codex along with other items including a pair of ivory anklets, a hand cross, the impression of Theodore's seal in wax, etc., from the Library of Humphrey Winterton offered by Maggs Brothers in 2003. Since then, Mac Lennan has been able to trace the provenance of the manuscript from the time it was taken in Ethiopia until the time he bought it in London. The Psalter and other items are listed in catalogue 1343, *From the Abbyssianian Expedition to the Mau Mau Insurrection: 100 Years of Military and Naval Operations in /Eastern and North-Eastern Africa (1860s–1960's): Books, Maps, Artifacts, Artwork, Photograhs, Manuscripts, Articles, Pamphlets and Ephemera from the Africana Library of Humphrey Winterton* (London: Maggs Bros Ltd, 2003), lot 50:

> These pieces were purchased at the Derwydd Mansion sale in 1998, their provenance being set out in the catalogue, they 'were brought from Magdala by Dr Rassam and presented by him to Captain Anderson (stepbrother of Mr Alan Stepney Gulston) in 1867; then given by him to Alan Stepney Gulson [sic].' Some of the items still retain the pink-ribboned descriptive labels made for them by Gulston.
>
> i/ Abyssinian Psalter. Described by Gulston as 'Early Christain Relic – A Service Book of the Psalms & case (brought from Magdala 1867 by Dr Rassam). It is in the ancient language of 'Amharic'. Manuscript with many added prayers.' Additionally, there is a inked note, 'Early Christian Service Book of Psalms in Amharic. The bible in Ethiopic & the Cross were taken from a dead Warrior after the fight at Magdala, 1867.' One hundred and seventy-four leaves of vellum with rubricated manuscript text in Ge'ez, sewn in quires of eight leaves, between wooden boards, the lower board split and with cord repair. In its leather carrying-case, worn, the handle snapped. Possibly C18th.

As the listing makes clear, Winterton had purchased the collection of materials including the Psalter from the Gulston estate offered by Sothebys a few years earlier. The psalter and other items are mentioned in 'Llandeilo-Fawr Meeting Report', *Archaeologia Cambbrensis* (1893), pp. 160–1 as part of an account of the association meeting at Derwydd House in which Mr Alan Stepney-Gulston presented several items. On page 160, it lists: 'Amharic MS. –Service-book in case. An early copy of the Book of Psalms, which was taken from the dead body of a priest after the battle of Magdala, 1867'. Elsewhere on the same page, the psalter and other objects are described as 'Abyssinian Curios' which had been 'brought from Magdala. . .by Dr Rassam, and presented by him to Captain Anderson, step-brother to Mrs Stepney-Gulston, in June 1867'. Rassam is, of course, the rather famous Dr Hormuzd Rassam, archaeological assistant to Henry Layard at the excavations of Nineveh and later emissary from the British Government to King Theodore in 1867, where he was taken captive and later freed as a result of the operation at Magdala.

21. Mac Lennan Codex 2
Psalter

Parchment, 170 x 145 mm, four Coptic chain stitches attached to two rough-hewn boards (front cover is broken in two places and loose from the binding; the back board is broken about 95 mm from the spine and stitched in three places), protection sheet + 21 quires + 2 single sheets and 3 single folios at the end, 173 folios (currently unnumbered), ff. 1r–150r one column, ff. 150v–168v two columns, Gəʿəz, 16th or 17th century.

Ff. 1r–168v: Psalter. See Bodleian Ms. Aeth. e.22 above.
1. Ff. 1r–127v : 151 Psalms of David.
2. Ff. 127v–142r: The Fifteen Canticles of the Prophets of the Old and New Testaments
   a. First Song of Moses (Exod. 15:1–19), ff. 127v–129r.
   b. Second Song of Moses (Deut. 32:1–21), ff. 129r–130v.
   c. Third Song of Moses (Deut. 32:22–43), ff. 130v–132v.
   d. Song of Hannah, mother of Samuel (1 Sam. 2:1–10), ff. 132v–133v.
   e. Prayer of Hezckiah (Isa. 38:10–20), ff. 133v–134r.
   f. Prayer of Manasseh, ff. 134r–135v.
   g. Song of Jonah (Jon. 2:3–10), ff. 135v–136r.
   h. First Song of the Three Children (Dan. 3:26–45), ff. 136r–137r.
   i. Second Song of the Three Children (Dan. 3:52–6), ff. 137r–137v.
   j. Third Song of the Three Children (Dan. 3:57–88), ff. 137v–138r.
   k. Song of Habakkuk (Hab. 3:1–19), ff. 138r–140r.
   l. Song of Isaiah (Isa. 26:9–20), ff. 140r–140v.

- m. Song of the Virgin Mary (*Magnificat*, Luke 1:46–55), ff. 140v–141r.
  - n. Song of Zachariah (*Benedictus*, Luke 1:68–79), ff. 141r–141v.
  - o. Song of Simeon (*Nunc Dimittis*, Luke 2:29–32), ff. 141v–142r.
3. Ff. 142r–150r: Song of Songs, divided into five sections.
4. Ff. 150v–163r: Praises of Mary, Wəddase Maryam, arranged for the days of the week: Monday, ff. 150r–151r; Tuesday, ff. 151r–153r; Wednesday, ff. 153r–155v; Thursday, ff. 155v–158v; Friday, ff. 158v–160r ; Saturday, ff. 160r–161r; Sunday, ff. 161r – 163r.
5. Ff. 163r–168v: Gate of Light, Anqäṣä bərhan.

Varia:
1. F. 169r: Some letters in their vowel order.
2. F. 169v: A few lines from the beginning of the hymn to Mary, 'I Glorify your Grace', እሴብሕ ጸጋኪ., in a crude hand.
3. F. 171v: The Gəʿəz alphabet from ሀ to ፕ.
4. F. 170r–171r and 172r–173v blank save for scrawls and scribbles.

Notes:
1. Damage has occurred to the upper fore-edge corner of the codex, from ff. 1 all the way through about f. 127. The upper portion of the pages are shrivelled and darkened and lend credence to the family story reported below.
2. F. 168v: Copied for Täsfa Mika'el, who donated it to the church of Däbrä Ad'ayä.
3. At the time of analysis, a small paper card lay between ff. 105 and 106 on which was written: [recto in a late-19th century/early 20th century hand] M J. Dearman Birchall—Leeds—Leeds Mercury—'The Weddase Maryam, or Encomium of the Blessed Virgin Mary in divisions for the days of the week, account of Theodore's Bible—M.S. taken at Magdala by Major Leveson;' [verso printed in a small cursive font] 'East Sussex Book Hawking Association, Willingdon Vicarage, Hurst Green.'
4. Accompanying the codex is a small piece of paper on which is written in a late 19th century hand: Early Christian Service book of Psalms in Amharic. 'The Bible in Ethiopia & the Cross were taken from a dead Warrior after the fight at Maqdala 1867.'
5. Accompanying the codex, the owner has a picture of Rev. Arthur Lewis and Miriam Vidal Lewis marked 'circa 1890.'

6. Accompanying the codex the owner has a handwritten statement which reads as follows: Ethiopic Psalter. The Emperor Theodore II (Kassa, ex. Shiflá, son of a minor chieftain) on 2nd Dec. 1866 in Gondor before his defeat by Lord Napier. After which he, Emperor Theodore, committed suicide. Given to my grandfather, Rev. A. Lewis, whose parish was in Dharmsala (circa 1890–1900?) (Kashmir) & Punjab by an officer who was in the Abyssinian expedition. Ethiopic Manuscript saved from the fire of one of the 40 churches plundered and set on fire by [the altercation described above.] The little book [codex 3 below] is also an Ethiopic manuscript.
7. Accompanying the codex, the owner has a statement. At the top of the paper is pasted an address label with the following printed on it: Lynes Court, 1 Lynes Yard, Bishop's Cannings, DEVIZES, Wiltshire SN102LS [then in handwriting] 01380–860401. To the right of the address label is the date: 11th Jan 2002. Underneath is written by hand: The enclosed manuscript (psalter?) and small testament? Are loaned by: Mrs Sarah Padwick, Linden House, London Road, Devizes, Wiltshire SN102DS, 01380–721595. Her grandfather is mentioned on the enclosed sheet about the books.
8. The codex is designated SGD S2 in the SGD Library of Ethiopian Manuscripts.

Rev. Arthur Lewis, an English gentleman and missionary in India, received this codex and Mac Lennan Codex 3 from Major Levinson who was part of the Magdala Expedition, 1867. The family history surrounding this codex is that Levinson saw that it was about to be consumed in flames and saved it from the burning debris. Within two months, the Magdala expeditionary force, which had been directed in the most part from the India Office of the British Foreign Service, returned to India. Levinson brought the codices from Magdala to India and gave it to the Rev Lewis. Rev. Lewis was missionary in Dharmsala, in Kashmir and in the Punjab, ca. 1890 to 1900 where, we assume, Major Levinson gave him the manuscripts. By 1904 he had returned to Chardstock and later became vicar of Portishead, Somerset, where he died. The manuscript passed to a granddaughter, Mrs Sarah Padwick (Linden House, London Road, Devizes, Wiltshire SN10 2DS). Dr Ian Mac Lennan bought the codices from Padwick in November 2003.

A Catalogue of Previously Uncatalogued Ethiopic Manuscripts in England

22. Mac Lennan Codex 3
Prayers of the Blessed Virgin Mary on Golgotha and The Mystagogia

Parchment, 75 x 43 x 17 mm, four Coptic chain stitches attached to two rough-hewn boards (front broken and repaired with three stitches), a leather protection strap passes down the spine and continues around the fore edge of the codex. Top margin 4 mm, bottom margin 13 mm, fore-edge margin 7 mm, gutter margin 3–4 mm, one column, Gəʿəz, 19th century. Small leather case with strap.

Ff. 1r–27r: Prayers of the Blessed Virgin Mary on Golgotha, ጸሎተ፡ እግዝእትነ፡ ማርያም፡ ዘሰኔ፡ ጎልጎታ፡. See 16. Cambridge University Library, Or. 2548 above and 19. Rylands Ethiopic MS 45 above.

Ff. 27v–39r: The Mystagogia, ትምህርተ፡ ኅቡአት፡. See 16. Cambridge University Library, Or. 2548 and 19. Rylands Ethiopic MS 45 above.

Ff. 39v–40r *Asmat* prayer to make the enemy speechless.
በስመ፡ አብ፡ ... ጸሎት፡ በእንተ፡ ጅጅጅናኤል፡ ፪፡ ጊዜ፡ ምርካኤል፡ ፪፡ ጊዜ፡ ብድፍናኤል፡ ፪፡ ጊዜ፡ ... ዶልል፡ ልቦሙ፡ ወእስር፡ ልሳኖሙ፡ ወዝጋህ፡ አፉሆሙ፡ እስር፡ እደዊሆሙ፡ ወአገሪሆሙ፡ ለጸርየ፡ ...

Miniatures, all in twentieth-century hand:
1. F. IIIv: An angel brandishing a sword.
2. F. IVr: An angel brandishing a sword.

Varia:
1. Ff. IIv–IIIr: *Asmat* prayer against headache.
   በስመ፡ አብ፡ በል፡ ኑፋ፡ ለፈናፍ፡ ፪፡ ጊዜ፡ ሰፈለፈናፍ፡ ፪፡ ጊዜ፡ ...
2. F. IVv: *Asmat* prayer against headache.
   በስመ፡ አብ፡ ... ጸሎት ፡ በእንተ ፡ ሕማም፡ ቁርፀት፡ በኔጋኮስ፡ ጸሎት፡ በእንተ፡ ሕማም፡ ውግአት፡ አአንተ፡ (sic) ረቢ፡ ...

Notes:
1. The codex is designated SGD S3 in the SGD Library of Ethiopian Manuscripts.

Regarding provenance, see under Mac Lennan Codex 2 above.

23. Mac Lennan Codex 4
Prayer against the Tongue of People

Parchment, 54 x 40 x 21 mm, two Coptic chain stitches attached to two rough-hewn boards, five quires, 32 folios, top margin 3 mm, bottom margin 5 mm, fore-edge margin 2–3 mm, gutter margin 2–3 mm, one column, Gəʽəz, 9 lines, 19th century. This miniature codex comes in an amulet case with a loop of leather through which to pass a string for wearing as an amulet.

Ff. 3r–31v: Prayer against the tongue of people, ጸሎት፡ በእንተ፡ ልሳነ፡ ሰብእ፡.
S. Grébaut, 'L'Hymne-invocation Lesâna sab'e', *Aethiopica. Revue philologique*, vol. 3 (1936), pp. 6–12; MG 59, pp. 271ff. See Strelcyn BL, 48.

Notes:
1. Ff. 1rv–2r and 32rv: blank.
2. F. 2v: a crude drawing of an angel with geometric boxes above and below.
3. F. 30r: the original owner's name was removed and replaced with Wäldä Gäbrəʼl Ahähu. See the same name written in pen in later hand on f. 31v.
4. The codex is designated SGD S4 in the SGD Library of Ethiopian Manuscripts.

Bought by Dr Ian Mac Lennan in Ethiopia in the Lalibela area, around 1997.

Chapter Two: Quire Maps and Notes

1. Bodleian MS Aeth. b.2
Seven Loose Folios with Illustrations
taken from One or Two Codices on the Saints

This 'manuscript' is not bound and is comprised only of loose folios.

2. Bodleian MS Aeth. d.9
The Miracles of the Blessed Virgin Mary

Two paper endsheets.

Protection Quire

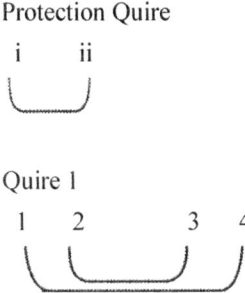

Quire 1

F. 3 has a hole near the outer edge. F. 4 has a hole near the upper edge. This quire contains the first work of the codex which is in a cruder and different hand than the main work. The columns are very uneven in this quire, e.g. f. 1r, column one is 70 mm wide while column two is 83mm wide.

Quire 2

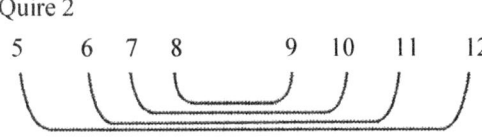

This quire contains the beginning of the main work of the codex. It is written in a fine hand in two columns. On f. 5r, lines 1, 2, 5, 6 in both columns are in red ink. On f. 6v, the shade of red ink turns very brown and shifts slowly back toward red by f. 8r. Several reinforcement strips are visible between folios 12 and 13.

Quire 3

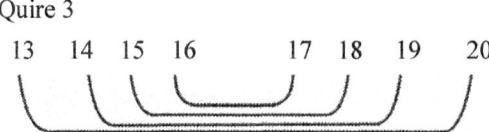

F. 13r has a quire number ፪ (two) written in the upper left corner in black ink. F. 18 has an oval hole 33 mm long near the inside margin; two smaller holes as well. No reinforcement strips are visible between ff. 20 and 21.

Quire 4

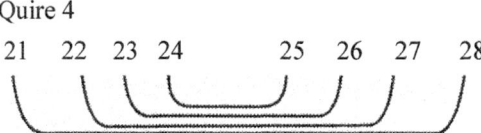

F. 21r has a quire number ፫ (three) written in the upper left corner in black ink. This quire number is written entirely in red ink. F. 22 has a hole in the centre column. F. 23 has a tear and stitching (25 mm) in the lower centre of the page. F. 24r contains two inserted texts over column one. The top one is in large pencil letters; the lower one is in red ink enclosed in a box with jagged ends. There is something similar over column two on f. 25v. Several reinforcing strips are visible between folios 28 and 29.

Quire 5

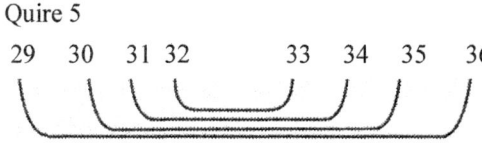

F. 29r has a quire number ፬ (four) in the upper left corner mainly in black ink, but with black lines reinforced in red ink. F. 31 has a tear and stitching (25 mm) on the upper edge. F. 32 has a large C-shaped tear and stitching (110 mm) near the outer edge. Several reinforcing strips are visible between ff. 36 and 37.

Quire 6

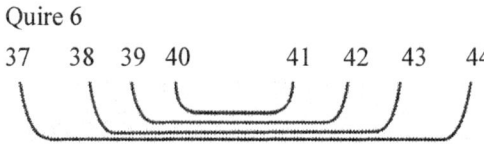

Quire Maps and Notes

F. 37r has the quire number ⲉ̄ (five) in the upper left corner. It is written all in red ink. Ff. 38 and 43 are cut off about 2 cm from the fore edge of the page, reducing the fore-edge margin. Several reinforcing strips are visible between ff. 44 and 45.

Quire 7

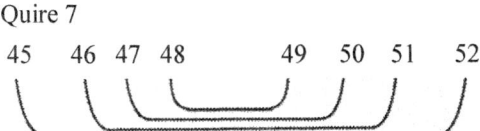

There is no quire number on f. 45r. There are no reinforcing strips between ff. 52 and 53, though the inside stitching of the quire can be seen clearly between ff. 48 and 49. Large portions of the vellum of ff. 50 and 51 are translucent.

Quire 8

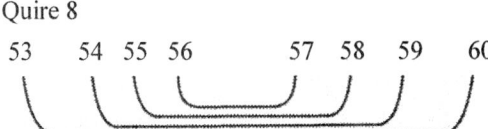

There is no quire number on f. 53r. F. 54 has a large oval hole (40 mm) near the fore edge. Ff. 59 and 60 are nearly translucent. F. 59 has a small hole in the upper fore edge of the page. Several reinforcing strips are visible between ff. 60 and 61.

Quire 9

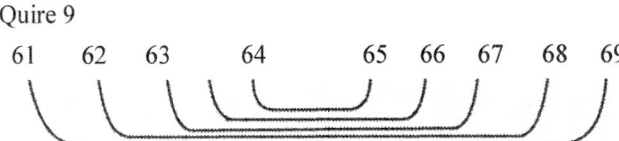

There is no quire number on f. 61r. A folio stub is visible between ff. 63 and 64. By folio stub we mean that the sheet has been cut in such a way that about 1 cm extends on one side past the centre fold. We do not think that these represent folios that were once present in the codex and which have been cut out. In all these cases, the text on the extant folios continues uninterrupted. Instead, we assume these to be intentional half-sheets (perhaps so as not to waste a smaller piece of vellum) inserted with the stub as a means of fastening the sheet into the quire. F. 61 has an oval hole (20 mm) near the bottom fore edge of the page. A folio stub is visible between ff. 63 and 64. F. 66 has an oval hole (20 mm) in the top centre of the page. F. 66 has a small tear and stitching on the centre of the page towards the spine.

Quire 10

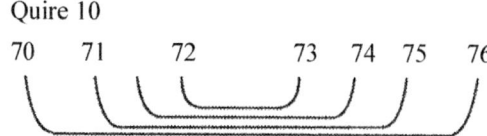

F. 70r has no quire number. A folio stub is visible between ff. 71 and 72. Sheets comprised of folios 70/75 and 71/76 are shorter than the other sheets by about 10 mm. F. 75 has a hole, tear and stitching in the lower, fore-edge corner. F. 76 has a small hole in the fore-edge margin. Several reinforcement strips are visible between ff. 76 and 77.

Quire 11

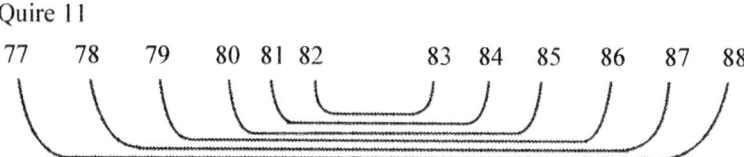

F. 77r has no quire number. Though the even number of folios is consistent with a simple quire of six sheets, there are problems in explaining this quire. Several of the folios are distinctive, either cut short (ff. 85 and 86), or else the vellum is very thick (ff. 82 and 83) or very fine (f. 80) or very translucent (f. 77). One would expect the other folios that make up the sheet to have the same characteristics. They do not. Thus, it would appear there are some mysteries in the structure of this quire which the current binding makes it impossible to solve. Several reinforcement strips are visible between ff. 88 and 89.

Quire 12

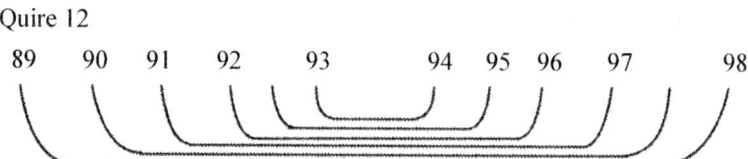

F. 89r has no quire number. There is a folio stub between ff. 92 and 93. The edge of a folio is barely visible, we believe, between ff. 97 and 98.

Two paper endsheets.

Quire Maps and Notes

3. Bodleian MS. Aeth. d.11
Hymns (Zəmmare) and Anthems (Mäwas'ət) for the Whole Year
with musical notation

Protection Quire

i   ii

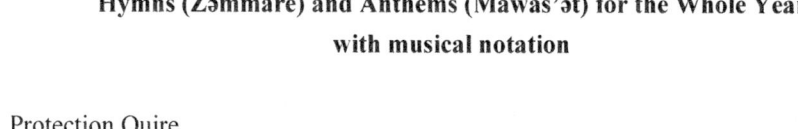

This sheet has been full prepared for text (margins, two columns, prickings and 26 lines) though it has no text.

Quire 1

1   2 3 4   5 6 7   8

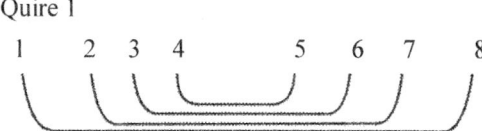

F. 2 has a small hole in the middle of the page. F. 3 has a hole in the lower fore edge of the page. F. 5 has a long tear and stitching (50 mm) on the fore edge. F. 6 has a small hole in the centre of the page. F. 7r, column one has thirty six lines of text, plus musical notations, written on a page marked out for 26 lines. The text in column two observes the lines.

Quire 2

9   10 11 12   13 14 15   16

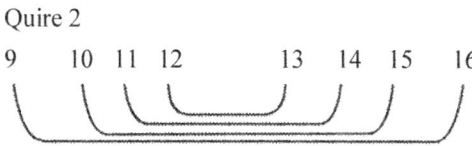

F. 10 has two small holes toward the outer margin. There is additional writing and musical notation above the main text on f. 14v, 15r and 15v. Cp. ff. 17v, 18r and 19r below and following. F. 16 has a small and a large hole near the spine at the top of the page.

Quire 3

17   18 19 20   21 22 23   24

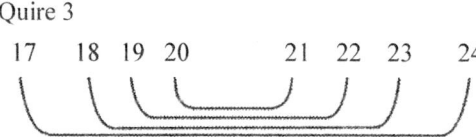

F. 21 has a tear and stitching (32 mm) near the fore-edge margin.

A Catalogue of Previously Uncatalogued Ethiopic Manuscripts in England

Quire 4

F. 25 has a small hole in the lower centre. F. 32 has a hole in the upper, outer edge. F. 32 v has a small symbol in the outer margin

Quire 5

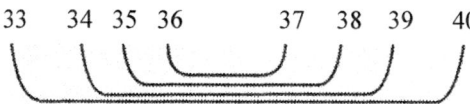

F. 37 has a tear and stitching (30 mm) near the outer, bottom edge of the page. F. 39r has a small symbol in the inner margin in black ink. It is 6 mm wide.

Quire 6

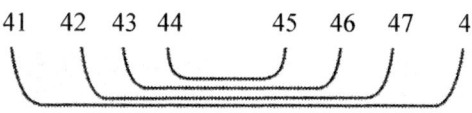

Quire 7

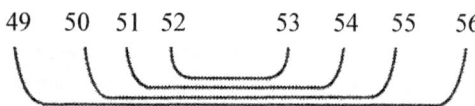

F. 51 has a small hole in the upper, centre portion of the page.

Quire 8

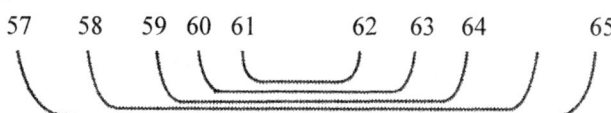

F. 58 is cut irregularly, being narrower and shorter near the centre of the book. F. 60 has a small hole in the bottom margin; a smaller hole is above. F. 61 has a small hole in the lower centre. A folio stub is visible between ff. 64 and 65.

Quire 9

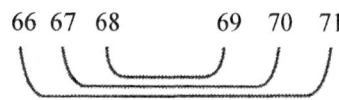

F. 68 has writing in modern ink pen in the lower margin. F. 69r, column 2, line 8 is the last of the base text.

4. Bodleian MS. Aeth. d.14
Antiphonary (*Dəgg^wa*) with musical notation

Protection Sheet

F. 1r : a strip of vellum ca. 35 mm wide has been laid over the outer edge of the folio and stitched onto the vellum sheet. Since the folio is fully intact, the purpose for this is unclear. F. 1 has a hole near the spine. The sheet has been fully prepared to receive text (3 columns per page, pricking and at least some lines scored on the folios), but was not used for the main text.

Quire 1

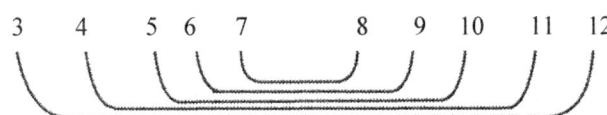

F. 3 is written in three columns and contains the opening of the work. There is writing without musical notation in the top third of the page (in all columns). Immediately below these is a *haräg* (of red and black) that extends across the page. The bottom half of the page (i.e. the text below the *haräg*) has lines in red ink on lines 1, 2, 5 and 6. This text (below the *haräg*) has musical notation. A line of text has been written above column one. F. 7 has a hole in the bottom centre of the page. F. 12 has a hole in the bottom fore edge of the page.

Quire 2

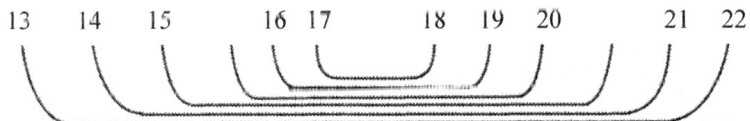

F. 13r has the quire letters/number in black letters with a circle of black and red dots around it. There is a folio stub between ff. 15 and 16 and between 20 and 21. F. 17 has a large hole (23 mm) in the upper centre. F. 22 has a hole in the upper fore edge of the page.

Quire 3

F. 23r has a quire number with red encircling it. F. 23r has writing in the upper margin. F. 24 has two holes on the bottom of the page. F. 25 has a hole, a tear and stitching in the lower fore edge. F. 26 has holes in the upper centre and lower centre of the page. F. 29 has four medium holes and several smaller ones in the outer column. F. 31 has a hole in the inner column.

Quire 4

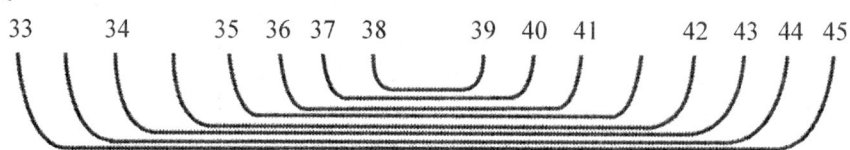

F. 33r has quire letters/numbers in the upper left corner. The first two letters are surrounded in small red dots. The third letter is much smaller and in red ink. F. 33 has a burn hole just above the inner column. A folio stub is visible between ff. 33 and 34 and between ff. 34 and 35 and between ff. 41 and 42. F. 37 has a huge (230 mm) tear and stitching along an irregular path in the lower fore edge of the page. F. 43 has a huge hole in the fore edge. F. 43r has musical notations above the text in only columns 1 and 2. The text in column three is in a larger (and perhaps different) hand. F. 44 has a hole in the upper outer edge. Ff. 44r and v are written in only two columns and have musical notation.

Quire 5

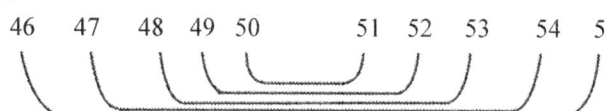

F. 46r has no quire number. F. 46 has a small hole in the outer column. F. 46r is the beginning of a new work with musical notation. Lines 1, 2, 3, 6, 7, 21 and 22 are in red ink. F. 47 has a large hole in the lower portion of the page. F. 48 the outer edge is cut off toward the bottom. F. 51 has two large holes in the lower fore edge. F. 51r, column 3, five lines below the bottom is a nice, small illustration of an ornamental cross made of red and black ink. It measures 15 x 12 mm. F. 52 has two holes centre and bottom. F. 54 has a small hole at the top. F. 55 has three holes in the lower portion, one of them large.

Quire Maps and Notes

Quire 6

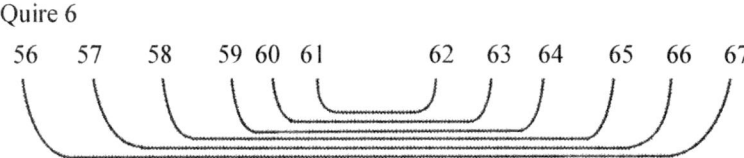
56 57 58 59 60 61   62 63 64 65 66 67

F. 56r has no quire number. F. 59 has two large holes on the inside column. F. 63 has a large hole near the spine. F. 66v is the end of the work. A small red and black *haräg* is located at the bottom of the third column. On f. 67r, only the first column has text. F. 67v has three columns of neat text without musical notation.

Quire 7

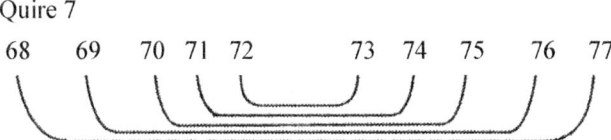
68   69   70 71 72   73 74 75   76 77

There is no quire number on f. 68r. F. 68r is the beginning of a new work with musical notation. Lines 1, 2, 5, 6, 20 and 21 in all three columns are written in red ink.

Quire 8

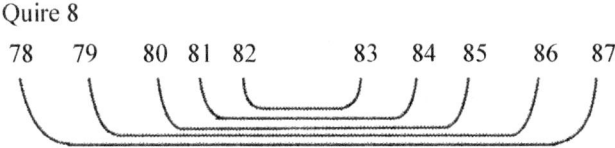
78   79   80 81 82   83 84 85   86 87

F. 78r may have quire letters/numbers. They are written in black ink beside the first line of text rather than in the usual space above the first line of text. F. 79 has a hole in the outer edge. F. 85 has a large hole in the outer column.

Quire 9

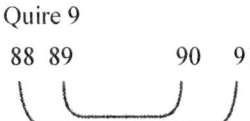
88 89   90   91

F. 88r has no quire number. F. 88 has a hole in the lower centre of the page. F. 89 has a large hole in the lower fore edge. F. 91r, columns one and two have text with musical notation; column three is without musical notation, though in a neat hand. The lower portion of column two is text in a very rough hand. F. 91v has neat text in columns one, two and three, but crude writing in the lower margin.

5. Bodleian Ms. Aeth. e.22
Psalter

Protection Quire

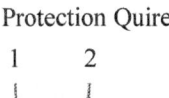

This protection sheet has not been prepared to receive text. F. 1r has a red stain that covers the bottom fore-edge quarter of the folio. In pencil in the middle of the page is says: 'Ms. Aeth. e. 22.'

Quire 1

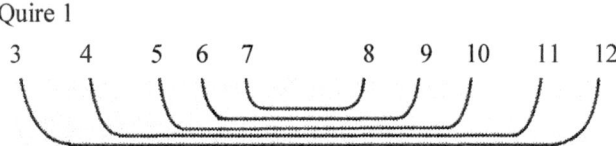

F. 3r begins the new work. The text is in a single column. The pages of text from ff. 3r through 129v are in one column. Every sentence ends at the right side of the page and with the sentence ending symbol in a distinctive form: . F. 3r has a *haräg* in black ink at the top with something like wings on either end. Lines 1, 2, (an interlinear line of text has been written between lines 4 and 5) 7, 8, 14, 15, and 18 are in red ink. F. 3 has white threads sewn into the upper fore edge of the page some 15 mm from the top. F. 8 has green threads sewn into the upper fore edge of the page some 15 mm from the top. F. 8v has a line of alternating black and red dots near the bottom. F. 11 has a small hole near the bottom fore edge of the text area.

Quire 2

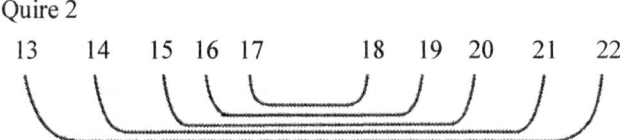

F. 14r has two lines of additional small text written in the lower margin. F. 15v has a line of black and red dots across the page. There is also interlinear writing. Interlinear writing on ff. 16r, 17v, 18r, 18v, etc. F. 22 has a small hole in the bottom margin. F. 22v has a line of red and black dots across the page.

Quire 3

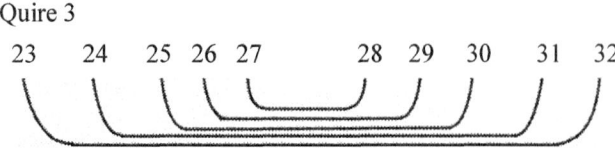

F. 25r has an erasure on line 13. Nothing has been written in the space. F. 26r has a line of interlinear text. F. 27 has a small burn hole near the bottom of the page. Ff. 27v and 28r have single words circled in pencil. F. 29r has a line of text in the upper margin. F. 29v has an erasure of the entire bottom line of text. Nothing is written in the space. F. 31v has a line of black and red dots across the page near the bottom. F. 31 has a yellow thread sewn into the upper fore-edge corner of the page some 15 mm from the top.

Quire 4

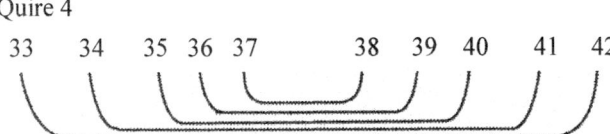

F. 35 has a small section of the lower fore-edge corner missing. F. 37 has two lines of text written in a later hand in ink pen. One is above the column; the other between lines 9 and 10. F. 38 has two sections of the outer edge of the page that are missing. One is in the upper fore edge; the other in the centre of the bottom. F. 39 has red and black threads sewn through the upper fore edge of the page some 15 mm from the top. F. 39r has a line of red and black dots across the page in the centre. F. 41v has three words written in a later hand in the inside margin of the text at the top of the page.

Quire 5

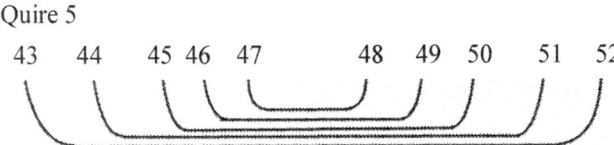

F. 44r has an interlinear line of text. F. 44v has a word written in the upper margin in large pencil letters. F. 44v has a line of red and black dots across the page in the centre. F. 47r has a word written in the upper margin in large pencil letters. F. 48r has a line of small text written in the lower margin.

Quire 6

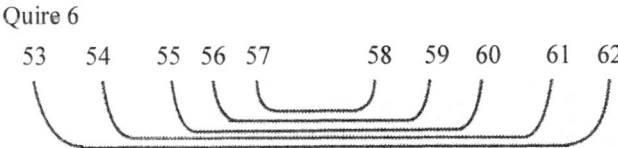

F. 53r has a line of red and black dots across the page in the centre. Ff. 58r – 61v have an extraordinary number of lines of text that begin with the letter ⟨ꝏ⟩. This continues even into the following folios.

Quire 7

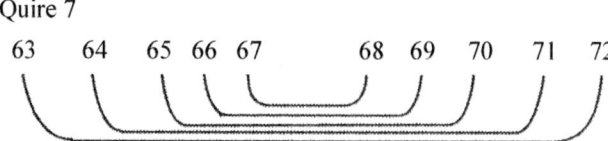

F. 63v has a word written in pencil in the upper column. F. 63v has a line of red and black dots across the page near the top. F. 64r has a water stain that affects but does not make illegible many letters on the upper portion of the page. ff. 65r and 65v each have a line of small text in the upper margin. F. 68 has a small hole in the fore-edge centre of the page. F. 69 has an interlinear line of text near the bottom. F. 71r has a line of red and black dots across the page near the top.

Quire 8

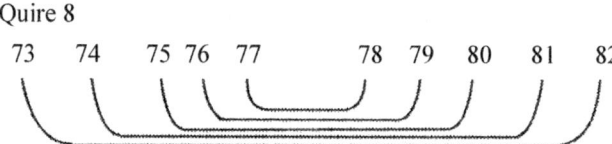

F. 76 has red threads sewn into the upper fore edge of the page some 13 mm from the top. F. 76r has a line of red and black dots across the page near the top. There are also lines of interlinear text. F. 77 has a small hole in the fore-edge margin.

Quire 9

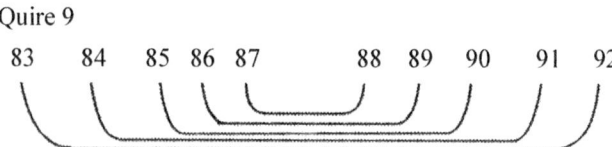

In three places on ff. 84r and v, the letter ⵉ has been added in front of the line of text. F. 85 has a large oval hole (25 mm long) near the bottom of the text area. F. 86v has an interlinear line of text. F. 87v has a word written twice in the upper margin in large pencil letters. F. 88 has red threads sewn into the upper fore edge of the page some 10 mm from the top. F. 88r has a line of red and black dots across the page near the top. F. 89 has three small holes in the vellum near the top. F. 90v has an erasure in the fourth line and text rewritten in the space. F. 91v has an interlinear line of text.

Quire 10

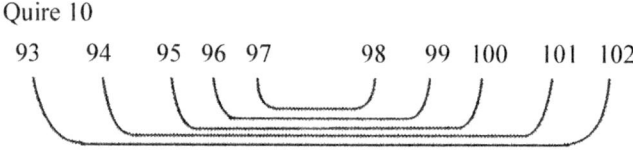

F. 98r has a line of red and black dots across the page near the bottom. F. 98v has an interlinear line of text. F. 99r has two lines of text in the upper margin. F. 99v has a word circled in pencil. F. 100 has a small hole near the spine in the centre. F. 100v

Quire Maps and Notes

has a word written in the upper margin in large pencil letters. F. 100v has a line of red and black dots across the page at the bottom. F. 101 has a hole at the fore edge.

Quire 11

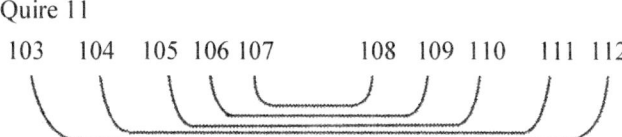

103   104   105 106 107   108 109 110   111 112

F. 103 has a small hole in the fore-edge centre of the page. F. 106 has a hole in the upper fore-edge corner of the page. F. 106r has a line of red and black dots across the page near the bottom. F. 111v has a word written in the upper margin in large pencil letters. There is also an interlinear line of text. F. 112r has a line of red and black dots across the page near the top. F. 112v has a line of small text written below the column of text.

Quire 12

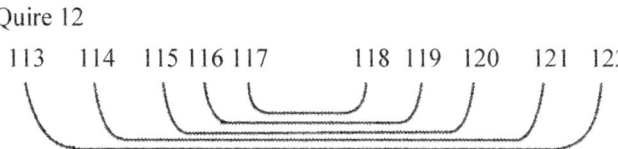

113   114   115 116 117   118 119 120   121 122

Ff. 120v and 121r has a long series of lines whose texts all begin with the same four letters and in which the second and fourth letters are in red ink. F. 121v has an interlinear line of text. F. 122r has an interlinear line of text as well as four lines of additional small text written in the lower margin.

Quire 13

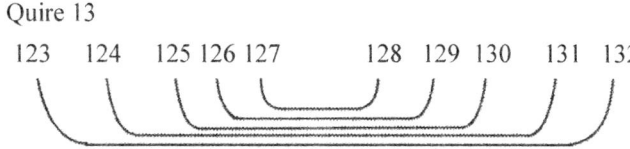

123   124   125 126 127   128 129 130   131 132

F. 123r has a line of red and black dots across the page near the bottom. F. 124v has four lines of additional small text written in the lower margin. F. 125 has a hole in the centre of the text area. F. 130r After 8 lines of single column text and a line of six symbols , a new text begins. It is laid out in two columns. Lines 1, 2 6, 7 and 11 in both columns are in red ink. F. 131 has a large hole on the inside margin and into the text area. F. 131v has some text circled in column two near the bottom.

Quire 14

133　　134　　135 136 137　　　138 139 140　　141 142
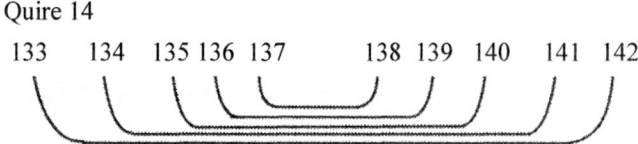

F. 134 has a hole in the centre column.

Quire 15

143 144 145　　　146　147　148
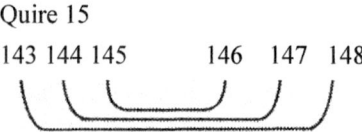

F. 146 has a hole in the upper part of the page near the spine.

Quire 16

149　　150
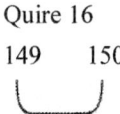

F. 149v The text ends in the middle of column two with two symbols ⟨symbol⟩ followed by a line of four more. The next two lines are erased, though some letters show through. Following are two lines of text in pencil. Then begins a longer text in a crude but trained hand which goes from the last seven lines of column two and onto ff. 150r and v.

6. Bodleian MS. Aeth. e.23
Psalter

Protection Sheet

　i　　1

F. i has been cut off such that it is only 30 mm wide. F. 1r centre top: 'MS Aeth. e. 23'. For discussion of other texts on this folio and 1v, see above.

Quire 1

2　　3　4　5　　　6　7　8　　9
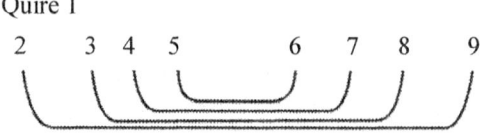

F. 2r is the beginning of the work. There is no *haräg*. Lines 1 and 17 (first and last) are in red ink. The text is in a single column. The pages of text from ff. 2r through 153ra are in one column. Every sentence ends at the right side of the page and with the sentence ending symbol ❖. New sentences are begun on the next line. The relatively large format of this codex leaves a lot of room in the right margins of the folios. There are water stains near the top centre of the codex in this quire, especially near the beginning (ff. 2–5). F. 4 has a hole in the lower outer corner. F. 6 has a hole in the upper centre. F. 8 has small holes in the outer centre (one of which is a burn hole) and one larger hole near the bottom close to the inner spine. F. 9 has two holes in the outer margin. F. 9v has a substantial section marker made up of two parallel lines going across the page in alternating red and black dots. The dots are connected such that they form one continuous line (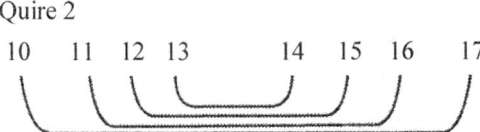). Since there is another form of red and black lines in this codex, we will refer to this as form one. Between the two lines are six of the standard symbols used for sentence endings in this manuscript ❖. The lines are about 8 mm apart.

Quire 2
10 11 12 13   14 15 16   17

Ff. 10 and 17 wore through their fold crease and have been reattached by stitching them to ff. 11 and 16 respectively. Rather than stitching with string, the stitching is done with a narrow strip (3 mm) of leather. F. 16 has a hole in the outer margin. F. 17 The vellum is quite thin and brittle and there is a tear from the top down into the text area.

Quire 3
18   19 20 21   22 23 24   25

F. 18r In the top margin a word is written. This folio also has a substantial section marker made up of two parallel lines going across the page in alternating red and black dots. The dots are in this pattern (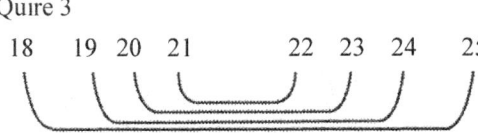). Between them are three of the standard symbols used for sentence endings in this manuscript ❖. F. 19 has a (burn?) hole in the lower, outer margin. F. 20 has a hole in the outer margin. F. 23r interlinear word above bottom line of text.

A Catalogue of Previously Uncatalogued Ethiopic Manuscripts in England

Quire 4

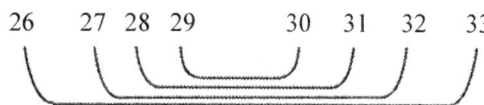

F. 27 has red thread sewn into the upper fore-edge corner of the page some 15 mm from the top. F. 27v has a substantial section marker made up of two parallel lines going across the page in alternating red and black dots. The dots are in pattern number one ( ). Between them are three of the standard symbols used for sentence endings in this manuscript ❖. F. 31 has a hole in the upper centre of the page. F. 33r has an erasure in line 10 with three words of text overwritten in a new hand.

Quire 5

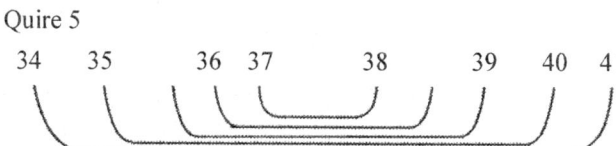

There are folio stubs visible between ff. 35 and 36 and between folios 38 and 39. F. 39r has a substantial section marker made up of two parallel lines going across the page in alternating red and black dots. The dots are in pattern number one (▬▬▬▬▬▬▬▬). Between them are three of the standard symbols used for sentence endings in this manuscript ❖.

Quire 6

42 43 44 45   46 47 48   49

F. 48 has three holes in it including one large one directly in the centre. F. 48 has red threads sewn into the upper fore-edge of the page at about 18 mm from the top.

Quire 7

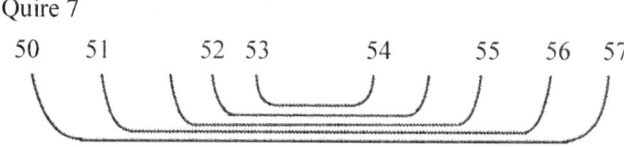

F. 51r has one line of text (line 16) that has a line drawn over it and under it. There are folio stubs visible between ff. 51 and 52 and between ff. 54 and 55. F. 52 has three small holes. F. 55 has red threads sewn into the upper fore-edge corner of the page about 15 mm from the top. F. 55v has a substantial section marker made up of two parallel lines going across the page in alternating red and black dots. The dots are in pattern number one (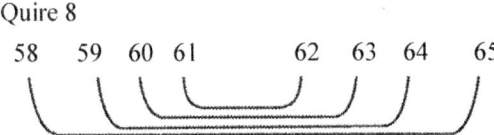). There are no symbols between the lines.

Quire 8
58   59   60   61   62   63   64   65

F. 59 has a large hole (32 mm) in the lower fore-edge portion. F. 63 has a hole and a tear at the bottom of the page.

Quire 9
66   67   68   69   70   71   72   73

F. 66 has a tear and stitching (35 mm) in the upper fore-edge corner. F. 66r has a substantial section marker made up of two parallel lines going across the page in alternating red and black dots. The dots are in pattern number one (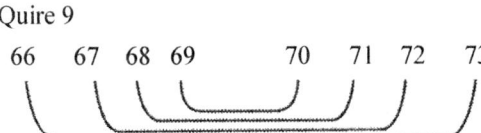). There are no symbols between the lines. F. 72 has a hole in the lower fore-edge portion of the page. F. 73 has a division marker written in (after the fact) between two lines of text. It consists of a single line of alternating red and black characters (< < < < < <) that extends the entire width of the text area.

Quire 10
74   75   76 77   78   79   80   81

There are folio stubs visible between ff. 75 and 76 and between ff. 78 and 79. F. 76 has a hole in the centre, inner portion of the page. F. 77v has a substantial section marker made up of two parallel lines going across the page in alternating red and black dots. The dots are in pattern number one (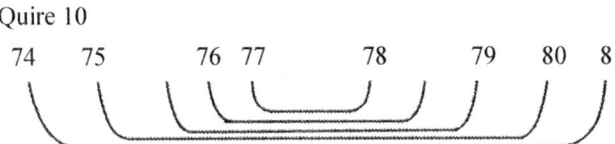). There are no symbols between the lines.

Quire 11
82   83   84   85   86   87   88   89

F. 83 has an erasure on line 14 and rewritten text of three letters in a different hand. F. 84 has a tear and stitching (42 mm) in the centre of the page. F. 86 has a hole in the upper, outer edge. F. 87 has a red thread sewn into the upper fore-edge corner about 20 mm from the top. F. 87v has a substantial section marker made up of two parallel lines going across the page in alternating red and black dots. The dots are in pattern number one (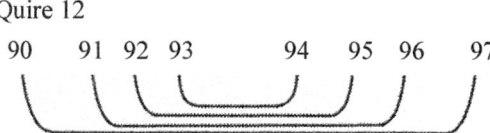). There are no symbols between the lines. F. 89v has an erasure (line 16) of the sentence ending symbol and the overwritten addition of a word.

Quire 12

90　91　92　93　　　94　95　96　　97

F. 94 has red thread sewn into the upper fore-edge corner of the page about 15 mm from the top. This folio also has a tear and stitching (40 mm) on the bottom of the page. F. 94r has a substantial section marker made up of two parallel lines going across the page in alternating red and black dots. The dots are in pattern number one (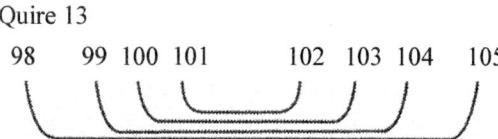). There are no symbols between the lines. Ff. 97v and 98r are tinged to a darker shade than the other folios.

Quire 13

98　　99　100　101　　　102　103　104　　105

F. 100 has a sizeable hole in the fore edge. F. 102 has a small hole on the inside margin. F. 102r has an erasure in line 13 and three words overwritten in a different hand.

Quire 14

106　107　　　108 109　　　110　111　　　112　113

Ff. 105v and 106r are tinged to a darker shade than the other folios. F. 106 has a long, irregular tear and stitching (100 mm) on the fore edge. There is a folio stub visible between ff. 107 and 108. There is also the bent remains of a folio stub visible between ff. 111 and 112. This stub has clearly worked its way back under the fold from its original place between ff. 107 and 108. F. 107r has an erasure (line 7) and overwritten text of three words in a different hand or pen. F. 108v has an interlinear line of text. F. 110 has red thread sewn into the upper, fore-edge margin about 15 mm from the top. F. 110r has a substantial section marker made up of two parallel lines going across the

Quire Maps and Notes

page in alternating red and black dots. However, this is not the same as in the other cases. In this case, 1) the lines are very close together (ca 3 mm); 2) they go only a portion of the way across the page, then a single line continues to the end of the page; 3) the dots that make up the line are not connected, nor are they as even as the ones in the previous lines, 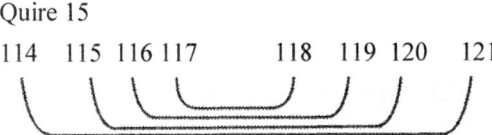. We will refer to this as line form two. There are no symbols between the lines. F. 112r has an interlinear word.

Quire 15
114   115 116 117   118   119 120   121

F. 117 has a crack 30 mm long in the parchment at the fore edge.

Quire 16
122   123 124 125   126   127   128   129

F. 122r has a line of dots in the second format 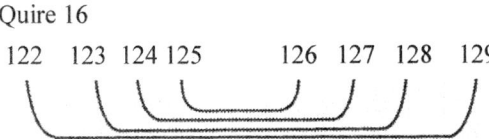. F. 122 has a large missing portion of the lower centre portion of the page and a tear that extends upward from the hole about 40 mm. F. 125 has red thread sewn into the fore edge of the page. This one is lower than the rest at about 60 mm from the top. F. 125r has a line of dots in the second format. F. 126 has a hole in the lower, fore-edge portion. F. 127 has a sizeable hole in the lower centre of the page. F. 127r has a line of text in the top margin in a rougher, though trained, hand. F. 128 has a hole in the lower fore edge. F. 128v has water stains at the top of the page. F. 129 has some portions of the leather missing at the bottom of the page.

Quire 17
130   131   132 133   134   135   136   137

F. 130r has an erasure without overwritten text. F. 130v has an interlinear line of text. There are folio stubs visible between ff. 131 and 132 and between ff. 134 and 135. F. 134v has a word with a line written above and below it. F. 137v has a substantial section marker made up of two parallel lines going across the page in alternating red and black dots. The dots are in pattern number one (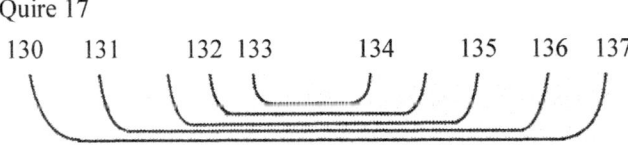). There are no symbols between the lines which are spaced about 10 mm apart.

A Catalogue of Previously Uncatalogued Ethiopic Manuscripts in England

Quire 18

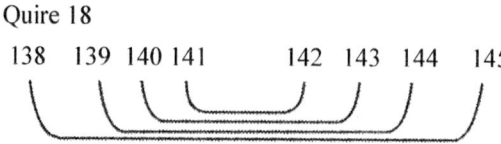
138 139 140 141   142 143 144   145

F. 141v has an erasure in line 16 with two words rewritten into the space in a different hand or pen. F. 143 has a small hole in the fore edge. F. 144v has an erasure and a rewritten word. F. 145r has an erasure and a rewritten two words in a different hand or pen.

Quire 19

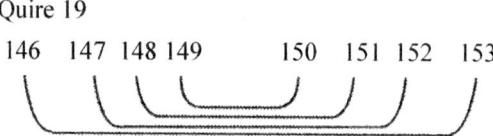
146 147 148 149   150 151 152   153

F. 146 is torn at the middle seam about 65 mm up the page from the bottom. F. 150r has some words through which lines have been struck. F. 153r has six lines of text in one column. Below this is a single line in form one (▬▬▬▬▬▬▬▬▬▬), followed by text in two column and in a much smaller hand. This text continues in two columns through f. 153v.

Quire 20

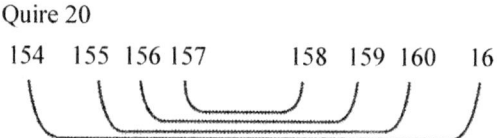
154 155 156 157   158 159 160   161

F. 154 begins a new text in one column and in the hand of the previous text (ff. 2r through 153r). The first line of text is in red ink. There are eight lines of text in two columns written in the upper margin of this folio. F. 155 has a small hole near the outer edge. F. 159 has a sizeable hole in the inside centre of the page. F. 161v has the conclusion of the work in one column. The next folio (which is also on a new quire) begins in two columns.

Quire 21

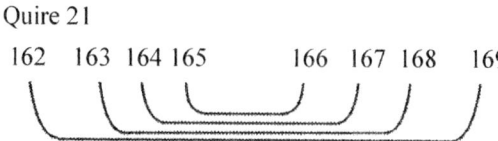
162 163 164 165   166 167 168   169

F. 162r begins a new work in two columns. Lines 1, 3, 15, and 17 in both column are in red ink. F. 165r has some words with lines drawn through them.

Quire 22
170 171

F. 171r, written in two columns, has a substantial section marker at the bottom of column one (after 11 lines of text). It is made up of two parallel lines going across the column width in alternating red and black dots. The dots are in pattern number one (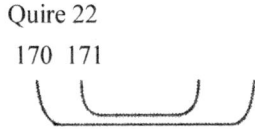). There are no symbols between the lines which are spaced about 10 mm apart and precisely on the lines scored in line with the prickings. There are two folio stubs visible between ff. 171 and 172. The first of these is about 15 mm wide and has the remnants of letters visible at the cut edge. The second is cut very close to the centre and has nothing visible on it.

Quire 23
172 173   174 175

F. 172v has several continuous words with lines written above and below them. Ff. 173v and 174r has interlinear lines of words. F. 175r has a single line of pattern number one (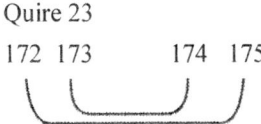) in column two, half way down the page. Three lines of text follow, then a line of black dots, then a body of 10 lines of text that extend into the lower margin. F. 175v has two columns of text in a different hand as well as crudely formed letters in the upper margin.

7. MS. Aeth. e.24
Antiphonary for Lent, Ṣomä Dəgʷa, with musical notation

Quire 1
i   ii   iii

F. i. has a tear and stitching (50 mm) in the fore edge. Neither of the sheets that make up this quire were prepared to receive text. There is the remains of a folio between ff. iii and 1. It is cut off at the centre of the page. There seems no way to tell if it once held writing.

A Catalogue of Previously Uncatalogued Ethiopic Manuscripts in England

Quire 2

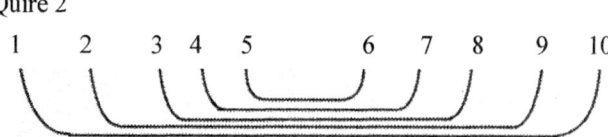

F. 1r begins the main work in two columns and with musical annotations. Lines 1, 2, 3, 9, 10, 11, 17, 18 and 19 in both columns are written in red ink. There are two lines of text in small letters (different than that of the text below) with musical notation in the upper margin, above the *haräg*. There is a crude *haräg* over column one in only black ink. A later hand has 'mirrored' the *haräg* in column one over column two in pencil. F. 3r has a hole in the upper, fore edge of the textblock. There is a text of three words with musical notation in the upper margin. This text is surrounded with a black line box. F. 3v has a minor section divider. It is interlinear. It consists of a line of dots, alternating red and black. These begin with dots going from the sentence divider symbol and rising up to the middle of the space between lines of text and going some distance, perhaps to the end of the column: 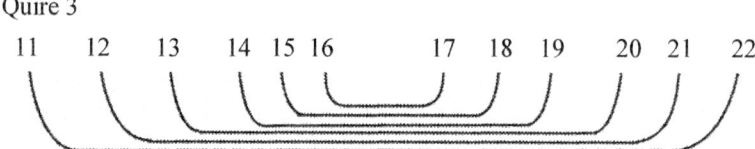. These dividers are rather frequent and another 20 of them appear between this point and f. 12r. At f. 12v and following, the symbol changes somewhat and is normally throughout the rest of the codex, but once or twice the form is

Quire 3

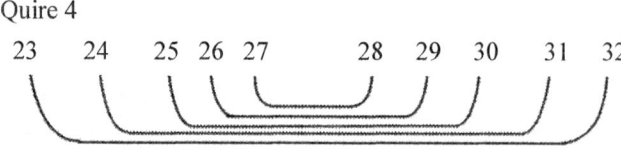

F. 13r has a *haräg* in the first column after the first five lines of text. Lines 6, 7, 18 and 19, in both columns, are written in red ink. F. 13 has a huge tear and stitching that runs perhaps 110 mm from the centre toward the fore edge and up the page. F. 15 has a small pencil scribbling in the lower margin. F. 16 has a deformation in the vellum on the outer edge of the page. F. 17 has a small hole in the upper fore-edge column. F. 19v has a pencil *haräg* drawn at the top of column two. Lines 1, 12, 13, 21 and 22 in column two only are written in red ink. F. 20 has a small tear and stitching in the lower fore-edge corner. F. 21 has small holes at top and bottom of the page.

Quire 4

F. 27r appears to begin a new work. Though there is no *haräg* on the page, lines 1, 2, 15 and 16 in both columns are written in red ink. F. 28r has two words written in the upper margin. F. 28 has a hole in the outer, lower margin. F. 29v has a word in the upper margin, surrounded in a black line box. F. 32v has a word in the upper margin, surrounded in a black line box.

Quire 5

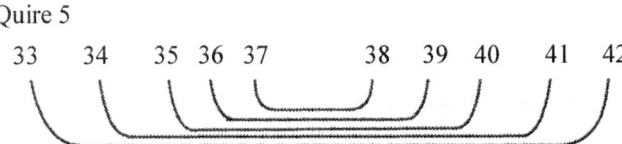

F. 33r has a word written in the upper margin. F. 33v, column two, lines 7, 8, 17 and 18 are in red ink. F. 35r has a line of almost illegible text in pencil in the upper margin. F. 39v has a word crossed out with two pencil lines. F. 40r has a word written in pencil in the upper margin. F. 41r has a word written in pen in the upper margin. Black lines are above and below, with word separator dots before and behind the word. F. 42 has a hole in the lower fore edge.

Quire 6

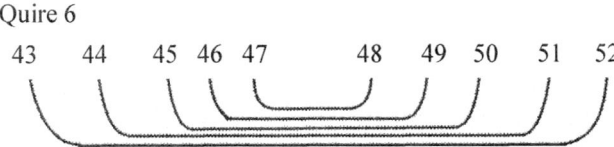

F. 43r has a section divider in column one after the first five lines of text. Two lines with connected, alternating black and red dots go across the column. They are comprised of the pattern ▬▬▬▬▬▬▬▬▬▬▬ . The two lines are about 4 mm apart. Between them are four modified sentence ending symbols that look like this: ❖⟶ . Two of these same symbols mark the end of the previous line. This section divider is followed by two lines (6 and 7) of text in red ink. F. 43v has two words in the top margin surrounded by a black line box. Ff. 45v and 46r has lines of text and musical notation in the upper margin. F. 47r has two words in the top margin surrounded by a black line box. F. 47 has a hole in the lower margin. F. 49 has a hole in the lower portion of the page. F. 50r has two words in the top margin surrounded by a black line box. F. 50r has several lines of text smeared in column two. The text is still legible. F. 51r has words and musical notation in the top margin. F. 52r has a word written in the top margin in green ink. The word has a word division symbol before and behind.

A Catalogue of Previously Uncatalogued Ethiopic Manuscripts in England

Quire 7

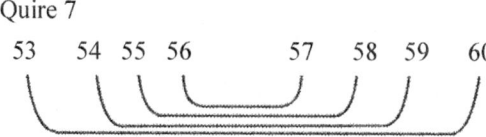

F. 53v has a line of text and musical notation written in the top margin. F. 56 begins a new text. Lines 1, 2, 15 and 16 in both columns are written in red ink. F. 57v has three words and musical notation in the top margin. F. 59 has a hole in the fore edge.

Quire 8

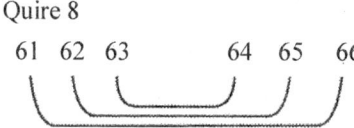

The folio is surrounded by a reinforcement strip. F. 61v has the conclusion of the text. A lot of text appears to have been erased from f. 61v, column two, the bottom half, through column two and onto the first dozen lines on f. 62r., thus, some 52 lines of text. Ff. 62v – 64v contain text in two columns, written with many red letters especially identical letters in the same position in subsequent lines (usually position one or two. The text is musically annotated. F. 66 has a large tear and stitching (ca. 85 mm). Ff. 65 and 66 have only a few letters on them.

8. Bodleian MS. Aeth. e.25
Psalter

Protection Sheet

This is a protection sheet taken from parchment prepared for another codex format. It has been lined, formatted for two columns, but top and bottom margins are both cut off. There is text now written on the folios, but only certain of the lines have been used, corresponding to a 'normal page', that is, margins have been left at top and bottom. The texts on ff. 1r, 2r and 2v are written by the same hand and are in one column. There two texts written on f. 1v. One, written in a different hand and written in brown ink, has employed the first column; the other, written in yet another hand and in black ink, is written in the second column. The text in the first column has been mostly erased through some process that has smeared much of the ink. Many letters are still visible. F. 1r has written in pencil in the upper fore-edge corner, next to the folio number: 'Psalms David'. At the bottom of the page, just below the Bodleian

Quire Maps and Notes

Library stamp is written in pencil 'MS. Aeth. e.25'. F. 2v has four lines of text written in the upper margin in two columns. There are four lines of text in column one and one line of text in column two. There is possibly the remains of several letters from a line above these lines of text, though the top portions have been cut off. This hand does not correspond to the hand in f. 1v, column two, though both are in black ink. This hand may represent the original hand for which the sheet was first made. Later this sheet was appropriated as a protection sheet for this codex.

Quire 1

3   4 5 6   7   8 9   10

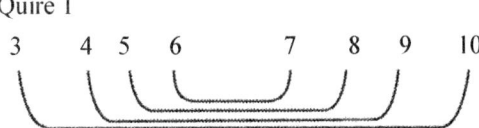

F. 3r has a line of text written in the upper margin, most of which has been erased. F. 3r contains the beginning of the work. There is no *haräg*, but lines 1, 2 and 18 are written in red ink. The text is written in one column and all sentences are written on a single line, with a sentence symbol divider at the end of each line. The relatively large format of this codex makes this unproblematic. Each psalm begins with a line of text in red ink, followed by a number at the beginning of the next line.

Quire 2

11   12 13 14   15   16 17   18

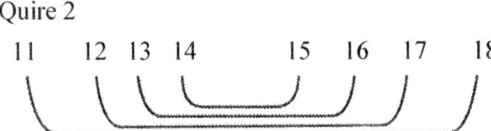

There is no quire number on f. 11r nor in the quires that follow.

Quire 3

19   20   21 22 23   24   25 26   27   28

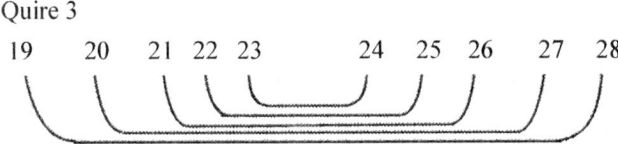

F. 23r has an interlinear addition of a word in a seemingly different hand. F. 27r has an erased line of text that has been overwritten in a different hand.

Quire 4

29   30   31 32 33   34   35 36   37   38

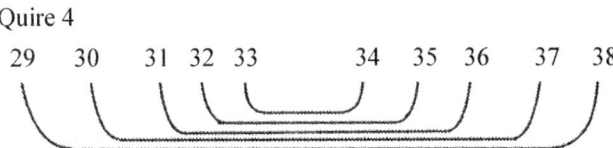

F. 32 The upper fore-edge corner has been torn off and reattached with stitching (40 mm). F. 33 has a tear and stitching (50 mm) in the bottom margin.

A Catalogue of Previously Uncatalogued Ethiopic Manuscripts in England

Quire 5

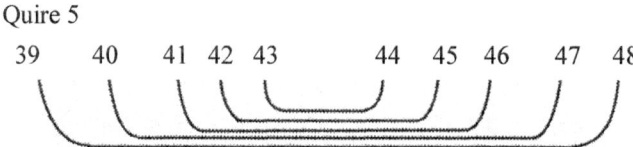

F. 39v has a very small interlinear word written above line 17. F. 40r has an interlinear word above line 1. F. 40v has an erasure with no overwriting (line 10), another erasure with overwriting (line 11), and an interlinear text of a couple of words above line 8. F. 41v has an interlinear line of text (at least two words long) above line 7 and a full line erasure and overwrite on line 12. F. 44v has an interlinear word above line 4. F. 45 has a small hole in the lower centre of the page. F. 45v has an interlinear word and an erasure and overwrite in line 3. F. 48v has a small interlinear word (above line 11) as well as words added in a different hand at the end of lines 2 and 3.

Quire 6

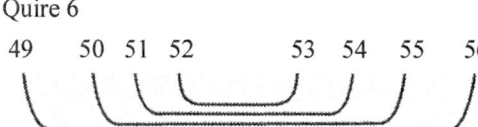

F. 50r has a correction (erasure, overwrite and interlinear addition) in line 9. F. 55 has red thread sewn into the upper fore-edge corner of the page some 20 mm from the top. F. 56v has a half line of text erased with no overwrite in line 4.

Quire 7

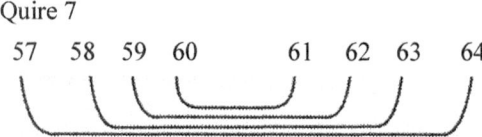

F. 57 has a small piece torn off of the fore-edge, lower corner. F. 59r has erasures of a few words and letters in lines 6, 7 and 8. Ff. 62v and 63r The red dots that are part of the sentence ending symbol ✤ have been left off. F. 63r has an interlinear word above line 14.

Quire 8

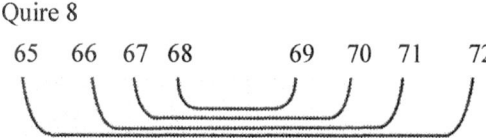

F. 65 has a red thread sewn in the upper fore edge of the page some 28 mm from the top and a blue thread sewn just below at about 45 mm from the top. F. 65r has an erasure, overwrite and substantial interlinear addition to line 8. F. 65v has a line across the page some four lines from the bottom. It is made up of alternating red and black dots in the form 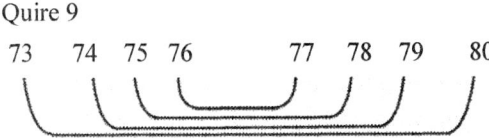, i.e. the dots do not touch. F. 68r has an erasure and overwrite of one word in line 4. F. 71 The outer edge of the page is cut irregularly.

Quire 9
73 74 75 76   77 78 79   80

F. 78v has an interlinear line of text above 10 which has been erased.

Quire 10
81   82   83   84 85   86

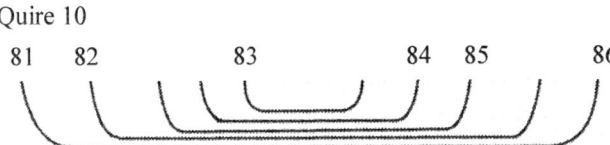

There is a large and a small folio stub visible between ff. 82 and 83. Other folio stubs are visible between ff. 84 and 84 and between ff. 85 and 86. The text on folio 83 (both r and v) is written in a different (more compact) hand on 22 lines to the page (the surrounding folios are written on 19 lines per page) and on vellum that appears to be a bit finer than the surrounding vellum. F. 83r has an interlinear addition of four words above line 4. F. 85v has an erasure and overwrite in a different hand in line 10. F. 86 has a blue thread sewn into the upper fore edge of the page some 57 mm from the top of the page. F. 86r has an erasure and overwrite in a different hand in line 13.

Quire 11
87   88 89 90   91   92 93   94

F. 87r has an interlinear word above line 16. F. 89r has a set of (erasure?) dots above and below an entire line of text (line 19). The text has not been erased. F. 90 has a small hole in the upper middle. F. 93 has a red thread sewn into the upper, fore edge of the page some 30 mm below the top. F. 93 has a hole on the fore edge of the page. F. 93r has a line of alternating red and black dots (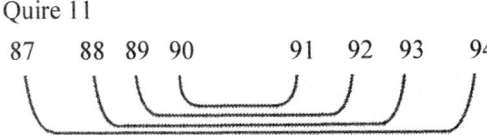) after the first five lines of text.

A Catalogue of Previously Uncatalogued Ethiopic Manuscripts in England

Quire 12

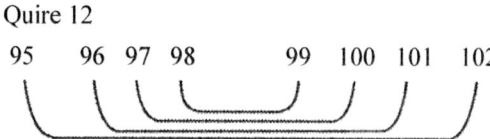

F. 95r has an interlinear line of text above line 6 with four words. F. 96 has two small holes in the upper inside of the page. F. 97r has an erasure and overwrite in a different hand in line 13. F. 98v has an erasure and overwrite in line 6. F. 99r has two lines of erasure and overwrite (lines 2 and 3). F. 99v has one line of erasure (the last line) with no overwrite. The sentence ending symbol is still visible. F. 101 has a small hole in the upper centre.

Quire 13

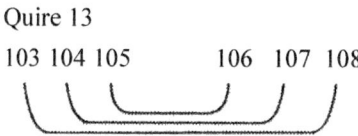

F. 103 has a hole near the bottom. F. 105v has an erasure in line 14.

Quire 14

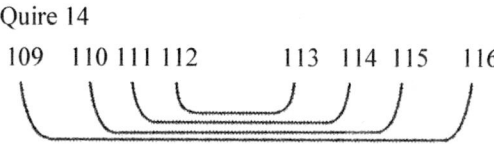

F. 109 has a small interlinear line of text (seven words) above line 19.

Quire 15

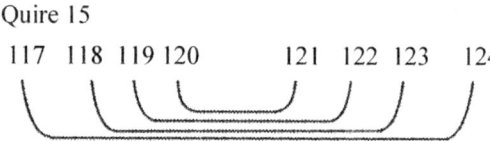

F. 119 has an interlinear line of text that appears to have been erased and overwritten. F. 121v has an interlinear word above line 17.

Quire 16

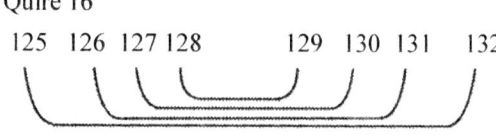

F. 125r has an erasure with no overwrite in line 14. F. 126r has an interlinear line of text and an erasure and overwrite in line 10. F. 128r has a line of erasure and overwrite in line 16. F. 129v has several erasures with no overwrite in lines 4, 16 and 18. F. 130r has text smeared in line 2. F. 130v has an interlinear word above line 4. F. 131v has added words after line 2 and above line 18.

Quire 17

133 134 135 136   137 138 139 140

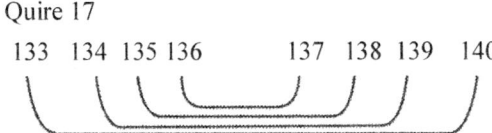

F. 134r has a significant section division after the first five lines of text, i.e. after the Psalms and before the Canticles. It comes in the form of two parallel lines written across the page. These are made up of lines of alternating black and red dots in the form ▪▫▪▫▪▫ ▪ ▫▪ ▫▪▫. The lines are about 5 mm apart (the width of the scraped lines). Between the two lines on far left, centre and far right are sentence divider symbols ❖. F. 135v has an interlinear word above line 8. F. 137v has an interlinear line of text above line 4. F. 138r has an erasure and overwrite in line 17. F. 140r has an interlinear word above a word crossed out with two ink lines in line 2.

Quire 18

141 142 143 144   145 146 147 148

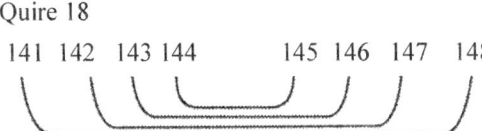

F. 141r has interlinear words above lines 3 and 15. F. 143v has interlinear letters above line 1. F. 144v has erasures and overwrites in lines 3, 11, 12 and 20. There are also interlinear words and letters above lines 4, 5, 12, 13 and 19. F. 145r has a large erasure and partial overwrite in line 6. There is also an interlinear word above line 7. F. 145v has erasures and overwrites in lines 16 and 20. F. 146r has interlinear words above line 2. There is also a significant section division at the bottom of the page, i.e. after the Canticles and before the Song of Songs. It comes in the form of two parallel lines written across the page. These are made up of lines of alternating black and red dots in the form ▪▫▪▫▪▫ ▪ ▫▪ ▫▪▫. The lines are about 11 mm apart (the width of two scraped lines). Between the two lines on far left, centre and far right are sentence divider symbols ❖. F. 146v begins the text written in two columns. There are several erasures and interlinear writing. F. 147r has interlinear text and an erasure. F. 147v has an erasure with overwrite, two interlinear words and a word in the margin between columns. F. 148r has erasures and interlinear words. F. 148v has erasures, overstrikes, interlinear words and two lines of text written in the upper margin.

Quire 19

149 150 151 152   153 154 155 156

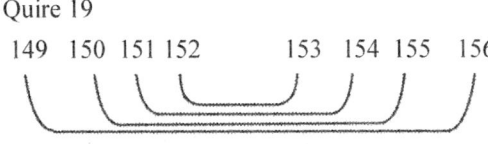

F. 149r has interlinear words, erasures, overstrikes and a line of text in the lower margin. F. 149v has erasures and interlinear text. F. 151r has a significant section division at the bottom of the page, i.e. after the the Song of Songs and before the Praises of Mary. It comes in the form of two parallel lines written across the column. These are made up of lines of alternating black and red dots in the form ▪▪▪▪▪▪▪▪▪▪▪▪. The lines are about 6 mm apart (the width of a scraped line). Between the two lines on far left, centre and far right are sentence divider symbols ❖. The centre symbol has no red dots in it. F. 151 has a tear and stitching (25 mm) on the fore edge of the page. Ff. 151v and 152r have some abrasions in which several words are letters are rendered illegible.

Quire 20

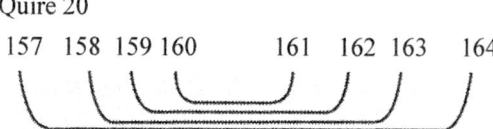

F. 159, col. 2, near the bottom, three sentence divider symbols (❖) appear at the end of the line. The following two lines of text are in red ink. F. 163r has some smeared ink. F. 164v has a line of text in a different hand in the upper margin.

Protection Sheet

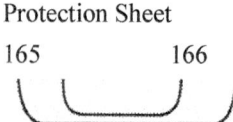

Folio stubs are visible between ff. 165 and 166 and after folio 166. F. 166r is written in two columns but in a different hand than the previous. F. 166v is written in a different hand.

9. Bodleian MS. Aeth. e.28
Harp of Praise, Arganonä Wəddase

Quire 1

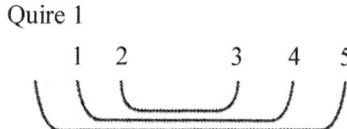

A folio stub is visible before folio one. F. 1 has blue thread sewn into the upper and lower corners of the sheet. These would appear to be the remains of threads to hold a cloth in place between f. 1v and 2r, both of which are covered with artwork. F. 1r contains three lines of writing in modern ink pen at the top centre. In the centre, in pencil is printed: '8072   MS Aeth. e. 28'. Just below is the stamp of the Bodleian library. Otherwise, there is no formal writing on f. 1r even though it is lined. F. 1v contains a full-page illumination. Three holy figures (with halos) stand side by side. The centre figure, a bit larger than the other two, has both hands upraised. The two figures flanking the central figure each have a sword in their right hand, tip pointing straight down. All three wear robes of elaborate geometric designs in black and red and white. F. 2r has the beginning of the main text on it in two columns. An elaborate *haräg* encloses both columns with designs in red, brown and black. The designs comprise the shape of a box that goes entirely around the text area and a pillar that connects bottom and top down the centre of the folio. Thus the two columns are entirely enclosed. Lines 1, 3, 5, and 10 in both columns are in red ink. F. 2v has an erasure in column 1, line 7. Nothing is written in the blank. F. 3v has an erasure in column 2, line 9. Nothing is written in the blank. F. 5v has erasures in column 1, lines 4 and 6. Nothing is written in the blank.

Quire 2

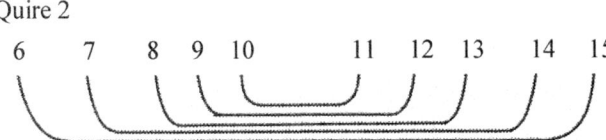

F. 6r has a quire number in the upper left corner: ፪ (two). F. 6r has an erasure in column 2, line 5. Nothing is written in the blank. F. 10 has a small portion torn out of the page at the bottom near the spine. F. 15v has an area of water damage that smears the ink and obscures much of column one.

Quire 3

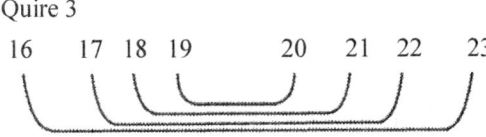

F. 16r has a quire number in the upper left corner: ፫ (three).

Quire 4

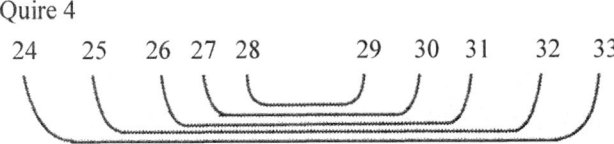

F. 24r has a quire number in the upper left corner: ፬ (four). F. 28r has an erasure in column one, line 16. It appears that the text has already been marked with erasure dots above and below the text. Some of these are still visible. F. 31r has an erasure in column one, line 6. Nothing is written in the blank. F. 33v has an erasure of text in red in column one, line 3. Nothing is written in the blank.

Quire 5

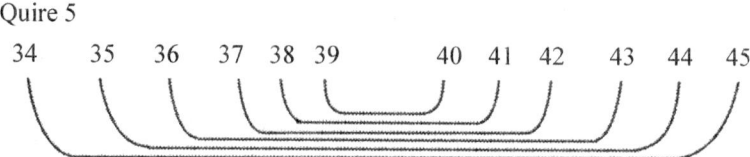

F. 34r has a quire number in the upper left corner: (five). F. 38r contains the end of the first work. There is a red and black *haräg* in the second column after the end of the text. There is red ink smeared beneath the *haräg*. There is also a substantial erasure of two lines (6 and 7) in column two. Nothing is written in the blank. F. 38 has coloured threads sewn through the outer edge of the page about 2 cm from the top. The threads are of red and black. F. 38v is a carpet page with a fairly sizeable (95 x 95 mm) square of geometric designs in red and black and white. F. 39r begins the next work. As before, the two text columns are surrounded by a box going around the outside and a pillar from top centre to bottom centre. Above the box enclosed in red dots is the text: ዘረቡዕ. F. 39r does not have the folio number written on it. Lines 1 and 3 in both columns are in red ink. F. 39 has a 'half moon' hole on the bottom centre. F. 41: the lower fore-edge corner of the page is missing. No text is affected.

Quire 6

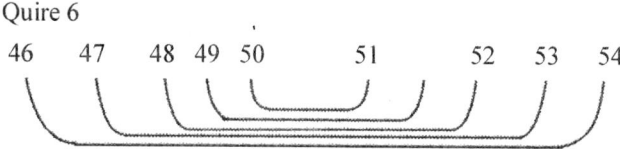

F. 46r does not appear to have a quire number in the upper left corner, though some portion of a letter in red ink is somewhat visible. There is a water stain that obscures whatever it is. In addition, this red letter is in a location slightly above the place that the quire number appears on the other quires in this codex. F. 49r has an erasure in column one, line 14. Nothing is written in the blank. A folio stub is visible between ff. 51 and 52. F. 54v has some scribbling in modern ink pen in the upper margin.

Quire 7

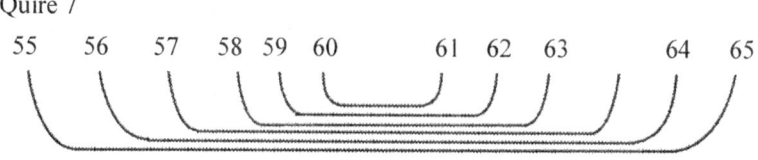

Quire Maps and Notes

F. 58 has a couple of sections of vellum missing in the lower margin. No text is affected. F. 58 has a red thread sewn into the upper corner of the page some 25 mm from the top. F. 58v has a small symbol between the bottom two lines of the first column. It is written in red ink with dimensions of 10 mm wide and 5 mm high. F. 61v contains the end of the current work, with a red and black *haräg* at the end of the text in column two. There is an erasure in column two, line 10 (just above the *haräg*). Nothing is written in the blank. F. 61 has red and black thread sewn into the upper fore-edge corner some 22 mm from the top. F. 62r begins a new work and has a colourful *haräg* of red, brown and black that dominates the page. Unlike the *harägs* in the two previous beginnings, this one does not continue around the bottom of the two columns of text. In a box at the very top appears the word በስመአብ. There is no folio number written on f. 62r. Lines 1, 3, and 11 in both columns are in red ink. There is a folio stub visible between ff. 63 and 64. F. 64v has a crude drawing of a prostrate figure in the bottom margin. It is written in pencil. F. 65v has a similar crude drawing in its lower margin as well as some other geometric designs (*haräg*?) in pencil.

Quire 8

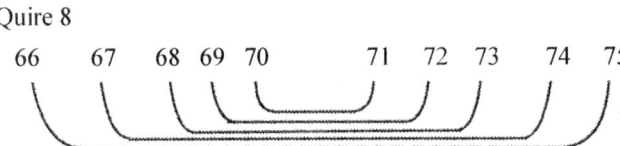

F. 70 has a small portion cut out of the lower fore-edge corner in a rectangle shape 13 x 35 mm. F. 70v has some (five) letters written in the fore-edge column in a line perpendicular to the base text.

Quire 9

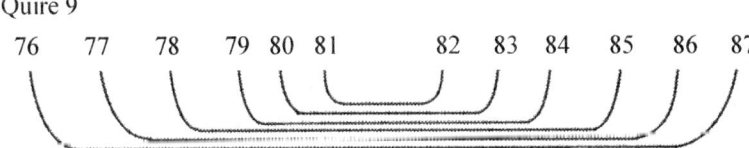

F. 79 has an erasure that, besides obscuring the text of two lines, produced a rather sizcablc hole in the vellum (10 mm in diameter). Read from the recto side, it is in column two, lines 15 and 16. Nothing is written in the space. As evidence that the hole was produced by the erasing action, we see that some of the text of the verso side has been rendered missing, i.e. the hole was not there when the base text was copied onto the vellum. F. 84 has an irregular and substantial portion of the bottom margin missing. F. 85 has two holes in the lower centre of the page. F. 85r has two lines erased, the bottom lines of both columns. F. 87 has a long narrow hole that developed after the text was copied down the vellum at the spine in the lower part of the page.

Quire 10

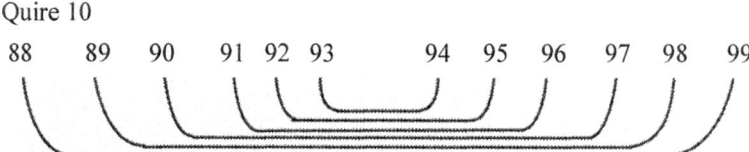

F. 89r has two large abrasions that obliterate about 20 letters in column one and perhaps four times that number in column two. F. 90 has red and black threads sewn into the upper fore-edge corner of the page some 20 mm from the top. F. 90v contains the last of the text of this work. Ten to twelve lines of text in column two have been erased. F. 91r begins a new work and has a colourful *haräg* of red, brown and black that dominates the page. Like the *harägs* around the first two beginnings, this one does continue around the bottom of the two columns of text. In a box at the very top appears a word. There is no folio number written on f. 61r. Lines 1, 3, and 10 in both columns are in red ink. F. 99v has ink pen scribbles in the lower margin and in the margin between columns of text.

Quire 11

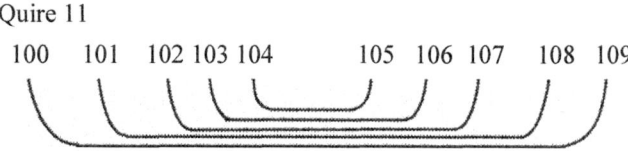

F. 100r has large letters scribbled in pencil in the lower margin. F. 100 has an irregular portion of the lower fore edge of the page missing (some 45 mm wide). F. 103 has a portion of the page missing in the lower inside portion of the page.

Quire 12

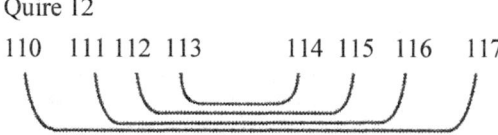

F. 110v has a small pen scribbling in the fore-edge margin. F. 116 has black threads sewn into the upper fore edge of the page some 13 mm from the top. F. 116v contains the last of the text of this work. There is an erasure in column two, line 15. Nothing has been written in the space. F. 117r begins a new work and has a colourful *haräg* of red, brown and black that dominates the page. Like the *harägs* around the first two beginnings, this one does continue around the bottom of the two columns of text. In a box at the very top appears a word. There is no folio number written on f. 117r. Lines 1, 3, and 9 in both columns are in red ink.

Quire Maps and Notes

Quire 13

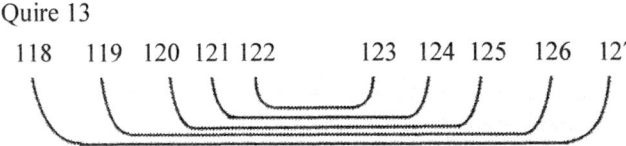

F. 119v has scuff marks on columns one and two, but the text is mostly legible.

Quire 14

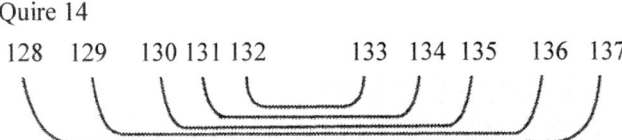

F. 130r contains the end of this work. There is a *haräg* of red and black designs at the bottom of column one. Column two has eight lines of text in it, seemingly in a different hand. The following letters (at least) seem to be formed differently than those in the other texts: ዉ, ሰ, ሙ, ት, etc. F. 130 has a black thread sewn into the upper and fore-edge corner of the page some 20 mm from the top. F. 130v has an elaborate 'carpet page' of geometric designs some 120 x 125 mm. There is no writing on the page. F. 131r begins a new work and has a colourful *haräg* of red, brown and black that dominates the page. Like the *harägs* around the first two beginnings, this one does continue around the bottom of the two columns of text. At the very top centre appears the word ዘእንደ. There is no folio number written on f. 131r. Lines 1, 2, 5, and 6 in both columns are in red ink.

Quire 15

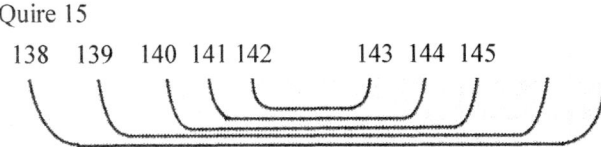

The remains of two cut-off pages are visible after f. 145. These are not folio stubs, but are simply cut off at the centre of the fold. F. 139 has a small ink pen scribble (two letters?) in the top margin. F. 143 has a blue thread sewn into the upper fore-edge corner some 20 mm from the top. F. 143v contains the end of this text with a small *haräg* of black, red and brown colours at the end of column two. F. 143v contains an erasure in column two, lines 2 and 3. Nothing is written in the space. F. 144 abruptly begins a new text without benefit of *haräg* or lines in red ink to indicate a new work. The writing is in a new hand, slightly smaller and more compact than the other hand, but still neat and trained. The text that begins on f. 144r continues through the end of the codex to f. 145v. There are several erasures in this work (f. 144r, col. 2, line 1; f.

144v, col. 1, lines 1 and 14; f. 145r, col. 1, line 17; and f. 145v, col. 1, line 12.). In none of them has text been written in the space. At the bottom of column one is a line of six symbols . Column two has three lines of text in a different and rougher (though not untrained) hand. There are some scribblings in pencil on the rest of the folio.

10. Bodleian MS. Aeth. f.19
Praises of Mary (Wəddase Maryam), Gate of Light (Anqäṣä bərhan), Hymns (Sälam) to Rufa'el

Front Cover
On the outside, in the lower right corner a small yellow piece of paper is affixed to the wood and on it is written, 'MS Aeth f 19'. On the inside front cover is written, 'MS Aeth f.19'.

Protection Quire

i ii   iii iv

On f. ir is written in pencil, 'MS Aeth. f. 19.'

Quire 1

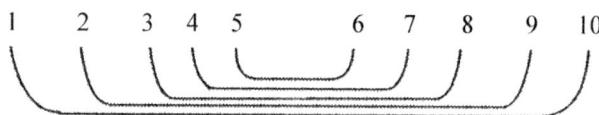

F. 1r has a quire number ፩ 'one' in the upper left corner. F. 1v has interlinear words. F. 2v has an entire interlinear line of text. F. 7v has a word with a black line above and below it.

Quire 2

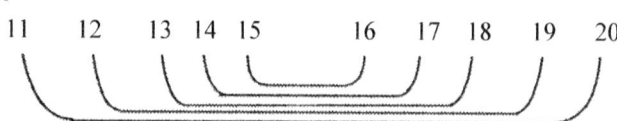

F. 11r has a quire number ፪, 'two', in the upper left corner. F. 14v has some black lines written above and below the last half of line nine and all of line ten.

Quire Maps and Notes

Quire 3

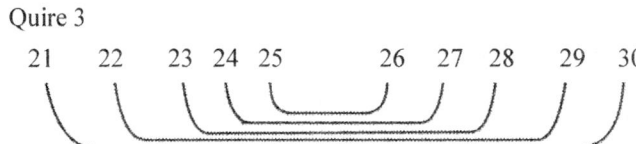

F. 21r has a quire number 'three' in the upper left corner. F. 21v has an erasure and three words overwritten in the space. F. 22r has two lines of text in red ink at the top of the folio. F. 22v has an interlinear word written in. F. 23r has three interlinear words written in. F. 25r has two lines of text in red ink in the middle of the page. v. 26v and 27r have interlinear words written in. F. 29r has a section divider after four lines of text. There follows a line across the page made up of alternating red and black dots with small spaces between them (). This line is followed by two lines of text in red ink.

Quire 4

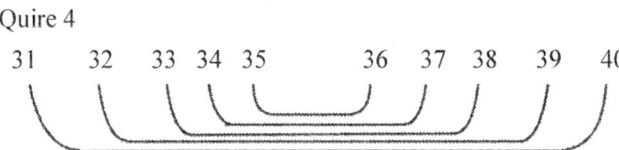

F. 31 r has the quire number ō 'four' in the upper left corner. F. 33 has irregular deformations along the lower fore edge and bottom edge of the page. F. 38r has a line of text written in the top margin. Ff. 38v and 39r have interlinear words written in.

Quire 5

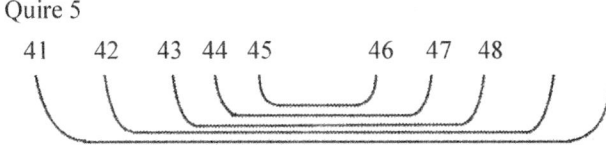

There is no quire number on f. 41. F. 42v has three words written in another hand in the upper margin. F. 43v contains the ending of the current text after five lines and two letters. This is followed by the completion of the 6th line of text and a seventh in another hand. F. 44 begins a new text. Lines 1 and 2 are written in red ink. Ff. 46v and 47r have a dark stained spot in their lower margins. F. 48 is the last folio of written text. The six folios that follow f. 48 are unnumbered.

Protection Quire

All of these folios are blank and unprepared for text (i.e. without columns, prickings and lines), except for the last which has written in English cursive, '48 folios'.

A Catalogue of Previously Uncatalogued Ethiopic Manuscripts in England

Back Cover
On the outside of the back cover, a couple of letters have been cut into the surface of the wood, they are difficult to decipher, but may be ታው.

11. Bodleian MS Aeth. f.20
Fragment from Gospel of John

This manuscript is a single sheet as described above.

12. Bodleian MS Aeth. f.21
Psalter

Protection Quire

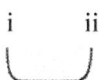

This sheet is pricked but neither columns nor lines have been etched in the vellum. There is no writing on any of the folios.

Quire 1

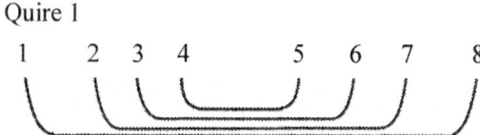

F. 1r begins the first work, the Psalms of David. There is a major *haräg* in red and black and a brown or yellow (perhaps in two different shades) that extends around three sides of the text block (top and two sides). These are filled with geometric patterns and weavings. The patterns in the side blocks incorporate several eyes. Lines 1, 2, 5, 6, 9, 10, 15, 16 and 18 are written in red ink. In this first work, the text is written in one column with one sentence per line. At the end of each line is the sentence ending symbol ❈. The handwriting is small and the lines many (26 to 27). With such a compact format, the objective of getting one sentence per line works in most cases. When it does not, and a word or two have to be placed on another line, this text is set off by a symbol '(' in red ink or sometimes two such symbols side by side, occasionally one in red and the other in black '(('. F. 6 has red threads (very much like yarn) sewn into the upper fore edge of the page some 15 mm from the top. F. 7r interlinear insertion above line 2.

Quire 2

9   10 11 12   13 14 15 16

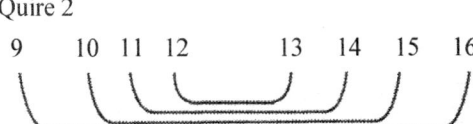

F. 10 has a hole in the upper midsection of the text block. F. 12r has an erasure and overwrite. F. 12 has red threads (very much like yarn) sewn into the upper fore edge of the page some 15 mm from the top. F. 13r has interlinear text. F. 16r has several examples of vertical columetric layout of the text, placing identical words in successive lines in the same place and in red ink.

Quire 3

17   18 19 20   21 22 23   24

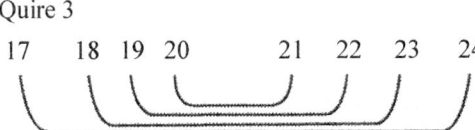

F. 18r has a major section divider. In the area between lines 3 and 4 is a string of symbols > > > > > > > > > > > > > > > > > > >. The last six letters of the line above are in red ink; the entire line of text below it is in red ink. F. 18 has red threads (very much like yarn) sewn into the upper fore edge of the page some 15 mm from the top. F. 23 has a hole in the lower portion of the textblock.

Quire 4

25   26 27 28   29 30 31   32

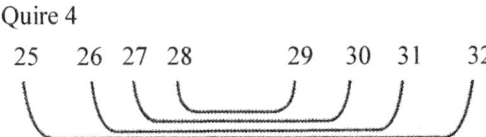

F. 26 has red threads (very much like yarn) sewn into the upper fore edge of the page some 18 mm from the top. F. 32 has red threads (very much like yarn) sewn into the upper fore edge of the page some 15 mm from the top.

Quire 5

33   34 35 36   37 38 39   40

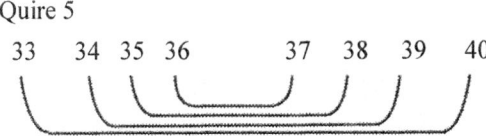

F. 37 has red threads (very much like yarn) sewn into the upper fore edge of the page some 15 mm from the top.

Quire 6

41 42 43 44   45 46 47 48

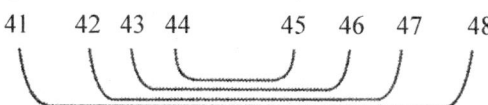

F. 45 has red threads (very much like yarn) sewn into the upper fore edge of the page some 19 mm from the top.

Quire 7

49 50 51 52   53 54 55 56

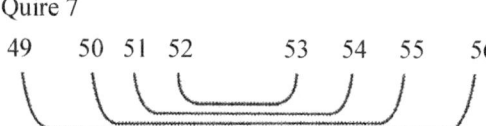

F. 54 has red threads (very much like yarn) sewn into the upper fore edge of the page some 9 mm from the top, and a little further in away from the outer edge than the location of the others. F. 54r has a major section divider. In the area between lines 3 and 4 is a string of symbols alternating red and black > > > > > > > > > > > > > > > > > > >. The last six letters of the line above are in red ink; the next line begins a new psalm with the entire line of text in red ink, followed by another partial line of red text.

Quire 8

57 58 59 60   61 62 63 64

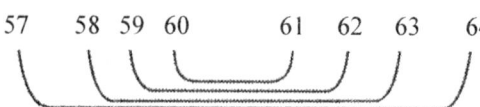

F. 60 has red threads (very much like yarn) sewn into the upper fore edge of the page some 15 mm from the top. F. 61 has a hole and some stitching at the top inside of the page. Between ff. 60 and 61 are several loose pieces of the red yarn.

Quire 9

65 66 67 68   69 70 71 72

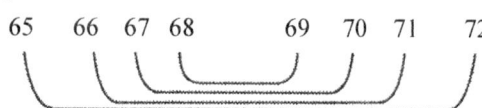

F. 65r has a major heading with a red and black and yellow *haräg* at the top of the page followed by three lines of text in red ink. F. 65 has red threads (very much like yarn) sewn into the upper fore edge of the page some 12 mm from the top. The thread attached to this one is particularly long. F. 66 has a hole (20 mm) in the fore edge. F. 67r has an interlinear line of text. F. 70 has two small holes in it. F. 71 has a hole in it.

Quire Maps and Notes

Quire 10

73　74　75　76　　77　78　79　　80

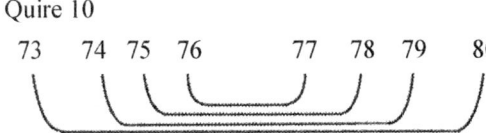

F. 74 has red threads (very much like yarn) sewn into the upper fore edge of the page some 15 mm from the top, but much closer to the edge than the others. Between ff. 76 and 77 are several loose pieces of the red yarn.

Quire 11

81　　　82　83　84　　85　86　　87　88

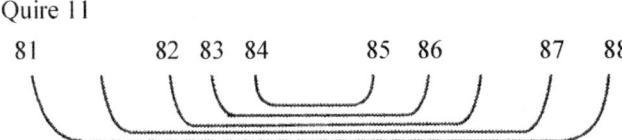

Folio tabs are visible between ff. 81 and 82 and between 86 and 87. F. 83 has red threads (very much like yarn) sewn into the upper fore edge of the page some 15 mm from the top. F. 85 has red threads (very much like yarn) sewn into the upper fore edge of the page some 15 mm from the top. F. 85r has an interlinear line of text. Ff. 87r and v have several examples of vertical columetric layout of the text, placing identical words and letters in successive lines in the same place and in red ink.

Quire 12

89　　90　　91　　92　　93　94　　95　96

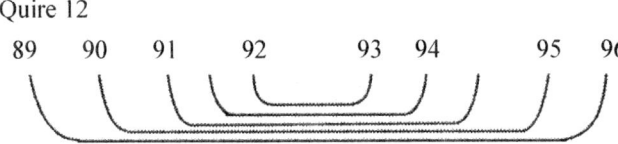

F. 90 has red threads (very much like yarn) sewn into the upper fore edge of the page some 18 mm from the top. F. 92v has two words of text written in the bottom margin in bigger black and rough letters. Ff. 94r and 95r have several examples of vertical columetric layout of letters. F. 95r has a section divider at the bottom of the page, a string of symbols alternating red and black > > > > > > > > > > > > > > > > > > >. F. 95 has red threads (very much like yarn) sewn into the upper fore edge of the page some 18 mm from the top. F. 95v begins the new work of the biblical canticles. There is a *haräg* at the top of the page followed by two lines of text in red.

Quire 13

97　98　99　100　　101　102　103　104

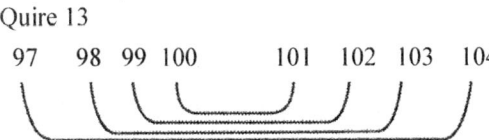

Ff. 103r and v have several fine examples of vertical columetric layout of letters and words.

Quire 14
105 106 107 108   109 110 111   112

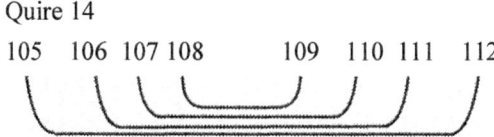

F. 106 has red threads (very much like yarn) sewn into the upper fore edge of the page some 18 mm from the top. F. 106v has the start of the new work, Song of Songs. There is a *haräg* of red and black after line three. This if followed by two lines of text in red ink. F. 110r has an interlinear word. F. 112r has the last 10 lines of the text of Song of Songs. The rest of the folio is blank as is the entirety of f. 112v.

Quire 15
113   114   115   116   117 118 119   120   121

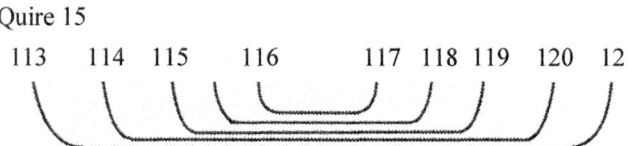

A folio stub is visible between ff. 115 and 116. F. 113r begins the new work, The Praises of Mary. There is a *haräg* of red and black at the top of the page. The text is written in two columns. Lines 1, 2, 5, 6, 9, 10, 17, 18, 21 and 22 in red ink in both columns. F. 117 has a large hole at the top of the page. F. 117r has a section divider in column 2, near the bottom. It is comprised of a line of alternating red and black symbols (> > > > > > > > > > > > > >) followed by a line of text in red ink.

Quire 16
122 123 124   125 126   127

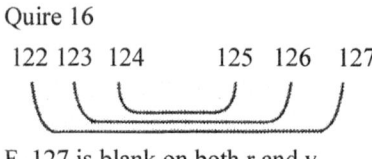

F. 127 is blank on both r and v.

13. Bodleian MS. Aeth. g.22
Book of Chants, *Zema*, with musical notation

There is a spine strap that extends around all of the folios and covers the spine. The ends extend across f. 1r by about 30 mm from the centre. In the back it goes even further, extending nearly the full width of the folio. The person designating folios counted the front part of the strap as folio i and the back part of the strap as f. 56. F. 56 has a long tear and stitching (43 mm) from centre to top. Through the spine is visible the impression of the three weavings that constitute the binding of the codex.

Quire Maps and Notes

On the spine is written (upside down in relation to the direction of writing in the codex): 'This book [illegible]'.

Quire 1

1　　2

Quire 2

3　　4　　　　5　6　7　　　　8　9　　　10　11　12

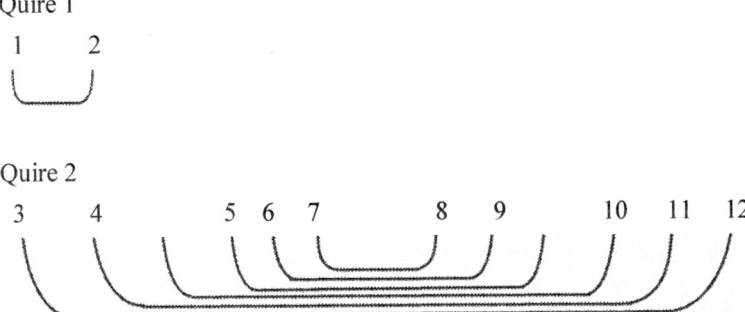

Folio stubs appear between ff. 4 and 5 and between ff. 9 and 10. F. 3r begins the new work, which is in one column. Lines 1, 2, 8 and 9 are in red ink (though not their musical notation). There is a line of text in a different hand in the top margin. F. 7 has a large tear and stitching (43 mm) from the centre to the fore edge of the page. F. 11r has a section division. After the first word of line 11, all the words in the line and in the next line are in red ink. Further, from the sentence ending symbol after the first word of line 11 rises a black and red dotted line that extends across the rest of the page between lines of text 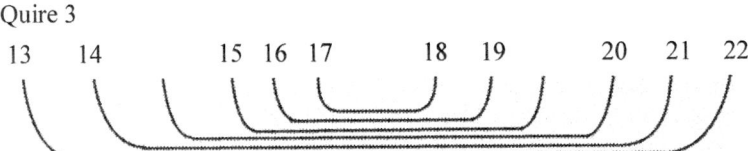 (hereafter 'rising full stop'). F. 12v has the rising full stop followed by two red letters.

Quire 3

13　　14　　　　15　16　17　　　　18　19　　　20　21　22

Folio stubs appear between ff. 14 and 15 and between ff. 19 and 20. F. 13v has the rising full stop followed by four red letters. F. 14v has rising full stop without the red dots and followed by two red letters. F. 16v has a rising full stop used as section divider followed by two red letters. F. 17v has a section divider. A line of alternating red and black ▪ ▫ ▪ ▫ ▪ ▫ ▪ ▫ ▪ ▫ dots run across the page just below the 12th line of text. This is followed by a full line of text in red. F. 18 has a small tear and stitching at the bottom of the page. F. 19v has a rising full stop section divider followed by two words and one letter in red ink. F. 21r has a rising full stop section divider followed by two words in red ink. F. 21v has a word in the upper margin. F. 22r has a rising full stop section divider followed by three words and one letter in red ink. F. 22v has two words written in the upper margin.

Quire 4

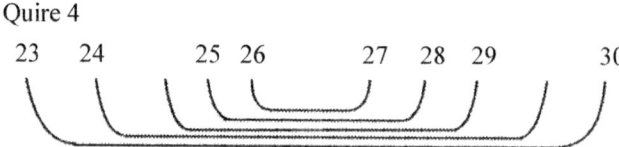

Folio stubs appear between ff. 24 and 25 and between fox 29 and 30. The sheet that is comprised of ff. 23 and 30 has been pricked along the bottom edge as well as in the normal fore edge. F. 23v has a section divider. A line of alternating red and black dots run across the page just below the third line of text. This is followed by two words of text in red ink. F. 24v has a rising full stop section divider followed by three words in red ink. F. 25v has a section divider. A line of alternating red and black dots run across the page just below the first line of text. This is followed by two words and one letter of text in red ink. F. 28v has a line of alternating red and black dots run across the page just below the first line of text.

Quire 5

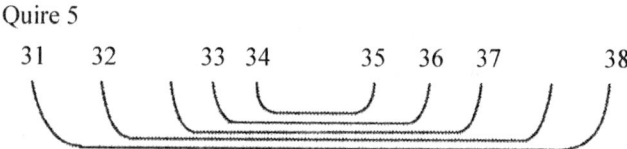

Folio stubs appear between ff. 32 and 33 and between ff. 37 and 38. F. 32r has a line of alternating red and black dots run across the page just below the first line of text followed by five letters in red ink. F. 35r has a line of alternating red and black dots run across the page just below the sixth line of text followed by four letters in red ink. F. 38v has a rising full stop section divider followed by two words in red ink.

Quire 6

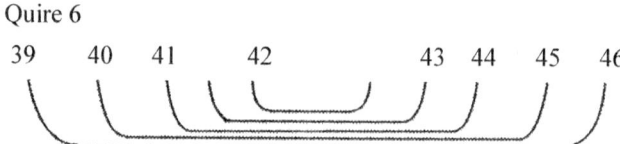

Folio stubs appear between ff. 41 and 42 and between ff. 42 and 43. F. 40v has a line of alternating red and black dots running across half the page under line 10. In this case there are no spaces between the dots. F. 42v has a major section divider. It has a line of alternating red and black dots running across three quarters of the page under line 9. The next two lines of text are in red ink.

Quire 7

47 48 49 50 51 52

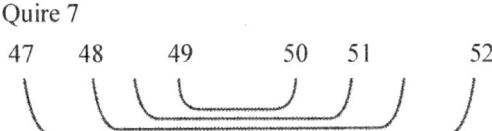

Folio stubs appear between ff. 48 and 49 and between ff. 51 and 52. F. 47r has a major section divider. It has a rising full stop followed by a word and a full line of text in red ink. The sheets that are comprised of ff. 47/52 and 49/50 have been pricked along the bottom edge as well as in the normal fore edge. F. 52v has a line of alternating red and black ▪░▪░▪░▪ ░▪░▪░▪ dots run across the page just below the twelfth line of text followed by four letters in red ink.

Quire 8

53 54 55

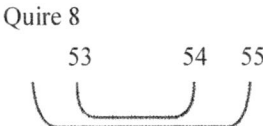

A folio stub is visible between ff. 52 and 53, although it is cut so close to the fold that it tends to pull over with fol 55. F. 53r is written in a larger format using more of the folio area for text block. None of the sheets in the final quire were prepared to receive text.

14. Bodleian MS. Aeth. g.23
Praises of Mary and Gate of Light, with musical notation

Quire 1

1 2 3   4 5 6

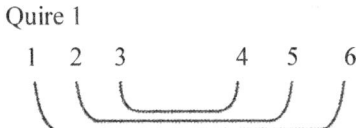

The bottom fore-edge portion of f. 1 has been torn off. F. 1r contains the beginning of the work. It is written with musical notation. There is a simple red and black *haräg* at the top of the page. Lines 1, 2, 5 and 6 are written in red ink. F. 2v has an interlinear text. F. 6v is badly water stained.

Quire 2

7 8 9   10 11 12

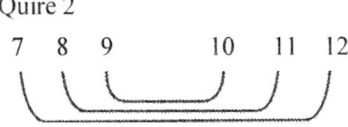

A Catalogue of Previously Uncatalogued Ethiopic Manuscripts in England

F. 7r is badly water stained. F. 8r has a word written in the bottom margin in a later hand. There is also an erasure in the same area of the folio.

Quire 3

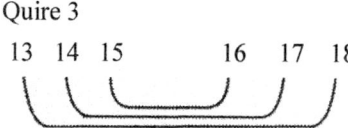

F. 13r has faded letters and water stain. F. 17v has fading and stains

Quire 4

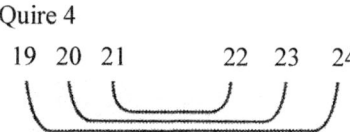

Ff. 18v and 19r are badly faded and water stained. F. 22r begins a new section (for Friday) and has a simple red and black *haräg* at the top of the page followed by two lines of text in red ink. Ff. 24v and 25r are badly faded and water stained.

Quire 5

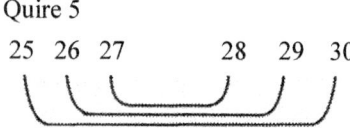

F. 26v has an interlinear line of text. F. 30r begins a new section of the text (for Sunday). There is a simple red and black *haräg* after the third line and this is followed by two lines of text in red ink. Ff. 30v and 31r are badly faded and water stained.

Quire 6

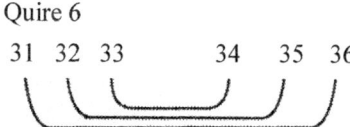

F. 34r contains the end of the first major work in the codex. The fourth line of text is but two letters. The rest of the line is given to five symbols ❖. The following lines of text on the same page are either in a different hand or a very different pen and ink.

Quire 7

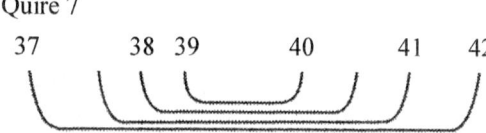

Folio stubs are visible between ff. 37 and 38 and between ff. 40 and 41.

Quire Maps and Notes

Quire 8

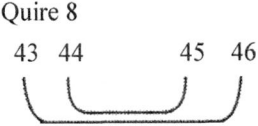

Ff. 42v and 43r are badly faded and water stained. F. 44v contains the end of Anqāṣā bərhan on the 9th line. This is followed by a line with 4 symbols ❖ in it. There are two lines of text in the lower margin in a different hand. Ff. 45 and 46 are filled with writing, but the text is in very poor condition with many letters completely illegible.

15. Cambridge University Library Or. 2547
Liturgical Chants, with musical notation

Protection Quire

i ii

Quire 1

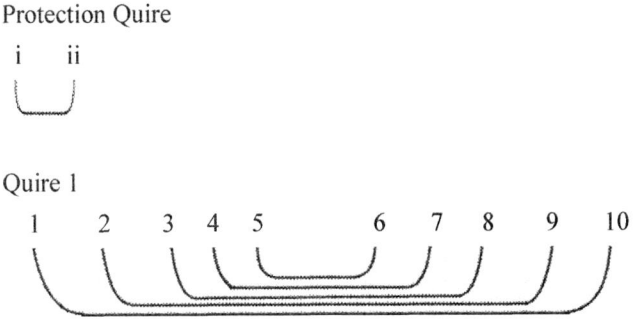

F. 1r begins the new work in one column of text. There is no *haräg*. Lines 1, 2, 5 and 6 are written in red ink. The text is written in rather small letters (2 mm high) and space left between the lines for the musical notation which is written in even smaller letters. The musical notation is made up of two elements: 1) letters (either single or double); and 2) lines. Some of the letters of the musical notation is written in red ink as are some of the lines.

Quire 2

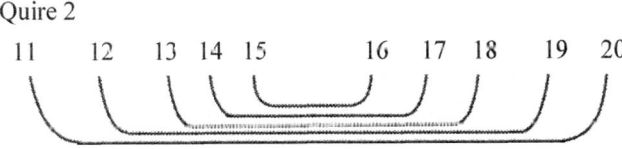

Ff. 20r and v have no musical notation.

Quire 3

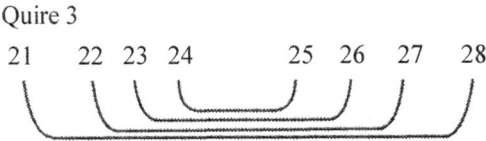

83

F. 21r begins the new work. There is no *haräg*. Lines 1, 2, 5 and 6 are written in red ink. There is musical notation, but all of it is in black ink.

Quire 4

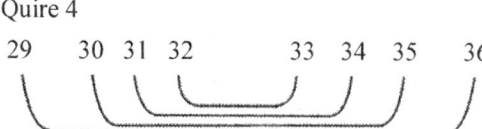

F. 33v begins the new work. There is no *haräg*. Lines 1, 2, 5 and 6 are written in red ink. All musical notation is in black ink.

Quire 5

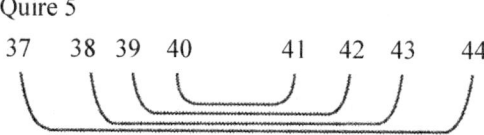

F. 44r contains the end of the work. There are 5 lines of text. The last of these is partial. The rest of the line is taken up with three sentence ending symbols ❈

Quire 6

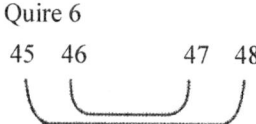

Ff. 45–6 are cut off 8mm and 12mm respectively from the centre. F. 47 is cut off ca. 22mm from the fore edge. F. 48 has the lower fore-edge corner of the folio cut off. A replacement piece of vellum in the shape of a triangle has been stitched in as a replacement. In this protection quire only f. 48r has any writing.

16. Cambridge University Library Or. 2548
Prayers of the Blessed Virgin Mary on Golgotha, The Mystagogia, and Hymn to Jesus

Protection Quire

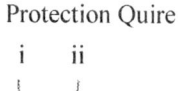

F. ir, pen trials and note: 'Səhin Sädalä is good'. F. iv. contains: 1) Beginning of prayer: Bäsəmä Ab Wäwäld wä-Mänfäs Qəddus ahadu Amlak, 'in the name of the Father, Son and Holy Spirit, one God. . . ;' and 2) Calendar of the days of the saints,

Quire Maps and Notes

from one to thirteen. F. iir, pen trials and miscellaneous letters. F. iiv, pen trials and name, Abba Mäzgäbu Jämärä.

Quire 1

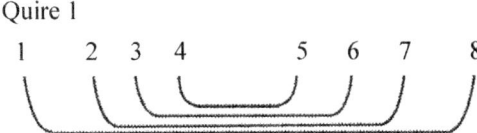

F. 1r begins the first work of the codex. It has a colourful *haräg* of black, red and green colours at the top of the page with columns running down each side of the text block to a base comprised of a small set of intertwined lines. Lines 1, 2, 6 and 7 are in red ink. F. 1v has an erasure in line 3 overwritten in a later hand in ink pen. F. 2r has four letters written in another hand in the bottom margin. F. 3v has a section marked: at the end of line 8 are two sentence ending symbols ✠ connected by three red lines and followed by other red and black lines and symbols. There are then two lines of text in red ink. F. 4r has two lines of text (lines 2 and 3) in red ink. F. 5r has a section marked: at the end of line 11 (the last line of the folio) are two sentence ending symbols ✠ connected by red and black lines and followed by other red and black lines and symbols. The next folio (5v) begins with two lines of text in red ink.

Quire 2

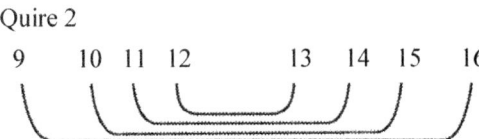

F. 9r. has a quire number ፪ 'two' in the upper left corner of the folio. As with all the quire numbers in this codex, it is located in an area above the first line of text and very close to the inner gutter (perhaps 3 mm away from the inner edge). It is surrounded by three sentence ending symbols, above, below and to the right. F. 16v has two letters in blue pencil in the lower margin.

Quire 3

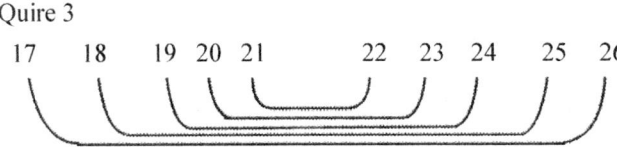

F. 17r. has a quire number ፫ 'three' in the upper left corner. It is surrounded by three sentence ending symbols, above, below and to the right. Ff. 17v and 18r have many markings in blue pencil: 15–20 letters along the top; lines along the bottom and some sort of woven design in the outer margin of 17v. F. 20r has an interlinear letter in another hand. F. 22r has a section marked: after the first letter of line 6 there are two sentence ending symbols ✠, the last one of which has black lines extending to the right. This is followed by two lines of text in red ink.

Quire 4

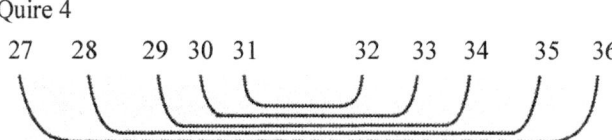

F. 27r has a quire number Ø 'four' in the upper left corner. It is surrounded not by three sentence ending symbols but by small red and black lines on all sides. F. 32v has four letters in blue pencil in the upper margin. F. 33r has the faint remains of markings in the blue pencil, mainly in the lower margin. F. 35r has a half dozen letters in black pencil in the bottom margin. These are continued in the upper margin of f. 35v. F. 35v has a blank space in the text on lines 10 – 11. It has not been erased, nor has anything been added. F. 36v has writing in a blue ink pen into a blank space left in line 6.

Quire 5

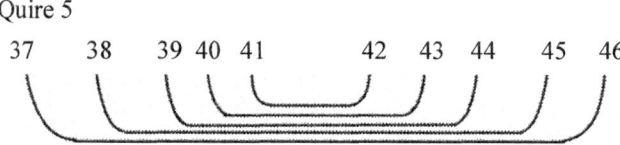

F. 37r has a quire number Ẽ 'five' in the upper left corner. It is surrounded by three sentence ending symbols and also several small red and black lines on all sides. F. 37r a section marked: at the end of the first line of text, there are two sentence ending symbols ✠, the last one of which has black lines extending to the right. This is followed by two lines of text in red ink. F. 42r has two interlinear letters, one in a crude hand in blue ink pen; the other in a neat small scribal hand. F. 42v has several words written in blue ink pen in a blank space in the text on line 6. F. 43r has two lines of text at the bottom in red ink. F. 44r has a blank space in line 1 and a large blank space in lines 9 and 10. In the latter is written in blue ink pen a full line of text. F. 44v contains the ending of the work with a line of three sentence ending symbols followed by blank space through the bottom of the page. In this space a later hand has written in blue ink pen three lines of text. F. 45 has a small white string sewn into the fore edge about 11 mm from the top of the page. F. 45r begins the new work. There is what is either a crude *haräg* of blue and pink or a text in pink letters that has been scribbled over in blue ink. Lines 1, 2, 5 and 6 are written in red ink.

Quire 6

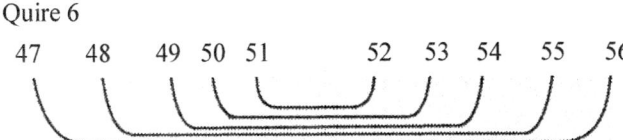

F. 47r has a quire number 𝌂 'six' in the upper left corner. It is surrounded by red and black lines and dots. F. 48v has interlinear letters. F. 53r has an interlinear word written above line 7.

Quire 7

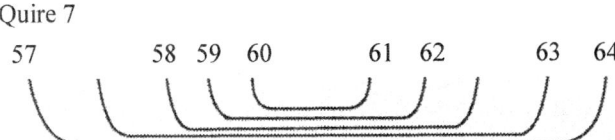

F. 57r has no quire number. There are two letters written in blue ink in the bottom margin. Ff. 57v and 58r have several words in blue ink written in the bottom margin. Folio stubs are visible between ff. 57 and 58 and between ff. 62 and 63. F. 58v has several words in blue ink written in the bottom margin. F. 59 has a hole lower portion toward the fore edge. F. 59r has a major division after line 2. There is a line with three sentence symbols in it, evenly spaced. Then, lines 4, 5, 8 and 9 are in red ink. F. 59r has a few words written in blue ink written between the symbols in line 3. F. 59v has a few letters written in the bottom margin. F. 61r has several smudged letters in the upper fore edge. F. 62v has a few letters written in the bottom margin.

Quire 8

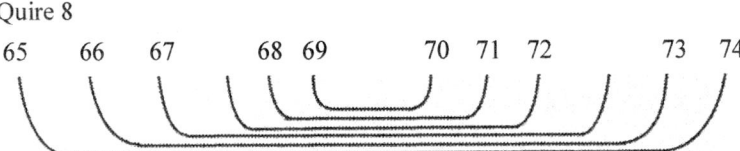

F. 65r has a quire number 𝌂 'eight' in the upper left corner. It is surrounded only by black lines and dots. F. 66r has an erasure and overwrite. Folio stubs are visible between ff. 67 and 68 and between ff. 72 and 73. F. 71 has a tear and stitching (25 mm) at the bottom gutter. F. 72v has an interlinear letter. F. 73r has an interlinear letter.

Quire 9

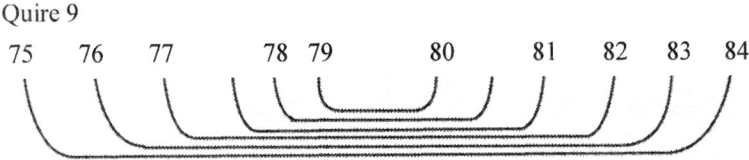

F. 75r has a quire number ፱ 'nine' in the upper left corner, surrounded by three sentence ending symbols ⁜, below, above and to the right. There is also an interlinear letter. F. 75v has an interlinear letter. F. 77v has an interlinear letter. Folio stubs are visible between ff. 77 and 78 and between ff. 80 and 81. F. 78r has an interlinear letter. F. 80r has two large blue letters in pencil in the bottom margin. Ff. 81v and 82r have large blue letters in pencil in their bottom margins. F. 82 has a small hole in the upper margin. F. 82r has an interlinear word above line 2. Ff. 82v and 83r have large blue letters in pencil in their bottom margins. F. 83v has large blue letters in pencil in the bottom margin. There is also a half-line of alternating red dots and small black lines between lines 9 and 10. F. 84r has a full line of alternating red dots and small black lines between lines 4 and 5 of the original text, as well as a similar line below the last line of text on the page. There is also an interlinear line of text in blue ink. F. 84v has a half-line of alternating red dots and small black lines between lines 8 and 9. The bottom three lines of text are in the same hand, but much smaller than the previous lines. There are two words of text in blue ink in the bottom margin.

Quire ten

85   86
_____/

F. 85r has a crude drawing of an angel. Ff. 85v – 86r are covered with pen trials.

17. Rylands Ethiopic MS 43
Daily Prayer Book, with musical notation

Quire 1

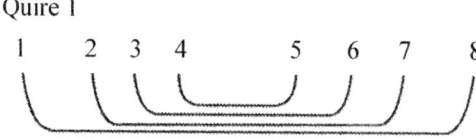

F. 1r contains the beginning of this work. The text is laid out in one column. Lines 1, 2, 5 and 6 are written in red ink. Many of the folios in this quire are very soiled. F. 6v contains a section division with three full stop symbols ⁂ at the end of line 8. F. 8r has a line of text in red ink.

Quire Maps and Notes

Quire 2

9   10 11 12   13 14 15   16

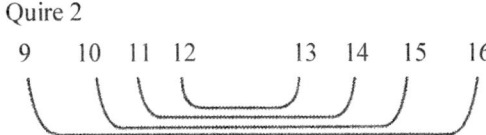

Many of the folios in this quire are very soiled. F. 13r has a line of text in red ink.

Quire 3

17   18 19 20   21 22 23   24

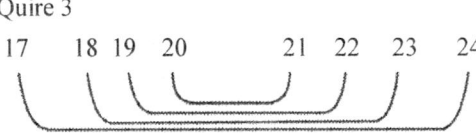

Many of the letters on f. 17r are smeared. F. 19r has a line of text in red ink. There is a section division at the bottom of f. 22v. A line of alternating red and black dots, of the form ▄▄▄▄▄▄▄▄▄▄, goes across the page. The next line of text (the first on f. 23r) is in red ink.

Quire 4

25   26 27 28   29   30 31   32

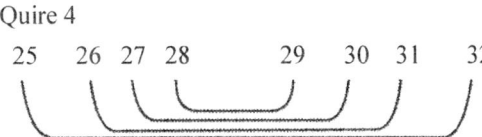

There is a section division at the bottom of f. 25v. A line of alternating red and black dots, of the form ▄▄▄▄▄▄▄▄▄▄, goes across the page. The next line of text (the first on f. 26r) is in red ink. Ff. 27v and 28r have smeared text near the bottom. There is a section division in the middle of f. 29r. Line 7 ends with three full stop symbols. This is followed by a line of alternating red and black dots, of the form ▄▄▄▄▄▄▄▄▄▄, going across the page. The next line of text is in red ink. F. 31 has a large hole.

Quire 5

33   34   35 36 37   38 39 40 41   42

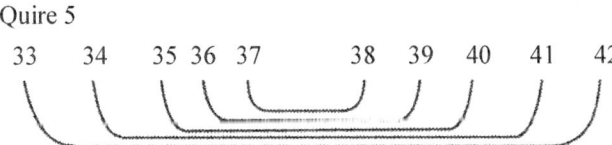

F. 33r begins a new quire and a new hand and a new text. The first line of text is in red ink. F. 34r has a line of text in red ink at the bottom. F. 35r has smeared lines of text at the bottom. F. 37r has a large area of smeared text. F. 39r has a large area of smeared text. F. 42r has a large area of smeared text.

A Catalogue of Previously Uncatalogued Ethiopic Manuscripts in England

Quire 6

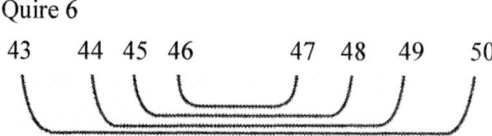

F. 45 is torn at the bottom near the gutter. F. 45v has a line of text circled with a black line. F. 48v has the end of the work after twelve lines. F. 49r has 10 lines of text in a different and crude hand.

18. Rylands Ethiopic MS 44
Daily Prayer Book and Funeral Ritual

Protection Quire

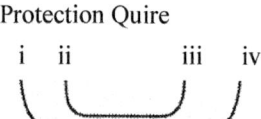

Both sheets have been cut at the gutter and re-stitched. In addition, f. 2 has been cut from the gutter to the fore edge and stitched. This quire has not been prepared for text. Though there is a set of prickings on the fore edge of f. iv, none of the others have prickings and none have been marked with columns or lines for text. The text in this quire is written in one column with red ink used for the names of saints and as part of the full stop symbol. There are sixteen lines of text on f. 1r, fourteen on f. 1v, twelve on ff. 2r and v, fourteen on f. 3r, thirteen on f. 3v, twelve on f. 4r and thirteen on f. 4v. The full stop symbol used is .

Protection Sheet

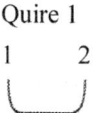

A folio stub is visible between ff. iv and v. It is the left-hand side of the sheet with f. v. The stub contains one marking on its 'recto' side. F. v has been cut from top to bottom in the centre and stitched together with a small flat strip of leather. F. v contains only pen trials.

Quire 1

1   2

This one-sheet quire has been trimmed along its bottom edge to be able to fit into the codex. The remaining bottom margin is smaller than normal. The top margin runs

Quire Maps and Notes

from 10–12 mm. The text on this quire is written in two columns. Red ink is employed at the top (column one, line one) and bottom (column two, line 14) of f. 1v and as part of some of the full stop symbols. Ff. 1v and 2r have interlinear insertions of a few letters

Quire 2

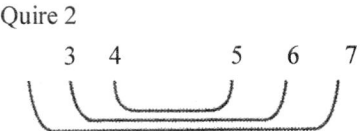

This three-sheet quire is missing one of its folios and the bottom has been trimmed to fit into the codex. The trim on this quire was not done with the same cut that trimmed quire one. The resultant bottom margin is completely missing and on a few folios (e.g. f. 7v) some of the letters are partly missing. The top margin in the quire is larger than that in the previous quire, 12–15 mm. The full stop symbol used in this quire is ❖. The left-side folio that once fitted with f. 7 to form a sheet is missing. There is no folio stub; f. 7 is loose. F. 3 is broken off at the line for the outside margin, about 15 mm from the fore edge. There is an interlinear insertion of a few letters. F. 5r has an erasure in col. one, line six.

Quire 3

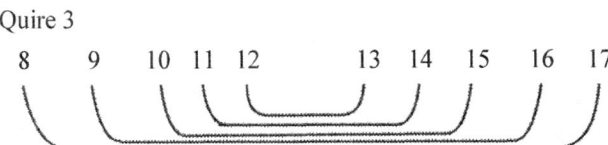

This quire is not from the same codex as the previous ones. The hand is different. The top margin is smaller than the previous quire. The text is laid out in one column. The full stop marker is usually ❖. Additionally, this quire is from the same source as those that follow. The subsequent quires are numbered with quire numbers in a sequence that presuppose this quire as the first. This quire begins a new work on f. 8r. Lines 1, 2, 5 and 6 are written in red ink. Red ink is used for sacred names and in writing numbers (the lines above and below the number) and in one and two-letter section markers.

Quire 4

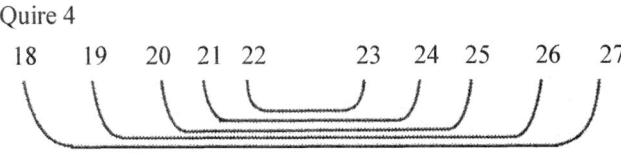

A Catalogue of Previously Uncatalogued Ethiopic Manuscripts in England

The trim along the bottom of this quire, is similar to, but not identical with, that of the quire before. The trim on this quire and the subsequent ones seems to be one made at a time later than the original production of the codex. The trims cut off most of the bottom margin and cut off portions of the bottom of the vertical lines that mark out the columns. These are usually complete in normal manuscripts. In the upper left corner of f. 18r is the quire number 'two'. It is located 3 mm from the gutter and 3 mm from the top of the page, i.e. well above the first line of text. F. 19r has an erasure in line 8. It has been filled in with two full stop symbols connected by horizontal black and red lines. F. 22r has two purple stains near the fore edge. F. 23r has a purple stain in the upper fore-edge corner. F. 24r has a purple stain in the upper fore-edge corner.

Quire 5

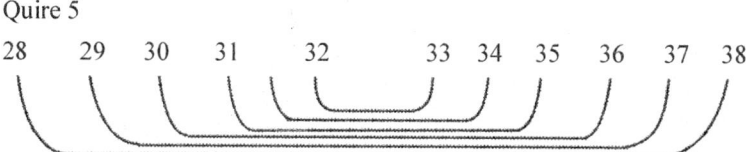

In the upper left corner of f. 28r is the quire number 'three'. F. 28v has an erasure into which three full stop symbols have been inserted, connected with black, crossing lines. F. 29 has an erasure at the top and at the conclusion of line three, there are three full stop symbols. The next line is written in red ink. F. 30v has an interlinear insertion of two letters in red ink. F. 31 has a tear and stitching (55 mm) from the gutter, arching outward and down to the bottom centre of the page. There is a folio stub visible between ff. 31 and 32. F. 34v has a heading in red text above the first line of text. F. 35 has a tear and stitching (50 mm) from the gutter directly out toward the fore edge. F. 37 has a hole in the bottom edge near the fore edge of the folio. The use of red and black full stop symbols is suspended between ff.. 29 r and 57r.

Quire 6

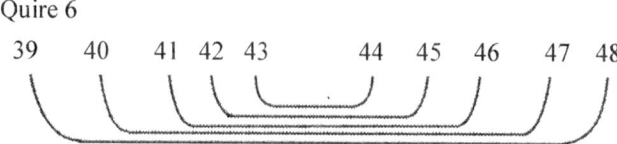

There is no quire number on f. 39r; however, the text is the smooth continuation of the text from 38v. The text on ff. 40v and 42v and 45r have been written in fifteen lines rather than the usual twelve lines of the folios before and after. F. 44r has fully two lines of erasures and overwrite.

Quire Maps and Notes

Quire 7

49　50　51　　52 53　　54　55　56　57　58　59

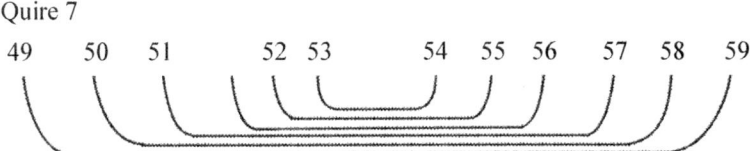

There is no quire number on f. 49r; however, the text is the smooth continuation of the text from 48v. There is a folio stub between ff. 51 and 52. F. 51v has nearly two lines of text in red ink. F. 50r has a word in the top line crossed out with three horizontal lines. Ff. 58v and 59r have several lines of erasures from between the current lines of text.

Quire 8

60　　　　61　62　　63　　64　65　　66　67　　68

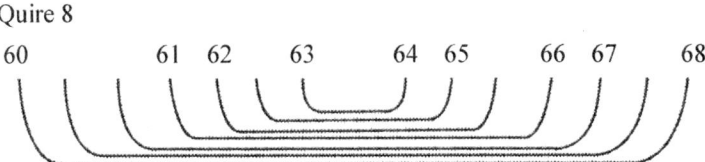

There is no quire number on f. 60r; however, the text is the smooth continuation of the text from 68v. A folio stub is visible between ff. 60 and 61 as well as the edge of an entirely cut off folio. Other folio stubs are visible between ff. 62 and 63 and between ff. 65 and 66. Another folio is entirely cut off between ff.. 67 and 68. F. 60v appear to be palimpsest, with the remains of several lines of text showing through. The same is true of f. 61r. There is a huge irregular tear and stitching that runs from top to bottom of f. 61. F. 64r has a section division after line three. There are two full stop symbols at the end of line three; line four is written in red ink. F. 66 has a large tear and stitching (60 mm) from gutter upwards toward the centre. Ff.. 67r and 68r appear to be palimpsest.

Quire 9

69　70　　　　　71

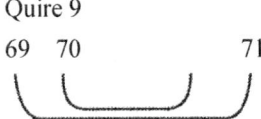

A folio stub is visible between ff. 70 and 71. F. 70r contains the end of the work with four and one half lines of text, followed by three full stop symbols and the rest of the page blank. F. 70v has fourteen lines of text. F. 71r is in a different hand and has seventeen lines of text with an eighteenth cut off and only partly visible near the gutter. F. 71v has a few lines of text, but they are too indistinct to decipher. They do not appear to be lined up with the scribed lines and marginal lines.

A Catalogue of Previously Uncatalogued Ethiopic Manuscripts in England

Quire 10

72   73   74   75

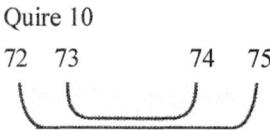

Both sheets in this quire have torn down the gutter from the top to nearly the first binding hole (30 mm). This quire has many differences from the prior ones. The text is laid out in two columns. The full page layout seems to be intact, i.e. the bottom of the sheet does not appear to have been trimmed into the bottom margin. The full stop symbol is used consistently and in the form ❖. The hand is similar to that in previous quires but not identical. F. 75r has interlinear words.

Quire 11

76   77   78   79

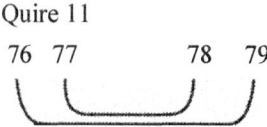

This quire has identical layout and scribal features as the previous. F. 77v has erasures. F. 79v has interlinear text.

Quire 12

80   81   82   83

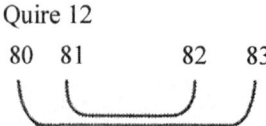

Both sheets in this quire have torn down the gutter from the top to the first binding hole. The quire employs a continuation of layout from the previous few quires. F. 80 has a word circled in black ink in column two.

Quire 13

84   85   86   87

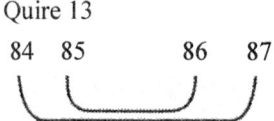

Both sheets in this quire have torn part way down the gutter from the top towards the first binding hole.

Quire 14

88   89 90 91   92   93   94   95

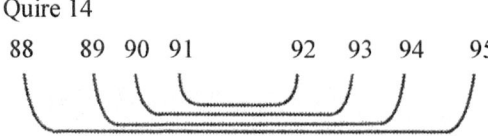

This quire is particularly mutilated. A reinforcement strip surrounds this quire. In addition, f. 89 has been cut off about 40–5 mm from the fore edge. The text is in two columns. F. 88r has a line of text in red above the first line of text in column one. F. 89r and v are blank. F. 90 has a small hole in the text area.

Quire 15

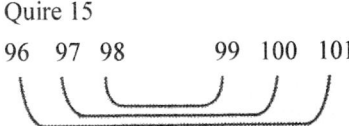

96 97 98   99 100 101

This quire and the one that follows (the last), have been trimmed on the fore edge with the same cut. This quire continues the format (two columns) of the previous.

Stops are frequently indicated by the use of the symbol ▌. F. 98 has a small hole near the fore edge. F. 99 has a hole near the gutter. F. 100 has a hole near the bottom centre.

Quire 16

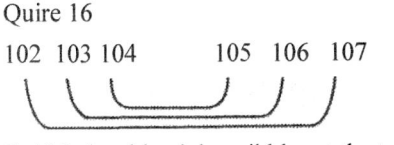

102 103 104   105 106 107

F. 105v has blue ink scribbles at the top.

19. Rylands Ethiopic MS 45
Prayers of the Blessed Virgin Mary on Golgotha

Protection Quire

i   ii

This sheet has not been prepared to receive text. There is a tear and stitching at the top of f. ii.

Quire 1

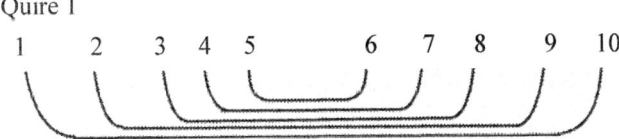

1   2   3   4   5   6   7   8   9   10

Ff. 1 r and v has been prepared for text, yet there is none on either side. F. 2r contains the beginning of the work. The first one and a half lines of text are in red ink. The text is laid out in one column of fourteen lines. F. 1r has a word surrounded by red dots (three above and three below) and partially erased. Red ink is used to indicate sacred names and in numbers (the red lines above and below the number) and in the full stop symbol which in this codex is usually 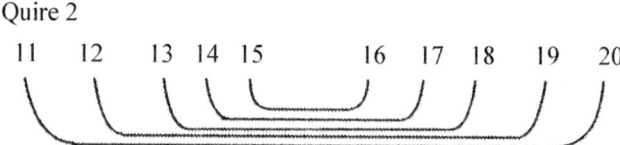, i.e. without an inner red dot. F. 5r has a black stain in the upper edge. F. 7v has interlinear letters.

Quire 2

In this quire, there are usually fifteen lines of text, with the fifteenth encroaching into the bottom margin. F. 13r has an interlinear word as well as black correction dots surrounding a word near the bottom of the page. F. 13v has red correction dots surrounding a word near the bottom of the page. F. 18v has black correction dots surrounding a word in line four.

Quire 3

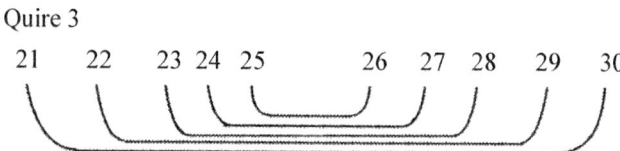

This quire lays out the text on fourteen lines. F. 23v has a word obliterated with ink in line three. There is a small piece of paper wrapped once around the binding string that appears between ff. 25 and 26. F. 29 has a hole in it in the lower text block.

Quire 4

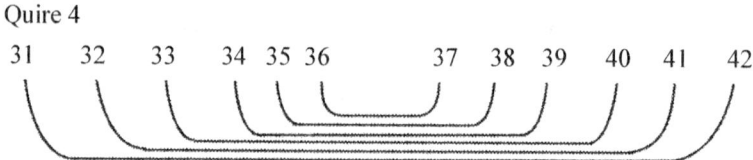

This quire lays out the text on fourteen lines. F. 32v has a black and red *haräg* (interwoven lines and geometric designs) after the ninth line. The line of text immediately following is in red ink. There is a word with red corrections surrounding it on lines 7/8. F. 35r has a word in red ink crossed out and written in above it between the lines. On f. 35v, the ink of several letters has flaked off. F. 38v has black correction dots around a word that has been partially erased. F. 40r has supralinear text. F. 42r has a word circled with a black ink line. F. 42v is devoid of writing.

Protection Quire

Quire Maps and Notes

This sheet has not been prepared to receive text. There is nothing written on the folios.

20. Mac Lennan Codex 1
Psalter

Protection Quire

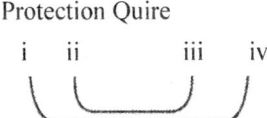

There is a reinforcement strip around the quire. Text is written on each folio of this protection quire. The writing on the quire is upside down in relation to the rest of the codex. The sentence ending symbol in this quire is ❖.

Quire 1

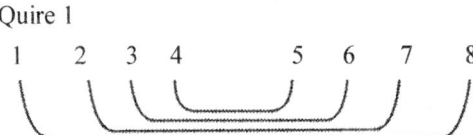

A reinforcement strip goes around this quire. F 1 has a tear and is repaired with stitching (17 mm) of red string. F. 1 has remains of a white string sewn into the upper, fore-edge corner of the page (5 mm from the top). F. 1 begins the new work. Lines 1, 2, and 18 are in red ink. There is no *haräg*. Text is in one column, with one sentence per line and ending with the sentence ending symbol ❖. F. 8r has an addition of 3 words of text at the end of line 8 in very small letters.

Quire 2

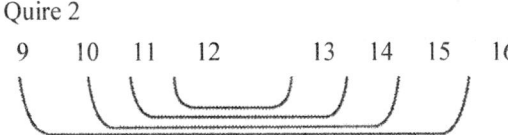

A reinforcement strip goes around this quire. F. 14r has an erasure and overwrite in line 16. F. 16 has remains of a white string and of a red string sewn into the upper fore-edge corner. F. 16r has an erasure and overwrite of a couple of letters in line 10.

Quire 3

A Catalogue of Previously Uncatalogued Ethiopic Manuscripts in England

A reinforcement strip goes around this quire. F. 23v has an erasure and overwrite in line 12.

Quire 4

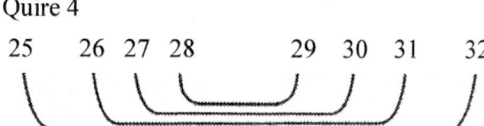

A reinforcement strip goes around this quire. F. 25 has remains of a red string sewn into the upper, fore-edge corner about 10 mm from the top. F. 26r has an erasure and overwrites in line 3 and 6.

Quire 5

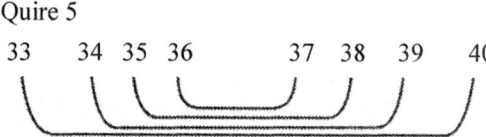

A reinforcement strip goes around this quire. F. 35 has remains of a green string sewn into the upper, fore-edge corner about 5 mm from the top. F. 36 has remains of a red string sewn into the upper, fore-edge corner about 10 mm from the top. F. 38 has a hole near the fore edge.

Quire 6

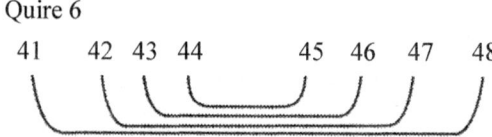

A reinforcement strip goes around this quire. F. 41v has an erasure and overwrite in line 8 as well as an interlinear line of text between lines 15 and 16. F. 42r has an erasure and overwrite of two words in line 8. F. 44 has remains of a green string sewn into the upper, fore-edge corner about 5 mm from the top. F. 47 has a hole in the parchment near the lower fore edge.

Quire 7

A reinforcement strip goes around this quire. F. 49v has an erasure in the centre of the folio. F. 51 has remains of two green strings, one in upper fore-edge corner, the other ca. 45 mm from the top on the fore edge. F. 52r has an erasure and overwrite of most of line 9. F. 53v has an erasure and overwrite of two words in another hand in line 19.

Quire 8

57   58 59   60   61 62 63   64

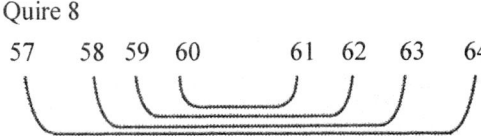

A reinforcement strip goes around this quire. F 57v has erasures and overwrites of a word or two in lines 4 and 6. F. 59v has an interlinear line of text between lines 11 and 12. F. 61 has remains of a white string sewn into the upper, fore-edge corner about 15 mm from the top. F. 63v has an interlinear half line of text between lines 18 and 19.

Quire 9

65   66 67 68   69   70   71   72

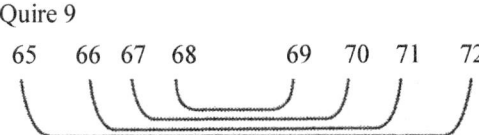

A reinforcement strip goes around this quire. F. 66r has erasure and overwrite in line 5. F. 72r has two lines of text in small letters in the upper margin.

Quire 10

73   74 75 76   77   78   79   80

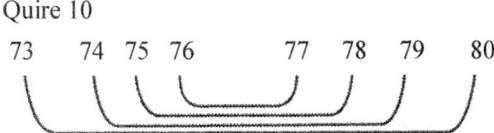

A reinforcement strip goes around this quire. F. 73 has remains of a red string sewn ca. 40 mm from the upper, fore edge. F. 73v has an interlinear line of text in red ink between lines 11 and 12. F. 76r has erasures and overwrites of letters. F. 77r has erasures and overwrites of words, most noticeably in line 4.

Quire 11

81   82 83 84   85   86   87   88

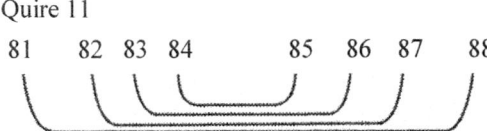

A reinforcement strip goes around this quire. F. 85r has interlinear words. F. 85v has a line of text with a line under and a line over it. F. 85r has an interlinear line of text above line 17. F. 86r has an interlinear line of text between lines 4 and 5. F. 88 has remains of a white string sewn ca. 40 mm from the upper, fore edge. F. 88v has an interlinear line of text between lines 1 and 2.

Quire 12

89   90 91 92   93   94 95   96

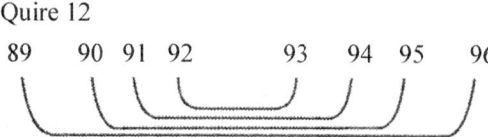

A reinforcement strip goes around this quire. F. 89r has an interlinear line of text between lines 6 and 7. F. 90r has erasures and overwrites of words. F. 94r has the last line of text circled. F. 94v has the first line of text circled.

Quire 13

97   98 99 100   101 102   103

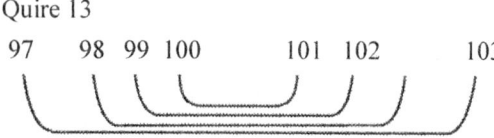

A reinforcement strip goes around this quire. A half sheet has been used and a folio stub is presumably present either between ff. 101 and 102 or between ff. 102 and 103, but because of the reinforcement strip, it cannot be determined which is missing. F. 103 has a hole in it near the lower fore edge.

Quire 14

104   105   106 107 108   109 110 111   112

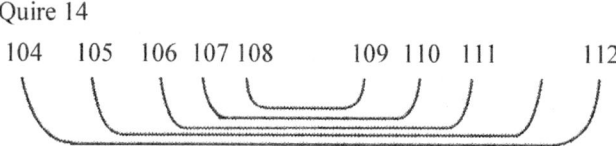

A reinforcement strip goes around this quire. A half-sheet has been used in the quire, but because of the reinforcement strip, it cannot be determined which folio is missing.

Quire 15

113   114 115 116   117 118 119   120

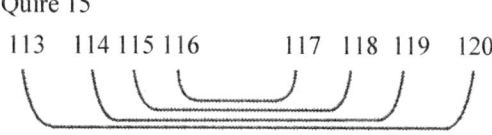

A reinforcement strip goes around this quire. F. 115 has a substantial thread sewn into the upper, fore edge 17 mm from the top. F. 118 has a substantial remnant of white thread sewn into the upper, fore edge of the folio. F. 119 has a substantial tear and stitching (75 mm) in the lower portion.

Quire 16

121 122 123 124   125 126 127   128

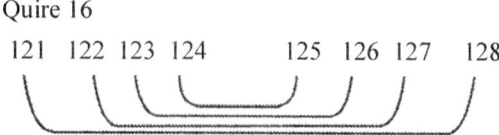

A reinforcement strip goes around this quire. F. 124 has a substantial and long (ca. 4 cm) remnant of thread sewn into the upper, fore edge only 3 mm from the top.

Quire 17

129 130 131 132 133 134 135 136 137

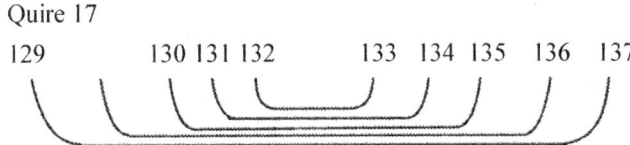

A reinforcement strip goes around this quire. A half sheet has been used in the quire somewhere between ff. 129 and 133, but because of the reinforcement strip, it cannot be determined which is missing. F. 131 has remnants of white thread sewn into the upper, fore edge of the folio, 13 mm from the top. F. 131v is blank below line 6, marking a major division. After the six lines of text are two parallel lines of alternating red and black dots in the form ▪▫▪▫▪▫▪▫▪▫▪▫. Between the two lines are three sentence ending symbols (✤), far left, centre and far right. A new work, the biblical Canticles, begins at the top of f. 132r with line one written in red ink.

Quire 18

138 139 140 141 142 143

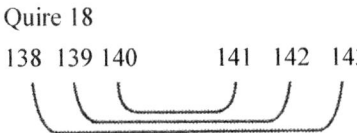

A reinforcement strip goes around this quire.

Quire 19

144 145 146 147 148 149 150 151 152

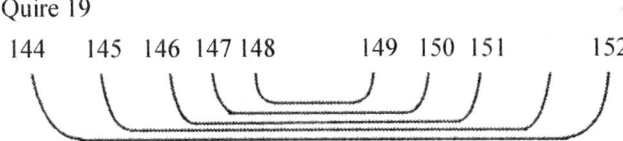

A reinforcement strip goes around this quire. A half sheet has been used in the folio somewhere between ff. 144 and 148 (with a corresponding folio stub somewhere between ff. 149 and 152), but because of the reinforcement strip, it cannot be determined which is missing. We have designated a location for a folio stub between ff. 151 and 152. F. 145 has remnants of white string ca. 5 cm from the upper, outer edge of the folio, about 40 mm from the top. F. 145r has a major division after line 8. There are two parallel lines of alternating red and black dots in the form ▪▫▪▫▪▫▪▫▪▫▪▫. Between the two lines are four sentence ending symbols (✤), evenly spaced. A new work, Song of Songs, begins immediately with a line of text in red ink. F. 151 has remnants of red string sewn into the upper, fore edge of the folio, about 8 mm from the top. F. 152v has a major division after line 5. There are two parallel lines of alternating red and black dots in the form ▪▫▪▫▪▫▪▫▪▫▪▫. Between the two lines are sentence ending symbols (✤), only one of which is currently visible on the

Quire 20

153 154 155 156 157 158 159 160

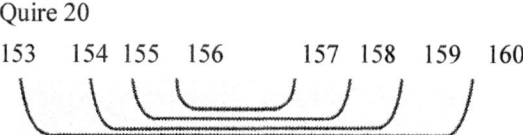

A reinforcement strip goes around this quire. A new work, Praises of Mary, begins on f. 153r. The text is in two columns. Lines 1, 3 in both columns are in red as well as line 6 in column one.

Quire 21

161 162 163 164 165 166 167 168 169

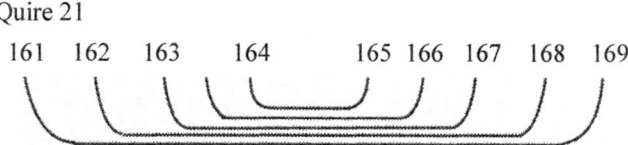

A reinforcement strip goes around this quire. A half sheet has been used in the quire, but because of the reinforcement strip, it cannot be determined which is missing. We have designated the space between ff. 163 and 164. F. 164v has a major division after column two, line 3. There are two parallel lines of alternating red and black dots in the form ▪⁖▪⁖▪⁖▪⁖▪⁖▪. Between the two lines are three sentence ending symbols (❖), evenly spaced. Immediately thereafter the new work begins with two lines of text in red ink. F. 169v contains the end of the current work at the bottom of the column one; column two is full of text from a very different hand. At the end of the first column is the division markers: two parallel lines of alternating red and black dots in the form ▪⁖▪⁖▪⁖▪⁖▪⁖▪. Between the two lines are three sentence ending symbols (❖), evenly spaced.

Quire 22

170 171 172 173

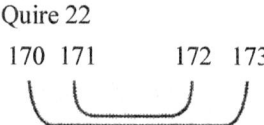

A reinforcement strip goes around this quire. The text in ff. 170rv is in a single column and written in a new hand. There are little, if any, margins. F. 171r contains one word. Ff. 171v–172r contain a running text in a new hand. F. 171v is full of text; there are eight lines of text on f. 172r. The bottom part of the folio has pen trials. F. 172v has pen trials. F. 173r contains two columns of text, each in a different hand, both of which are rough. The inner column is in black ink; the outer column is in brown ink. F. 173v is blank.

21. Mac Lennan Codex 2
Psalter

Quire 1

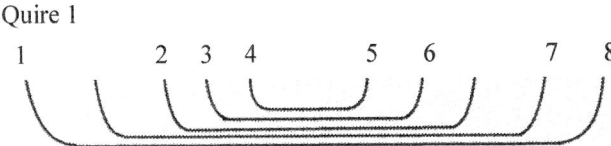

Folio stubs are visible between ff. 1 and 2 and between ff. 6 and 7. F. 1r begins the new work with lines 1 and 2 in red ink. There is one column of text. All sentences are on one line ending with the sentence ending symbol ❖. F. 1v has an erasure without overwrite. F. 4 has two small holes near the bottom of the page. F. 5r has an interlinear line of text near the bottom of the page. F. 8r has a major section division. After line 8, there are two parallel lines of alternating red and black dots of the pattern ▪▫▪▫▪▫▪ ▫▪▫▪▫▪. Between the two lines are 7 sentence ending symbols ❖ evenly spaced. F. 8v has an interlinear line of text.

Quire 2

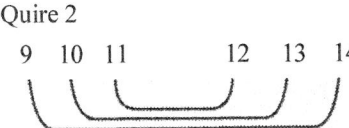

F. 9r has an erased line with some overwrite. F. 12r has an interlinear line of text as well as erasures and overwrites. F. 13r has an erased line with overwrite.

Quire 3

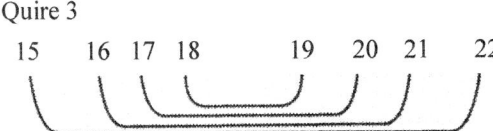

F. 20 has a tear and stitching (25 mm) at the top. F. 22v has a division marker. After line 12, there are two parallel lines of alternating red and black dots of the pattern ▪▫▪▫▪▫▪ ▫▪▫▪▫▪ .

Quire 4

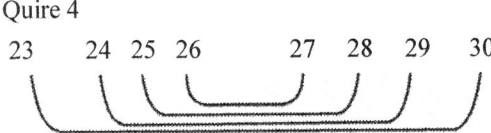

F. 24r has an interlinear line of text. F. 26 has a large tear and stitching (100 mm) in the lower portion of the page. F. 28 has a large, irregular tear and stitching at the bottom of the page.

Quire 5

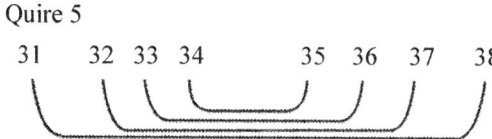

F. 31v has an interlinear line of text and erasures. F. 32 has two small holes. F. 33v has a division marker. After line 16, there are two parallel lines of alternating red and black dots of the pattern ▪ ▪ ▪ ▪ ▪ ▪ ▪ ▪ ▪ ▪. F. 35 has small holes in it. F. 38 is wrinkled and shrivelled somewhat. The wrinkling and shrivelling get more severe over the next several pages. There is a tear with stitching (40 mm) at the bottom of the page.

Quire 6

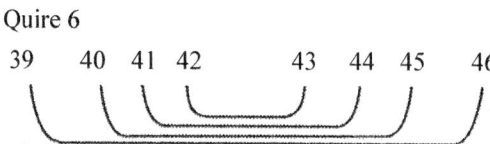

F. 39 has two tears and stitching at the bottom of the page. F. 41 has a tear and stitching (30 mm) at the bottom of the page. There is also interlinear text. F. 42r has a division marker. After line 7, there are two parallel lines of alternating red and black dots of the pattern ▪ ▪ ▪ ▪ ▪ ▪ ▪ ▪ ▪ ▪.

Quire 7

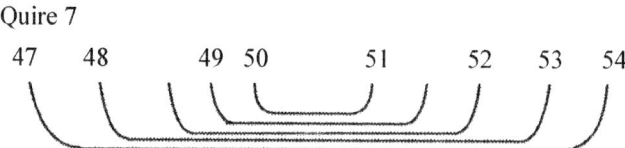

Folio stubs are visible between ff. 48 and 49 and between ff. 51 and 52. F. 52 has several erasures and overwrites of words.

Quire 8

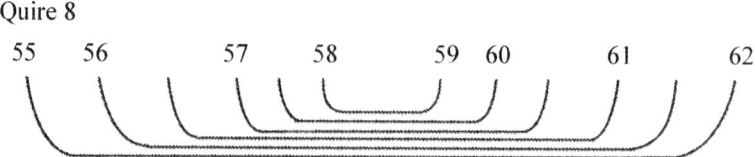

Folio stubs are visible between ff. 56 and 57, between ff. 57 and 58, between ff. 60 and 61, and between ff. 62 and 62. F. 57v has a major division marker. After line 10, there are two parallel lines of alternating red and black dots of the pattern

Quire Maps and Notes

▪▫▪▫▪▫▪▫▪▫▪▫. There are six sentence ending symbols ✤ evenly spaced between them. F. 60 has a large tear and stitching (70 mm) in the upper fore edge.

Quire 9

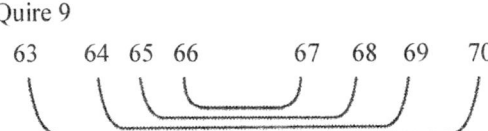

F. 65 has a large (25 mm long) burn hole near the centre top. F. 69r has a major division marker. After line 14, there are two parallel lines of alternating red and black dots of the pattern ▪▫▪▫▪▫▪▫▪▫. There are five sentence ending symbols ✤ between them, evenly spaced. F. 70 has a tear and stitching in the lower fore edge of the page.

Quire 10

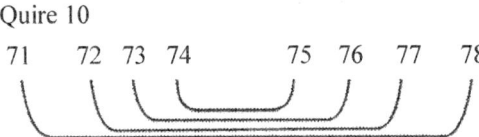

F. 74r has an interlinear line of text. F. 77v has a major division marker. After line 20, there are two parallel lines of alternating red and black dots of the pattern ▪▫▪▫▪▫▪▫▪▫. There are six sentence ending symbols ✤ between them, evenly spaced.

Quire 11

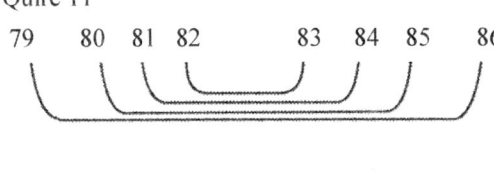

Quire 12

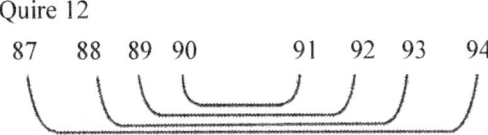

F. 87 has a tear and stitching (20 mm) in the lower fore edge. F. 87v has an interlinear line of text.

Quire 13

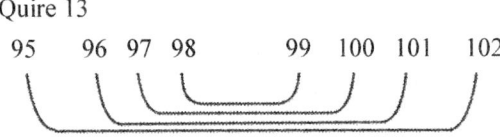

F. 95r has text written in the fore-edge margin in a different hand. F. 97 has a hole. F. 97r has erasures and overwritten words in a different hand. F. 97v has erasures and overwritten lines in a different hand. F. 99v has erasures with overwritten letters and interlinear letters in a different hand. F. 102 has a tear and stitching near the lower gutter edge.

Quire 14

103   104 105 106   107 108 109   110

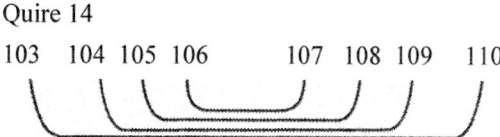

F. 107r has a section in which eight lines of text are written in the space normally given to five lines of text.

Quire 15

111   112 113 114   115 116 117   118

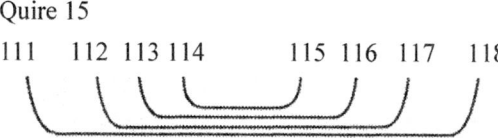

F. 111 has a tear and stitching (30 mm) near the bottom fore edge. F. 112 has two holes in it. F. 114 has a long, irregular tear with stitching (100 mm) near the bottom.

Quire 16

119   120   121   122   123 124   125 126

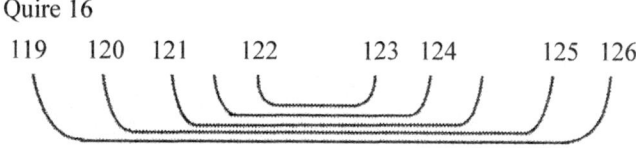

F. 120v has a division marker. After line 12, there are two parallel lines of alternating red and black dots of the pattern ▪▪▪▪▪▪▪ ▪▪▪▪▪. F. 121 has two holes near the top centre. Folio tabs are visible between ff. 121 and 122 and between 124 and 125. F. 124 has a huge tear and stitching (180 mm). F. 125 has a small hole in the upper fore-edge margin.

Quire 17

127   128 129 130   131   132 133   134

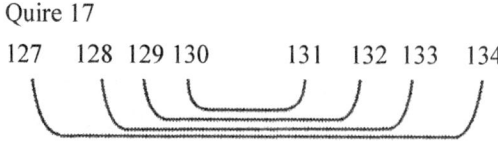

F. 127r has columnar writing of identical letters in red ink. F. 127v has a division marker. After line 14, there are two parallel lines of alternating red and black dots of the pattern ▪▪▪▪▪▪▪ ▪▪▪▪▪. F. 130r has interlinear line of text.

Quire Maps and Notes

Quire 18
135   136 137 138   139   140 141   142

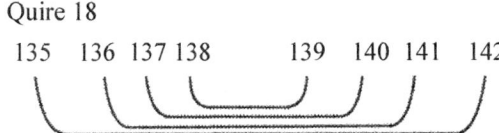

F. 135 has a hole in the centre. F. 137v and f. 138r have many examples of columnar writing of identical letters in red ink. There is also a column of erasures of a recurrent letter without overwrites on f. 137v. F. 138r has an interlinear line of text. F. 142 has a green thread sewn into the fore edge of the page some 42 mm from the top. F. 142r has a division marker. After three lines of text there is a single line made up of alternating red and black dots in the pattern ■■■■■■■■■■■■.

Quire 19
143   144 145 146   147 148 149   150

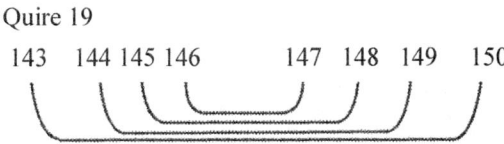

F. 143v has several erasures and an interlinear line of text. F. 144r has an interlinear line of text. F. 147v has an interlinear line of text and several erasures and overwrites. F. 149 has a tear and stitching (30 mm) near the upper page near the gutter. F. 150r has a major division. After 15 lines of text in a single column, there is a single line made up of alternating red and black dots in the pattern ■■■■■■■■■■■■. Below this line are fully 10 sentence ending symbols ✤ evenly spaced. Then follows a new work. It is written in two columns. Lines 1 and 2 of both columns are written in red ink.

Quire 20
151   152 153 154   155 156 157   158

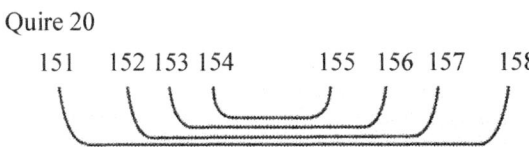

F. 154 has a burn hole near the bottom centre. F. 155 has a burn hole near the bottom centre. F. 155v begins a new work with four lines of red ink in both columns. F. 158 apparently came loose and is now sewn with a stitch onto the next quire

Quire 21
159   160 161 162   163 164 165   166

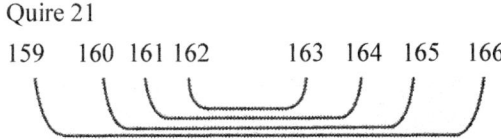

F. 161 has a tear and stitching in the lower gutter area. F. 162r has 14 lines of small text written in the fore-edge margin in small letters. F. 163r, column two has seven

and a half consecutive lines in red ink. F. 166r has several lines and words erased and overwritten.

One folio
167
There is at least one missing folio between f. 167 and f. 168.

Quire 22
168 169

F. 168v has a major division. After the 10th line in the first column, there are two parallel lines of alternating red and black dots in the pattern ▪▪▪▪▪▪▪▪▪▪▪. Above the top line are three sentence ending symbols and between the two lines are four sentence ending symbols, evenly spaced. The text that follows is in a different hand and continues into column two. F. 169r has large pen trials. F. 169v has a text in large crude letters.

Single folio
170
F. 170rv have what may be the start of crude drawings, but are more probably just random markings.

Protection Sheet
171 172

F. 171 has a large tear and stitching running down the centre of the folio. F. 171r has a crude drawing to the right of the tear. F. 171v has 10 lines of alphabet practice. F. 172r contains a crude drawing and several pen trials. F. 172v has several geometric patterns.

Single folio
173
F. 173 is not prepared for writing with lines. 173r has a few words at the bottom fore edge of the folio; f. 173v has only a few random letters.

22. Mac Lennan Codex 3
Prayers of the Blessed Virgin Mary on Golgotha and The Mystagogia,

Quire 1

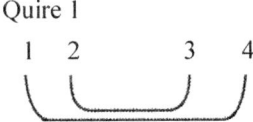

F. 1r and v blank. F. 2r pen trial. F. 2v – 3r, *Asmat* prayer. F. 3v – 4r, Painting of two angels.

Quire 2

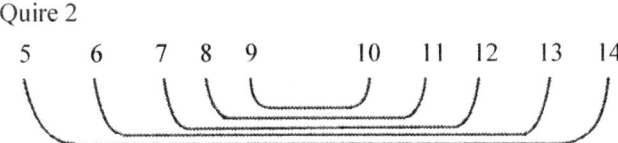

F. 5 begins new work. Text is in one column. There is a small *haräg* of red and black at the top. Lines 1, 2, 5 and 6 are in red ink.

Quire 3

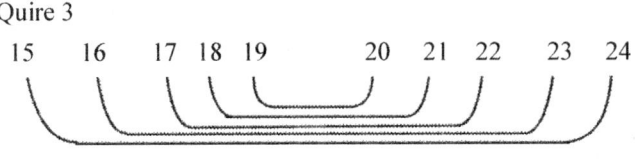

Quire 4

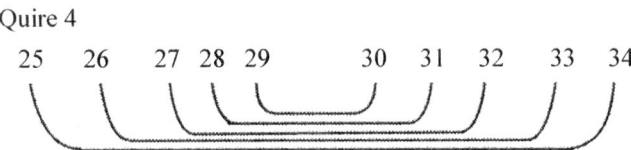

F. 31 has a green thread sewn into the upper fore edge about 8 mm from the top of the page. F. 31r has erasures in the bottom two lines. F. 31v begins a new text. There is a simple *haräg* of red and black. Lines 1, 2, and 6 are in red ink.

Quire 5

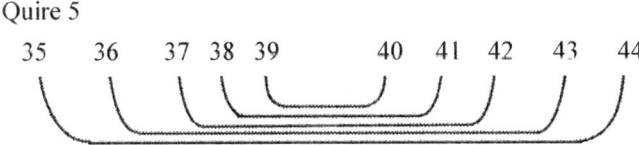

F. 37 has a hole in the upper centre. F. 43r has the ending of the work. There are 8 lines of text. The last word is in large black letters. There are two blank lines. There are about four rows of four sentence ending symbols ❖, thus, 16 in all. F. 43v and 44r are in another hand. F. 44v is blank.

23. Mac Lennan Codex 4
Prayer against the Tongue of People

Quire 1

1 2

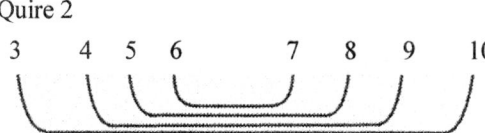

This sheet is not prepared for text. F. 1r v and 2r blank. F. 2v has the crude drawing of an angel with geometric boxes above and below.

Quire 2

3 4 5 6 7 8 9 10

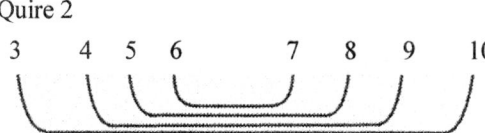

F. 3r is the beginning of the work. Lines 1, 2, 5 and 6 are in red ink. There are 9 lines of text in a single column

Quire 3

11 12 13 14 15 16 17 18

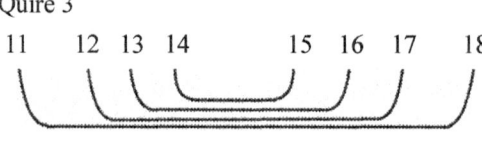

Quire 4

19 20 21 22 23 24 25 26

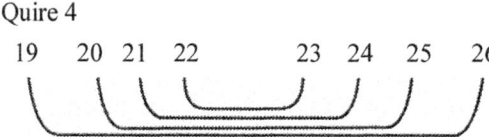

F. 25 has a hole in the lower area near the gutter.

Quire 5

27 28 29 30 31 32

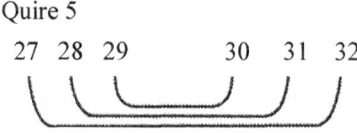

F. 30r the original owner's name was removed and replaced with Wäldä Gäbrə'l Ahähu. There is writing in ink in the lower margin. F. 31v has the name Wäldä Gäbrə'l Ahähu in pen in later hand. F. 32 blank.

Appendix One: Additional Information on the Bodleian Manuscripts

The Bodleian library has two additional sources of information on the manuscripts. The first of these is the information provided on a 3 x 5 card in the card catalogue of the reading room. In the same room is a small binder with the following title on the front: 'List of Arch. O.: Some Armenian and Hebrew Uncatalogued Manuscripts. Corrections to Ethiopic Manuscripts. MARGOLIOUTH Syriac Manuscripts'. In this appendix we provide from those two sources the information relevant for the fourteen Ethiopian manuscripts. Below we refer to the former as the card catalogue; the latter as the reading room list.

1. Bodleian MS Aeth. b.2

Card catalogue
'Seven vellum folios of illuminations in the Gondarene style. c. 1850 [Acqd 1986].'

2. Bodleian MS Aeth. d.9
The Miracles of the Blessed Virgin Mary

Card catalogue
    'Miracles of the BVM. 17th/18th c. ? 98ff.'

Reading room list
    XIXth cent.; vellum; 195 x 250 mm.; 98ff.; 20 lines to a page; written in two columns; mediocre hand; binding – stamped leather over wooden boards, repaired in Europe.

Miracles of the Virgin Mary

ff. (5ra – 97vb) – Miracles of Our Lady Mary, መጽሐፈ፡ተአምሪሃ፡ ለእግዝእትነ፡ማርያም, seventy four in number. Incomplete.

Remarks.
1. (ff. 1ra – 4v) A fragment of another ms. containing the Miracles of the Virgin Mary written in a poorer hand; the rubra have not been filled in.
2. (f. 2v) – In the lower margin two impressions of an oval seal with an illegible inscription. Between the two seals the name ምኒልክ is written in pencil.
3. The name of the owner, added in a second hand, was Wäldä Iyäsus.

3. Bodleian MS. Aeth. d.11
Hymns (Zəmmare) and Anthems (Mäwas'ət) for the Whole Year with musical notation

Card catalogue
Zimmare and Mewasiit, with musical notations. / 18th c. ii, 70ff.

Reading room list
XIXth cent.; vellum; 185 x 230mm.; 70ff.; 25 lines to a page; written in two columns; binding – wooden boards.

Zəmmare – Mäwas'ət

(ff. 1ra – 48vb and 54vb – 69rb) Hymns Zəmmare and antiphons Mäwas'ət for the whole year, with musical notation. Beginning
መዝሙር፡እምዮሐንክ፡እከኩ፡ዮሐንክ፡ዘጸድቃን፡ወሰማዕታት፡ዘሰር ብት፡ ዘዋዜማ፡ወዘሥሰ. . . .

2. (ff. 49ra – 54va) ከብሔተ፡ነግህ written in a second hand.

Remarks.
1. (Two front fly–leaves, ff. 69v – 70r, 71r–v) Blank.

Additional Information on the Bodleian Manuscripts

2. (f. 70v) Two notes in Amharic concerning the selling of the manuscript by *qes* Fəsha Gäbrä Həyät to *Marigeta* A'əmro Gäbrä Mädhən.

4. Bodleian MS. Aeth. d.14
Antiphonary (*Dəgg^{w}a*) with musical notation

Card catalogue

Fol. 1r – 2v: awaits description; 3r – 43r: Zemaré; 43v – 44v: awaits description; 45r – 45v: awaits description; 46r – 62r : Arganona Maryam; 62v – 63v: from life of Abuna Abereham; 63v – 66v: awaits description; 67v: donations [? To the church], witnesses, &c.; 68r – 80v: Me'eraf; 80v – 91r Mawades; 91v: Awaits description.

19th cent. 91ff.

Reading room list

XVIIIth – XIXth cent.; vellum; 220 x 265 mm.; 91ff.; 24 lines to a page; written in three columns in a very nice räqiq script, with musical notation; binding – wooden boards, repaired in Europe. / Dəgg^{w}a / ff. 3ra – 91ra The hymn book Dəgg^{w}a

Remarks.
1. The title Dəgg^{w}a appears written in a second hand on f. 3r in the upper margin, and in the Amharic note, f. 91r, see below Remark 5.
2. The manuscript belonged to Tewosalos and his teacher Arkä Səllus. The name of the owner's father was Asahel, that of his mother Ermon and that of his sister Ya'abbi Kəbra (ff. 43rb and 66vc).
3. (ff. 43r, v, 67r; 91v) Probationes calami, graffiti, etc.
4. (f. 91rc) Sälotä haymanot (Creed).
5. (f. 91rb) A note added in big cursive characters, in Amharic, during the reign of Haylä Səllase; an oath stating that this Dəgg^{w}a will pass, after the death of Wäldä Qirqos to abba Yamanä Bərhan
6. [sic] (f. 67ra) Three notes in Amharic: a. evaluation of a mullet, b. repayment of a slave, c. inventary [sic].

A Catalogue of Previously Uncatalogued Ethiopic Manuscripts in England

5. Bodleian Ms. Aeth. e.22
Psalter

Card catalogue

Psalms, Cantacles, etc. / 17th/18th c.? 150ff

Reading room list

XIXthe cent.; vellum; 120 x 170 mm.; 150 ff.; 23 lines to a page; written in one column, ff. 130r – 149v in two columns; binding – wooden boards covered with linen; the manuscript is contained in a double leather case (*mahdär*)

Psalter

1. (ff. 3r – 112r) <u>Psalms</u>. The titles of the chapters are the new ones.
2. (ff. 112r – 123r) The Canticles of the Prophets of the Old and the New Testaments.
3. (ff. 123r – 130r) Song of Song divided into five sections.
4. (ff. 130ra – 144ra) <u>Wəddase Maryam</u> arranged for the days of the week.
5. (ff. 144ra – 149vb) <u>Anqäsä bərhan</u>.

Remarks.
1. (ff. 149vb – 150vb) Praise of the Virgin Mary, ደዪድክዋ፡መላእክት፡ በግርያም... Incomplete.
2. (f. 149vb) – The name of an owner, Wäldä Səgab, in pencil.

6. Bodleian MS. Aeth. e.23
Psalter

Card catalogue

Amharic
Psalms [in red & black on goatskin]
17th c? 175ff.

Reading room list

XVIIth – XVIIIth cent.; vellum; 900 x 950 mm. [we do not know how to account for these numbers which are clearly wrong] ; i + 175ff.; 19 lines to a page; nice

Additional Information on the Bodleian Manuscripts

handwriting in one column ff. 162r – 175v in two columns; binding – wooden boards.

Psalter

1. (ff. 2r – 137v) Psalms, all bearing one title:
2. (ff. 138r – 153r) The Canticles of the Prophets of the Old and the New Testaments.
3. (ff. 154r – 161v) Song of Songs divided into five sections.
4. (ff. 162r – 171ra) Wəddase Maryam arranged for the days of the week.
5. (ff. 171rb – 175rb) Anqäṣä bərhan.

Remarks.
1. (Front fly-leaf r) A note concerning a marriage, in Amharic; Annunciation, in Geez; v – Three prayers, in Geez. All hardly legible.
2. (ff. 153ra – 154b) – In the upper margin, written later in two columns räqiq - Mälkə' to Gäbrä Mänfäs Qəddus.
3. (ff. 175rb – vb) Genealogies. At the end: a note in Amharic of religious contents.
4. The owner was Mäzgäbä Səllase (f. 175rb).

7. MS. Aeth. e.24
Antiphonary for Lent, Ṣomä Dəg^{w}a, with musical notation

Reading room list

XVIIIth – XIXth cent.; vellum; 130 x 185 mm.; 66ff. + two front fly-leaves; in one column in a nice räqiq with musical notation; binding – stamped leather over wooden boards.

Somä dəgg^{w}a

(ff. 1ra – 61va) Somä dəgg^{w}a, antiphons for the Fast of Lent.
(ff. 62va – 64rb) Table of halleluiahs (index of type meloshes).
(f. 64v) A hallelujah prayer with musical notation. Beginning
ዝንቱ፡በእኪ፡በእሲ፡እግዚ.ብሔር፡. . .

A Catalogue of Previously Uncatalogued Ethiopic Manuscripts in England

Remarks.
1. (Fly-leaf i r–v) Graffiti; a rudimentary drawing in pencil.
2. (Fly-leaf iir) Graffiti; a drawing in pencil representing a buste [sic] of a woman.
3. (Fly leaf iii r and v) Two miniatures representing a priest keeping the cross in one hand and the mäq^wamiya in the other.

8. Bodleian MS. Aeth. e.25
Psalter

Reading room list

XVIIIth cent.; vellum; 166ff.; 170 x 190 mm., fly-leaves ff. 1–2 and 166 160 x 190 mm.; ____ [blank space written in by hand] lines to a page; written in a good hand in one column, ff. 146v – 165r in two columns; binding – wooden boards.

Psalter

1. (ff. 3r – 134r) Psalmes. The titles of the chapters are the new ones.
2. (ff. 134r – 146r) The Canticles of the Prophets of the Old and the New Testaments.
3. (ff. 146va – 151rb) Song of Songs divided into five sections.
4. (ff. 151va – 161va) Wəddase Maryam arranged for the days of the week.
5. (ff. 144ra – 149vb) Anqäṣä bərhan. The last two sentences are missing. End: . . . ደስረደ፡ጋጤ፡አተነ፡በብዝ፡ጋ፡ሣዝሀሉ፡መም፡ሕረቱ።

Remarks.
1. (ff. 1r and 2r, v) Fragment of Psalmes in a second hand.
2. (f. 1vb) Magical prayer.
3. (f. 166r) Fragment of a prayer.
4. The owner was Täklä Maryam (f. 166vb).

9. Bodleian MS. Aeth. e.28
Harp of Praise, Arganonä Wəddase

No notes in either card catalogue or reading room list.

10. Bodleian MS. Aeth. f.19
Praises of Mary (Wəddase Maryam), Gate of Light (Anqäṣä bərhan), Hymns (Sälam) to Rufa'el

Card catalogue

[Awaits description] / [Acqd. 1966] iv. 48ff.

Reading room list

XXth cent.; vellum; 95 x 130 mm.; 48ff. + vi fly-leaves; 17 lines to a page; written in one column; binding – wooden boards.

Wəddase Maryam – Anqäṣä bərhan – Sälam to Rufa'el

1. (ff. 1r – 29r Wəddase Maryam arranged for the days of the week.
2. (ff. 29r – 43v) Anqäṣä bərhan
3. (ff. 44r – 48v) Sälam to Rufa'el (Chaîne, *Répertoire*, 215)

Remarks:
(Fly-leaves 1–vi) blank

11. Bodleian MS Aeth. f.20
Fragment from Gospel of John

No notes in either card catalogue or reading room list.

12. Bodleian MS Aeth. f.21
Psalter

No notes in either card catalogue or reading room list.

A Catalogue of Previously Uncatalogued Ethiopic Manuscripts in England

13. Bodleian MS. Aeth. g.22
Book of Chants, *Zema*, with musical notation

Card catalogue

Part of the Ethiopic hymnary (in Ge'ez), with musical notation
n.d. [Acqd 1959] i, 58ff.

Reading room list

XIXth – XXth cent.; vellum; 70 x 100 mm.; 58 + 1ff.; 14 lines to a page; written in one column with musical notation, in a current hand; binding – wooden board.

"Chants d 'école" - Kəstät zä-aryam

I. (ff. 3r – 44v) "Chants d 'école" (Velat, Me'eraf, I, 34–68).
   1. (ff. 3r – 12r) Mästägabə'.
   2. (ff. 12r – 17v) Arba't.
   3. (ff. 17v – 25v) Aryam.
II. (ff. 44v – 55r) Kəstät zä-aryam (Velat, ibid. 190–203).

Remarks.
1. (ff. 1 – 2) Fly-leaves.
   a. (f. 1r) Ornamentation, graffiti.
   b. (f. 2r) Miniature of St. Michael.
   c. (f. 2v) Probatio calami.
2. (f. 55v). Beginning of the First Epistle of St. John.
3. (ff. 56r, 57r) Graffiti.
4. (f. 57v) Magical prayer. Recipe for making an amulet.
5. (f. 57v) Graffiti, an rudimentary drawing.

14. Bodleian MS. Aeth. g.23
Praises of Mary and Gate of Light, with musical notation

Card catalogue

[Awaits description] / [Acqd 1965] 46ff.

Reading room list

XIXth cent.; vellum; 75 x 100 mm.; 46ff.; 14 lines to a page; written in one column; with musical notation, European binding.

Wəddase Maryam – Anqäṣä bərhan

1. (ff. 1r – 34r) Wəddase Maryam arranged for the days of the week
2. (ff. 34r – 46v) Anqäṣä bərhan.

Remarks:
1. F. 1 is badly damaged.
2. (ff. 45r–46v) – A prayer. Ff. 45r and 46r are almost illegible. The end is missing.
3. On the front fly-leaf in paper: 'To the Bodlean Library Signed P. Borrelli. 16/2/65'.
4. On the internal face of the back cover – 'Ex libris P.M. Borrelli'.

Appendix Two: A Study of Bodleian MS Aeth. b.2

Folio One

420 x 382+ mm. Three sides of the sheet are fairly straight. One side is roughly cut. It seems clear that this was the side toward the spine. Using this as the key, it would appear that the folio number has been put on the verso side of the page. However, we will refer to the sides (r and v) according to the library's designation. The parchment has been prepared for text. Nineteen prickings are visible on the fore edge and 19 lines have been scored across the folio from the gutter to the fore-edge margin. The top and bottom prickings for columns are visible. There are column lines for two columns of text. The bottom margin is 93 mm from the bottom of the page; the fore-edge margin is 75–8 mm; the top margin is 55 mm (the top line is set about 62 mm from the top edge). The margin between columns is 35 mm. The inside margin is where the cut was made out of the codex. One small tab still remains that looks as though it extended all the way to the fold. This would make the inside margin at 35 mm. On the verso side, there are seven examples of the symbol ❈. Four of them designate the ending of a sentence. The other three are part of a section close. This is found in the bottom of column two and is made up of two parallel lines of alternating red and black dots with three symbols between (left, centre and right).

Red ink is used in the following ways: 1) as part of the sentence ending symbol; 2) as part of the section divider; 3) in writing of the names of the saints on both recto and verso.

Folio Two

420 x 387+ mm. Three sides of the sheet are fairly straight. One side is roughly cut. It seems clear that this was the side toward the spine. Using this as the key, it would appear that the folio number has been put on the verso side of the page. However, we will refer to the sides (r and v) according to the library's designation. The parchment has been prepared for text. 19 prickings are visible on the fore edge and 19 lines have been scored across the folio from the gutter to the fore-edge margin. The top and bottom prickings for columns are visible. There are column lines for two columns of text. The bottom margin is 90 mm from the bottom of the page; the fore-edge margin is 75–80 mm; the top margin is 55 mm (the top line is set about 62 mm from the top

edge). The margin between columns is 33–5 mm. The inside margin is where the cut was made out of the codex. At the very bottom, one small tab still remains that looks as though it extended all the way to the fold and around it. This would make the inside margin at 35 mm. On the verso side, there are fourteen examples of the symbol ▪▪/▪▪. Eleven of them designate the ending of a sentence. The other three fill up the space between the end of the last line of text and the margin edge. There is no red ink used on the verso side. The hand is also a different hand than that on folio one. There are three blocks of text on the recto side: one at the top describing the picture, one at the bottom describing the picture and one on a banner as part of the lower picture. Only the text on the banner uses any red ink. The banner presents two pages or columns of text. There are eight lines of text. Lines 1, 2, 5 and 6 are written in red ink, as though this were the beginning of a work in an Ethiopian book.

Red ink is used in the following ways: 1) as part of the title page of a work (represented on the banner). The other uses of coloured ink are for illumination on the recto side.

Folio three

422 x 387+ mm. Three sides of the sheet are fairly straight. One side is roughly cut. It seems clear that this was the side toward the spine. Using this as the key, it would appear that the folio number has been put on the verso side of the page. However, we will refer to the sides (r and v) according to the library's designation. The parchment has been prepared for text. Nineteen prickings are visible on the fore edge and 19 lines have been scored across the folio from the gutter to the fore-edge margin. The top and bottom prickings for columns are visible. There are column lines for two columns of text. The bottom margin is 85 mm from the bottom of the page; the fore-edge margin is 80 mm; the top margin is 65 mm to the top line (there is no writing on the lines. The margin between columns is 34 mm. The inside margin is where the cut was made out of the codex. Thus, it is impossible to tell what the inner margin was. There are currently 32 mm of margin. The recto side has a text block that describes the picture. In it there are three examples of the symbol ⁝. At the end of the text block are four examples of the symbol ❖.

Red ink is used in the following ways: 1) as part of the sentence ending symbols; 2) in writing of the names of the saints. The hand on the recto side is not the same as the hand on the verso side.

Folio four

420 x 387+ mm. Three sides of the sheet are fairly straight. One side is roughly cut. It seems clear that this was the side toward the spine. Using this as the key, it would appear that the folio number has been put on the verso side of the page. However, we will refer to the sides (r and v) according to the library's designation. The parchment has not be prepared for text. There is a scoring line or some other scored line that runs across the top of the vellum. Moving from outer edge to gutter, it rises from 18 mm from the top at the outer edge to around 8 mm at the gutter side. There is a tear and stitching (22 mm) visible near the upper fore edge of the folio. There are two small holes and one larger hole in the vellum. The recto side has no text on it. The verso side has three words of text written in an orientation upside down to that of the recto side, plus pen scribbles in large letters in an orientation the same as the recto side.

Neither red ink nor any other coloured ink except black is used on this folio.

Folio five

417 x 392 mm. Three sides of the sheet are fairly straight. One side is roughly cut. It seems clear that this was the side toward the spine. In this case, the folio number has been put on the recto side of the page. The parchment has been prepared for text. 19 prickings are visible on the fore edge and 19 lines have been scored across the folio from the gutter to the fore-edge margin. The top and bottom prickings for columns are visible. There are column lines for two columns of text. The bottom margin is 90 mm from the bottom of the page; the fore-edge margin is 75 (top) – 82 (bottom) mm; the top margin (there is no text on the lines) is 64 mm. The margin between columns is 35 mm. The inside margin is where the cut was made out of the codex. One small tab still remains that looks as though it extended all the way to the fold. This would make the inside margin at 35 mm. On the recto side there are 20 small texts at various places around the numerous illustrations. In none of these texts except for the one in the extreme upper left corner is there any use of red ink. In all of the texts the sentence divider is the symbol ⁖. On the verso side, there are 8 lines of text above the illustration. In this text there are several examples of the symbol ⁝ . At the end of the text, the remainder of the eighth line of text contains 8 examples of the symbol ❈.

Red ink is used in the following ways: 1) as part of the sentence ending symbol ⁝ ; 2) as part of the section divider ❈; 3) in writing of the names of the saints on both recto and verso.

A Catalogue of Previously Uncatalogued Ethiopic Manuscripts in England

Folio six

422 x 388+ mm. Three sides of the sheet are fairly straight. One side is roughly cut. It seems clear that this was the side toward the spine. In this case, the folio number has been put on the recto side of the page. The parchment has been prepared for text. 19 prickings are visible on the fore edge and 19 lines have been scored across the folio from the gutter to the fore-edge margin. The top and bottom prickings for columns are visible. There are column lines for two columns of text. The bottom margin is 89–92 mm from the bottom of the page; the fore-edge margin is 80 mm; the top margin (there is no text on the lines) is 60 mm. The margin between columns is 35 mm. The inside margin is where the cut was made out of the codex. In several places, the cut appears to extend nearly all the way to the centre fold. The inside margin is measurable at 35 mm. On the recto side there is one small text describing the illustration at the top of the page. There is one example of a sentence divider in the form of the symbol ⁚⁚. It has no red ink in it. On the verso side, there are 7 lines of text beside the main character in the illustration. There are three examples of the sentence divider in the form ⁚⁚ with two further examples of the same symbol in the remainder of the seventh line.

On this folio, red ink (in this case, almost brown) is used in the text only to designate the name of the saint. Beyond that it is used as colour paint for a few items in the illustrations.

Folio seven

422 x 385+ mm. Three sides of the sheet are fairly straight. One side is roughly cut. It seems clear that this was the side toward the spine. Using this as the key, it would appear that the folio number has been put on the verso side of the page. However, we will refer to the sides (r and v) according to the library's designation. The parchment has not been prepared for text. There is a scoring line or some other scored line that runs across the top of the vellum from the gutter side to about the centre of the folio, rising slightly from 8 mm from the top until it hits the top of the page at the centre. Neither the recto side nor the verso side has any text written on it.

There is one small instance of red ink in the bottom right side of the recto side: seven very small marks (no higher than 2 mm) that appear to be the beginnings of colour added to the fore-edge margin of the illustration.

The Relationships of the Folios to One Another

Two lines of evidence suggest that the folios all came from the same codex. First, the sizes of the folios are consistent with having come from one codex. Second, those that have been prepared to receive text (all but folios 4 and 7) are prepared in exactly the same way (two columns, 19 lines, margins of identical size). This last piece of evidence does not apply to folios 4 and 7 which have their own unique relationship.

Several lines of evidence substantiate the idea that folios 4 and 7 originally made up one sheet. First, neither is prepared for text (all the rest of the folios are). Second, the general measurements coincide (though this is true of all the folios). When placed side by side with their gutters together, three further observations can be made. Third, skin sides and hair sides correspond. Fourth, the general appearance of the vellum (particularly on the inside of the sheet) look very similar in terms of their shade, colouring, wear, etc., though not in terms of the usage markings on the outside of the sheet (f. 4v has some very noticeable wear and stain marks on it, while f. 7r does not). Fifth, and most conclusive, is the scoring line that begins on the outside of folio 4 and ascends to meet the scoring line on the gutter edge of folio 7 (at precisely 8 mm from the top) and extends to the middle of folio seven. These codicological observations line up with observations about the style of artistry in the illuminations on the two folios. Several observations of this kind indicate the same artist on the two folios: 1) the formation of the wings on the two winged characters; 2) the hood around the face of the two winged characters, etc.

The best piece of evidence to try to pair up any of the other folios would be the scored lines for text on the folios.

One compelling piece of evidence points to the fact that folio 3 has no partner sheet among the remaining four folios. Whoever scribed the lines across the sheet, did not carry lines 2–11 and 13 across the gutter, while lines 1, 12 and 14–19 were carried across the gutter. All of the other folios are scored across the gutter.

Another piece of useful evidence goes beyond the mere fact of the scoring of lines for text, to the observation of the side of the folio on which the sheet was scored. If we lay the final four sheets gutter side to the left, the scoring of the lines looks like this:

    Folio one: top
    Folio two: bottom
    Folio five: top
    Folio six: top

When looked at in this way, the scoring of folios would have to be on opposite sides in order for them to be from the same sheet. Thus, the only possibility is for folio two to line up with one of the remaining three. But, in fact, none of these line up. Thus, of the seven folios, only two (folios four and seven) came from the same sheet.

List of the Manuscripts by Shelf Mark

1. Bodleian MS Aeth. b.2
2. Bodleian MS Aeth. d.9
3. Bodleian MS. Aeth. d.11
4. Bodleian MS. Aeth. d.14
5. Bodleian Ms. Aeth. e.22
6. Bodleian MS. Aeth. e.23
7. Bodleian MS. Aeth. e.24
8. Bodleian MS. Aeth. e.25
9. Bodleian MS. Aeth. e.28
10. Bodleian MS. Aeth. f.19
11. Bodleian MS Aeth. f.20
12. Bodleian MS Aeth. f.21
13. Bodleian MS. Aeth. g.22
14. Bodleian MS. Aeth. g.23
15. Cambridge University Library Or. 2547
16. Cambridge University Library Or. 2548
17. Rylands Ethiopic MS 43
18. Rylands Ethiopic MS 44
19. Rylands Ethiopic MS 45
20. Mac Lennan Codex 01
21. Mac Lennan Codex 02
22. Mac Lennan Codex 03
23. Mac Lennan Codex 04

List of the Manuscripts by Date

Several of the codices are composite, containing quires from different hands and different times. Consequently, the same codex may be listed in more than one century.

15th Century
    11. Bodleian MS Aeth. f.20

16th Century
    21. Mac Lennan Codex 2

17th Century
    6. Bodleian MS. Aeth. e.23
    9. Bodleian MS. Aeth. e.28
    18. Rylands Ethiopic MS 44, ff. 3r–7v
    20. Mac Lennan Codex 1

Early-18th Century
    18. Rylands Ethiopic MS 44, ff. 88r–107v

18th Century
    3. Bodleian MS. Aeth. d.11
    4. Bodleian MS. Aeth. d.14
    8. Bodleian MS. Aeth. e.25
    17. Rylands Ethiopic MS 43
    18. Rylands Ethiopic MS 44, ff. 1r–2v
    19. Rylands Ethiopic MS 45

Late-18th Century
    18. Rylands Ethiopic MS 44, ff. 8r–87v

Late-18th, Early-19th Century
    2. Bodleian MS Aeth. d.9

A Catalogue of Previously Uncatalogued Ethiopic Manuscripts in England

19th Century

    5. Bodleian Ms. Aeth. e.22

    7. Bodleian MS. Aeth. e.24

    12. Bodleian MS Aeth. f.21

    14. Bodleian MS. Aeth. g.23

    22. Mac Lennan Codex 3

    23. Mac Lennan Codex 4

Mid-19th Century

    1. Bodleian MS Aeth. b.2

Late-19th, Early 20th Century

    16. Cambridge University Library Or. 2548

20th Century

    10. Bodleian MS. Aeth. f.19

    13. Bodleian MS. Aeth. g.22

    15. Cambridge University Library Or. 2547

    18. Rylands Ethiopic MS 44, ff. ir–ivv(erso)

Index of Works

A guide for singing in the various styles, 4
Angels Praise Her, Yewedsewa Mäla'ekt lä Maryam, 24
Angels Praise Her, Yəwedsəwa Mäla'ekt lä Maryam, 6
Antiphonary (Dəggʷa) with musical notation, 4, 43, 113
Antiphonary for Lent, Ṣomä Dəgʷa, with musical notation, 9, 57, 115
Asmat prayer, 11, 19, 34, 109
Chant Kəstät zä-aryam, 19
Chants, *Zema*, with musical notation, 19, 78, 118
Daily Prayer Book, 25, 88, 90
First Epistle of St. John, 19
Funeral Ritual, *Mäṣḥafä Gənzät*, 25, 90
Gate of Light, Anqäṣä bərhan (*see also*, Psalter), 14, 25, 72, 117
Gate of Light, Anqäṣä bərhan, with musical notation (*see also*, Psalter), 20, 81, 118
Gospel of John, 15, 26, 74, 117
Harp of Mary, Arganonä Maryam, 4
Harp of Praise, Arganonä Wəddase, 11, 66, 116
Hymn to Jesus, Mälkə'a Iyäsus, 23, 84
Hymn to Mary, 29
Hymns (Sälam) to Rufa'el, 117
Hymns (Zəmmare) and Anthems (Mäwas'ət) for the whole year, 3
Hymns (Zəmmare) and Anthems (Mäwas'ət) for the Whole Year, 41, 112
Hymns (Zəmmare) with musical notation, 4, 9
Hymns to Gäbrä Mänfäs Qəddus, 8
Hymns to Rufa'el, Sälam to Rufa'el, 14
Hymns to the Four Creatures, 29
King Herod and the Killing of the Innocents, 4
Life of Abunä Abrəham, 4
Liturgical Chants, with musical notation, 20, 83
Mäwädəs, with musical notation, 4
Mə'əraf, with musical notation, 4
Miracles of the Blessed Virgin Mary, 3, 37, 111
Missal, Qəddase Maryam, 26
Mystagogia, 23, 34, 84, 109
Orthodox Faith, Retu'a Haymanot, 26
Praises of Mary, Wəddase Maryam (*see also*, Psalter), 14, 72, 117
Praises of Mary, Wəddase Maryam, with musical notation (*see also*, Psalter), 20, 24, 81, 118
Prayer against the Tongue of People, a.k.a., Hymn-Invocation Lesanä Säb', 35, 110
Prayer to Mary, Sälotä Maryam, 26
Prayers of the Blessed Virgin Mary on Golgotha, 23, 27, 34, 84, 95, 109
Psalter, 5, 7, 10, 17, 28, 31, 46, 50, 74, 97, 103, 114, 116, 117

Index of Names

2nd Viscount Rennell of Rodd, 11
A'əmro Gäbrä Mädhən, 113
Abba Gäbrä-Mädhən, 23
Abba Giyorgis, 13
Abba Mäzgäbu Jämärä, 24, 85
Abunä Abib, 8
Abunä Abrəham, 4
Abunä Amoṣ, 2
Abunä Märqorewos, 1
Abuna Wäldä Libanos, 29
Arkä Səlus, 4
Asahel, 4, 113
Beck, Dr B.E., 24
Booth, Richard, 25
Borrelli, P.M., 20, 119
Cliffe, Mrs, 27, 28
Däjazmach Hailu, 1
Dennison, Mary Annette, 18
Devil, Satan, 1, 2
Ermin, 4
Ewosṭatewos, 1
Ewos(atewos, 2
Fəsha Gäbrä Həyät, 113
Fogg, Sam, 12, 13
Forbes, Lesley, 13
Fowler, H.A.B., 3, 6
Gäbrä Amlak, 24
Gäbrä Egziabher, 24
Gäbrä Krəstos, 1
Gäbrä Mänfäs Qəddus, 1, 8, 13, 115
Gädlä Tsadqan, 1

Getatchew Haile, Professor, x
Ground Hornbill painter, 13
Hale, Colonel, 15, 16
Isitrfos, 21
Kane, Dr Thomas L., 5
La'əkä Maryam, 11
Leveson, Major, 33
Lewis, Rev. Arthur, 33
Liqä Guba'e Wäldä Giyorgis, 1
Mac Lennan, Dr Ian, v, vii, 30, 33, 35
Mäzgäbä Səllase, 8, 115
Minio-Paluello, Dr A., 19
Padwick, Mrs Sarah, 33
Picken, Laurence, 22
Rassam, Dr Hormuzd, 31
Säbänä Giyorgis, 1
SGD Library of Ethiopian Manuscripts, x, 30
Täklä Haymanot, 1, 2, 13
Täsfa Mika'el, 32
Tewosalos, 4, 113
Thornton's Bookshop, Oxford, 3, 9
Wälätä Kidan, 24
Wäldä Ṣäga-Ab, 6
Wäldä Gäbrə'l Ahähu, 35, 110
Wäldä Iyäsus, 3, 112
Wäyzaro Warka, 1
Wigan, Bernard, 15
Wingate, Sir F.R., 8
Yä'abi Kəbra, 4

Description of Plates

Plate 01: Bodleian MS. Aeth. b. 2, f. 3r (used by permission Bodleian Library, University of Oxford), showing an illumination of the Ethiopian saint, Gäbrä Mänfäs Qəddus.

Plate 02: Bodleian MS. Aeth. d. 9, f. 5r (used by permission Bodleian Library, University of Oxford), showing: 1) the beginning of a new work with lines 1, 2, 5 and 6 written in red ink; 2) the name of Mary written in red ink; 3) space at the top of the folio left, presumably, for a *haräg*; and 4) the stamp of the library at the bottom of the folio.

Plate 03: Bodleian MS. Aeth. d. 11, f. 8r (used by permission Bodleian Library, University of Oxford), showing: 1) the text with musical notation; 2) marginal notation; 3) clear vertical lines scribed for the layout of the text block.

Plate 04: Bodleian MS. Aeth. d. 14, f. 46r (used by permission Bodleian Library, University of Oxford), showing: 1) the text block in three columns; 2) the beginning of a new work with lines 1, 2, 5, 6, 20 and 21 written in red ink; text and musical notation; and 4) clear prickings on the fore edge of the folio.

Plate 05: Bodleian MS. Aeth. e. 22, f. 130r (used by permission Bodleian Library, University of Oxford), showing: 1) the end of the *Song of Songs* at the top of the folio (which, along with the *151 Psalms of David* and the fifteen *Biblical Canticles*, is always written in one column); 2) full stop symbols used to mark division; and 3) the beginning of *Praises of Mary* (which, along with *Gate of Light*, is always written in two columns).

Plate 06: Bodleian MS. Aeth. e. 23, f. 87v (used by permission Bodleian Library, University of Oxford), showing: 1) two parallel lines of alternating red and black dots used as a section divider between psalms (typically placed after every tenth psalm); 2) marginal lectionary notation; 3) remnant of red string (used as a navigation system with strings corresponding to the various divisions of the Psalter) in the upper fore-edge corner.

Plate 07: Bodleian MS. Aeth. e. 24, f. 13r (used by permission Bodleian Library, University of Oxford), showing: 1) text and musical notation; 2) a one-column haräg marking the beginning of a new work; 3) the new work indicated by lines

8, 9, 20 and 21 written in red ink in both columns; 4) a huge tear with repair stitching; 5) marginal liturgical notation.

Plate 08: Bodleian MS. Aeth. e. 25, f. 134r (used by permission Bodleian Library, University of Oxford), showing the division between the Psalms and the Biblical Canticles.

Plate 09: Bodleian MS. Aeth. e. 28, ff. 1v–2r (used by permission Bodleian Library, University of Oxford), showing the distinctive illumination work of the so-called 'Hornbill Artist.'

Plate 10: Bodleian MS. Aeth. f. 19, ff. 21v–22r (used by permission Bodleian Library, University of Oxford), showing: 1) the quire number 'three' on f. 22r; 2) the prickings on f. 21; and 3) the four chain stitches visible between quires.

Plate 11: Bodleian MS. Aeth. f. 20, ff. 1v–2r (used by permission Bodleian Library, University of Oxford), showing: 1) the abrasion strip down the centre where the sheet was affixed to Col. Hale's book; 2) the layout of the text blocks; and 3) the marginal navigation and lectionary systems.

Plate 12: Bodleian MS. Aeth. f. 21, f. 113r (used by permission Bodleian Library, University of Oxford), showing the prickings, lines, and *haräg* as well as the lines of text written in red ink (to indicate the first folio of a new work).

Plate 13: Bodleian MS. Aeth. g. 22, ff. 42v–43r (used by permission Bodleian Library, University of Oxford), showing text and musical notation, a section division (with line of alternating black and red dots and with two lines of text written in red ink), and a folio stub in the gutter.

Plate 14: Bodleian MS. Aeth. g. 23, f. 22r (used by permission Bodleian Library, University of Oxford), showing string from the new binding, text with musical notation, two lines of text written in red ink and a simple *haräg*.

Plate 15: Cambridge University Library, Or. 2547, ff. 36v–37r (used by permission of the Syndics of Cambridge University Library) showing: 1) an erasure and overwrite of the name of the latest owner in blue ink on f. 36v, line 6; 2) the quire number 'five' at the top, inside of f. 37r; 3) the beginning of a new work with lines 2, 3, and 8 written in red ink; and 4) a distinctive sentence ending symbol.

Plate 16: Cambridge University Library, Or. 2548, ff. 36v–37r (used by permission of the Syndics of Cambridge University Library), showing: 1) text and musical notation; 2) text and musical notation; 3) small numbers in inner margin indicating for the worshipper to sing the line 2 or 3 times.

Plate 17: Rylands Ethiopic MS 43, front cover and f. 1r (used by permission, John Rylands Library of Manchester University), showing: 1) the binding

Description of Plates

attachment to the covers (visible in the gutter); 2) the beginning of a new work with lines 1, 2, 5 and 6 written in red ink; 3) the stitching of the cracked board (lower fore edge); and 4) text with musical notation.

Plate 18: Rylands Ethiopic MS 43, ff. 1v–2r (used by permission, John Rylands Library of Manchester University), showing text with musical notation and water stains.

Plate 19: Rylands Ethiopic MS 43, ff. 32v–33r (used by permission, John Rylands Library of Manchester University). The left side (f. 32v) shows the final page of *The Angels Praise Her*; the right side (f. 33r) shows the beginning of *The Gate of Light* in a new hand.

Plate 20: Rylands Ethiopic MS 43 in leather carrying case (*mahdär*) with strap (used by permission, John Rylands Library of Manchester University).

Plate 21: Rylands Ethiopic MS 44, spine (used by permission, John Rylands Library of Manchester University). The spine shows some of the evidence of the composite nature of the codex.

Plate 22: Rylands Ethiopic MS 44, ff. 7v–8r (used by permission, John Rylands Library of Manchester University). Folio 8r contains the beginning of the primary work in the codex. We can also see text layout in both one and two-column formats.

Plate 23: Rylands Ethiopic MS 27, left, and Rylands Ethiopic MS 45, right (used by permission, John Rylands Library of Manchester University). Ethiopian manuscripts come in all shapes and sizes. Rylands Ethiopic MS 45 represents those on the small end of the scale.

Plate 24: Rylands Ethiopic MS 45, f. 2r (used by permission, John Rylands Library of Manchester University), showing the beginning of the major work in this codex and red correction dots used around the partially erased word in line eight.

Plate 25: Mac Lennan Codex 1 (used by permission, Dr Ian Mac Lennan), showing codex, carrying case and hand-written note by Alan Stepney-Gulston.

Plate 26: Mac Lennan Codex 1, spine (used by permission, Dr Ian Mac Lennan).

Plate 27: Mac Lennan Codex 1, ff. 152v–153r (used by permission, Dr Ian Mac Lennan), showing the end of Song of Songs in one column, the beginning of Praises of Mary in two columns and the note of ownership between.

Plate 28: Anklets from Ethiopian soldier or priest sharing the same provenance as Mac Lennan Codex 1, along with Gulston note to that effect (used by permission, Dr Ian Mac Lennan).

A Catalogue of Previously Uncatalogued Ethiopic Manuscripts in England

Plate 29: Iron hand cross (used by permission, Dr Ian Mac Lennan) from an Ethiopian soldier or priest sharing the same provenance as the Mac Lennan Codex 1, along with a Gulston note which says: 'This cross was held to be extremely sacred. Wherever it was placed up, it at once constituted that spot a place for all religious ceremony brought from Maqdala 1867 by Dr Rassam'. Dr Mac Lennan considers it likely that the attribution of these powers to the hand cross is the result of a confusion that developed somewhere early in the process of acquiring the codex and bringing it to England. Those powers are more appropriately attributed to the sacred *tabot* that was part of the same lot and which Dr Mac Lennan purchased and returned to Ethiopia.

Plate 30: Mac Lennan Codex 2, ff. 137v–138r (used by permission, Dr Ian Mac Lennan), showing the tenth Biblical Canticle laid out with a columetric format in which the successive letters that make up the first word of each line are written in alternating red and black ink and form a uniform column when viewed vertically.

Plate 31: Mac Lennan Codex 3, cover and protection flap (used by permission, Dr Ian Mac Lennan). Note the small size of the codex.

Plate 32: Mac Lennan Codex 3, ff. 27v–28r (used by permission, Dr Ian Mac Lennan), showing a simple *haräg* at the top of f. 27v and the start of the new work.

Plate 33: Mac Lennan Codex 4, cover and amulet case (used by permission, Dr Ian Mac Lennan).

Plate 34: Mac Lennan Codex 4, ff. 8v–9r (used by permission, Dr Ian Mac Lennan), showing text and two chain stitches between quires in the gutter.

Plates

A Catalogue of Previously Uncatalogued Ethiopic Manuscripts in England

Plate 1: Bodleian MS. Aeth. b. 2, f. 3r.

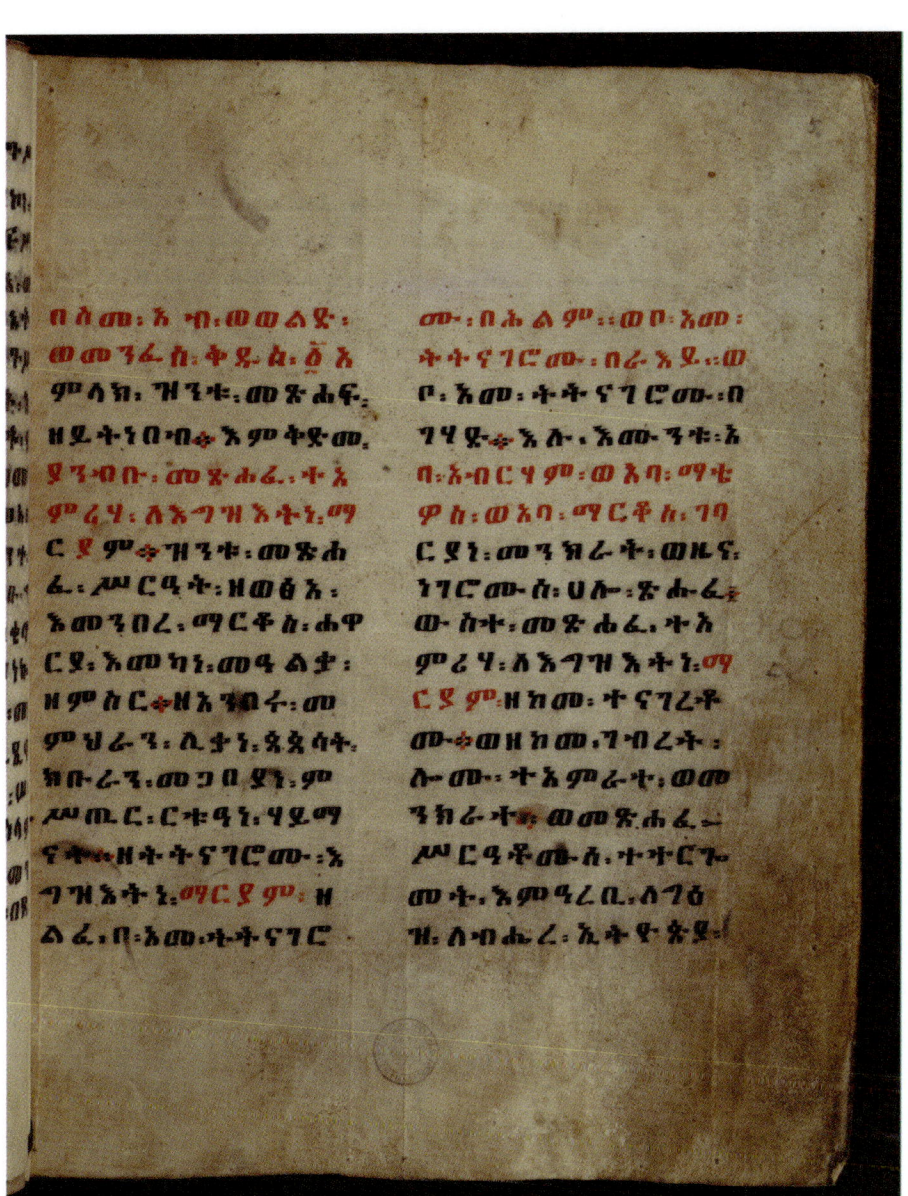

Plate 2: Bodleian MS. Aeth. d. 9, f. 5r.

A Catalogue of Previously Uncatalogued Ethiopic Manuscripts in England

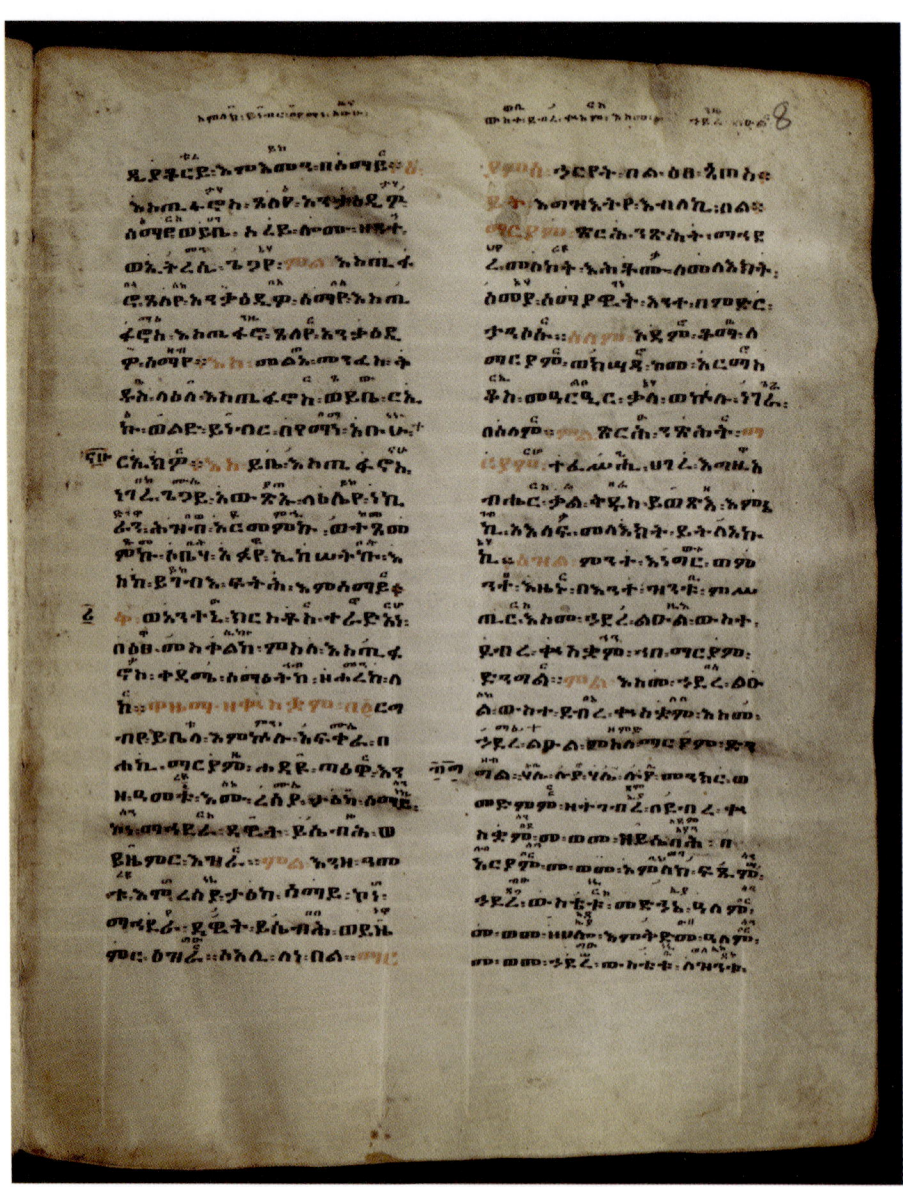

Plate 3: Bodleian MS. Aeth. d. 11, f. 8r.

Plate 4: Bodleian MS. Aeth. d. 14, f. 46r.

A Catalogue of Previously Uncatalogued Ethiopic Manuscripts in England

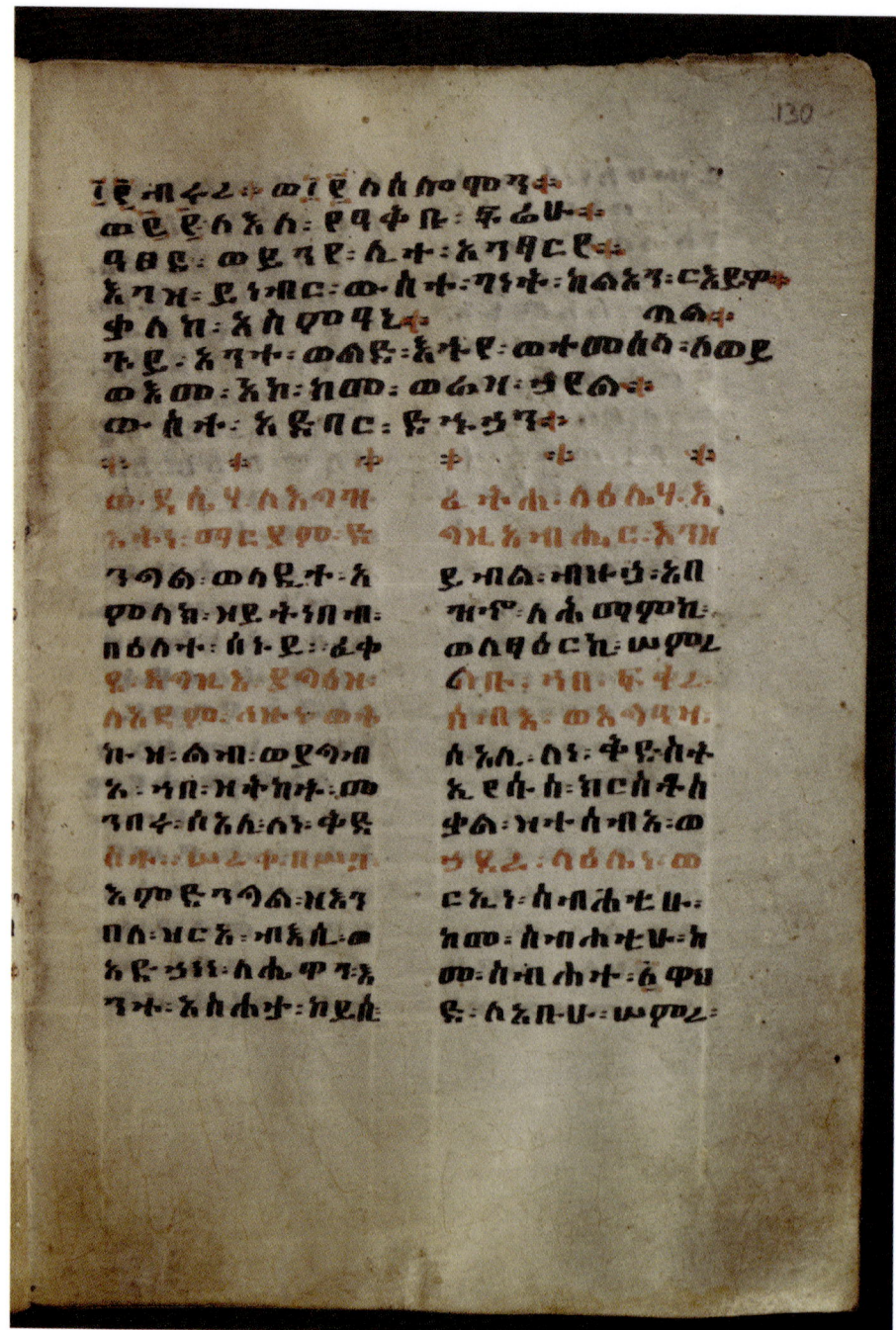

Plate 5: Bodleian MS. Aeth. e. 22, f. 130r.

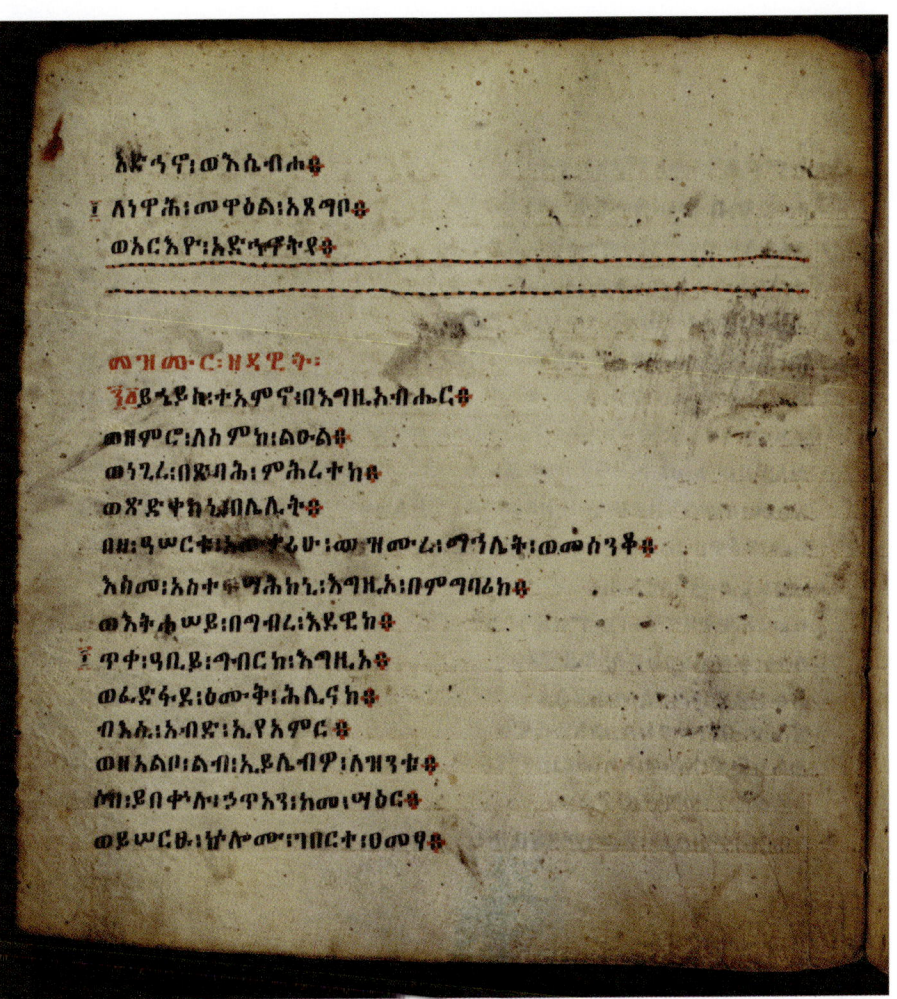

Plate 6: Bodleian MS. Aeth. e. 23, f. 87v.

A Catalogue of Previously Uncatalogued Ethiopic Manuscripts in England

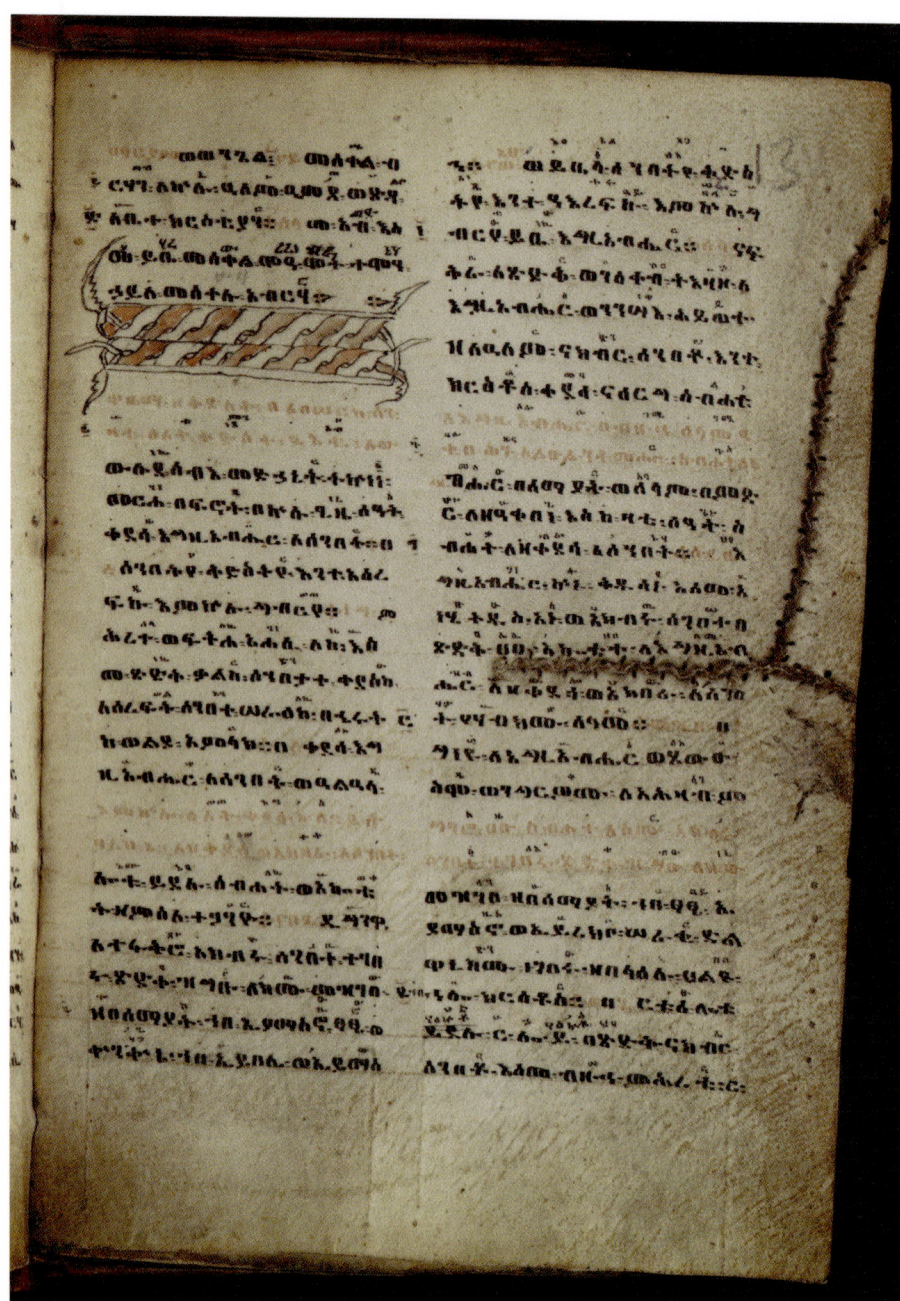

Plate 7: Bodleian MS. Aeth. e. 24, f. 13r.

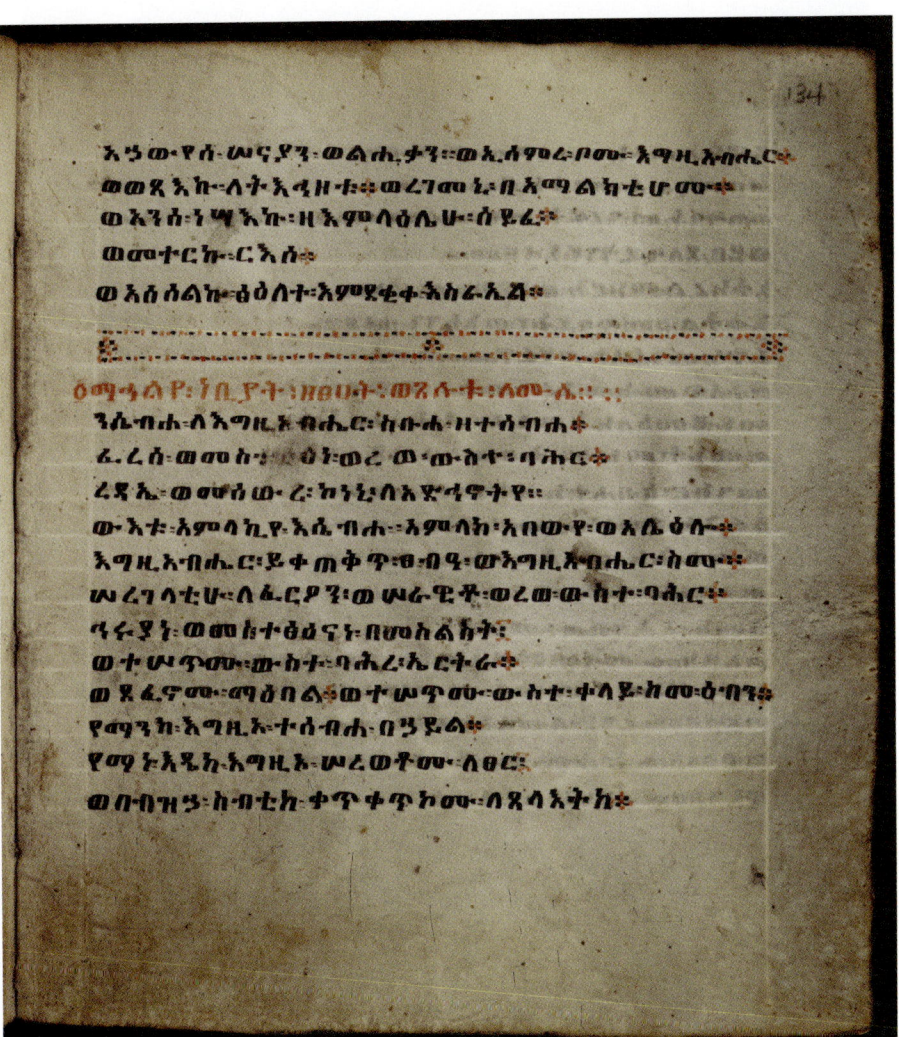

Plate 8: Bodleian MS. Aeth. e. 25, f. 134r.

A Catalogue of Previously Uncatalogued Ethiopic Manuscripts in England

Plate 9: Bodleian MS. Aeth. e. 28, ff. 1v–2r.

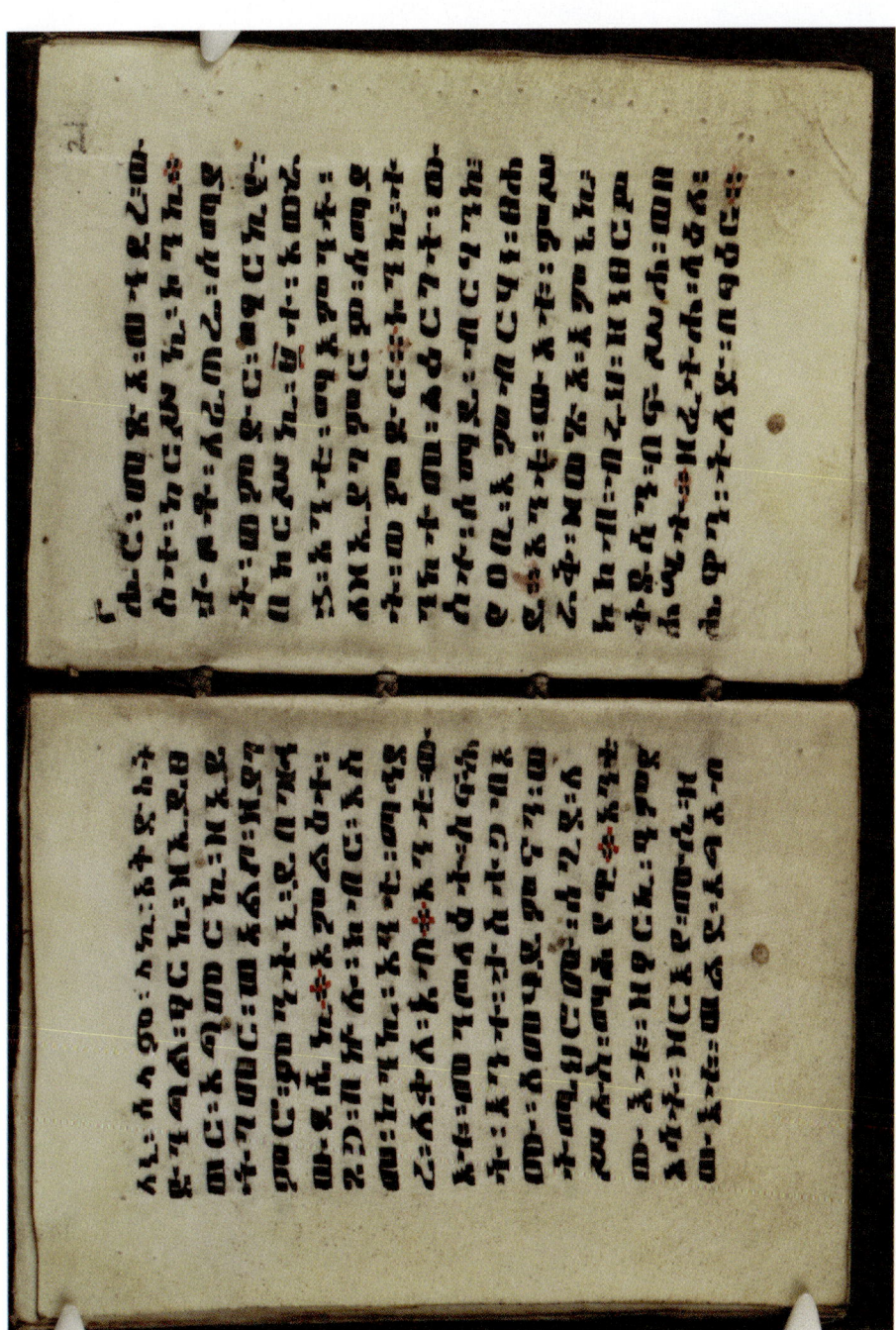

Plate 10: Bodleian MS. Aeth. f. 19, ff. 21v–22r.

A Catalogue of Previously Uncatalogued Ethiopic Manuscripts in England

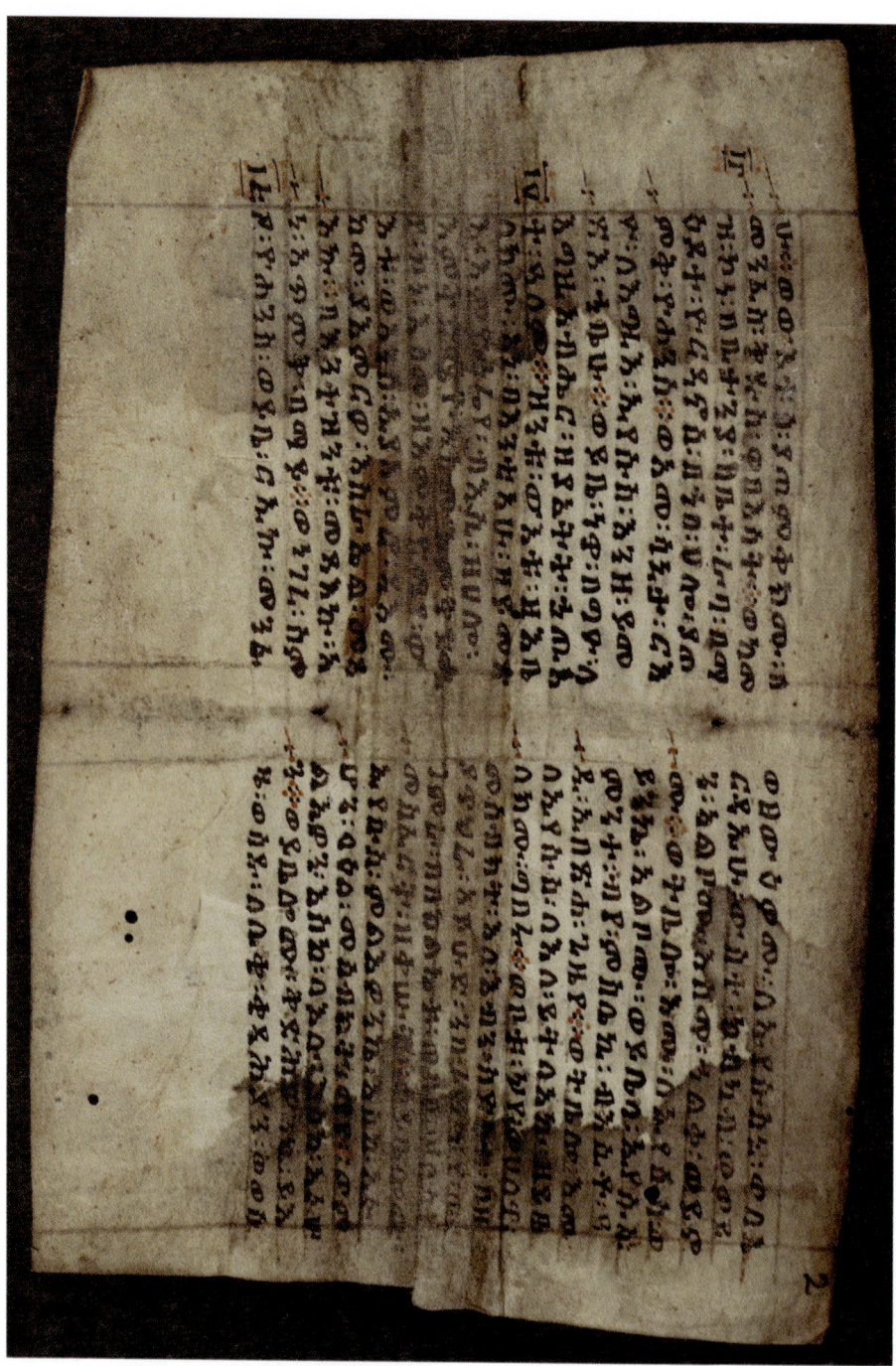

Plate 11: Bodleian MS. Aeth. f. 20, ff. 1v–2r.

Plate 12: Bodleian MS. Aeth. f. 21, f. 113r.

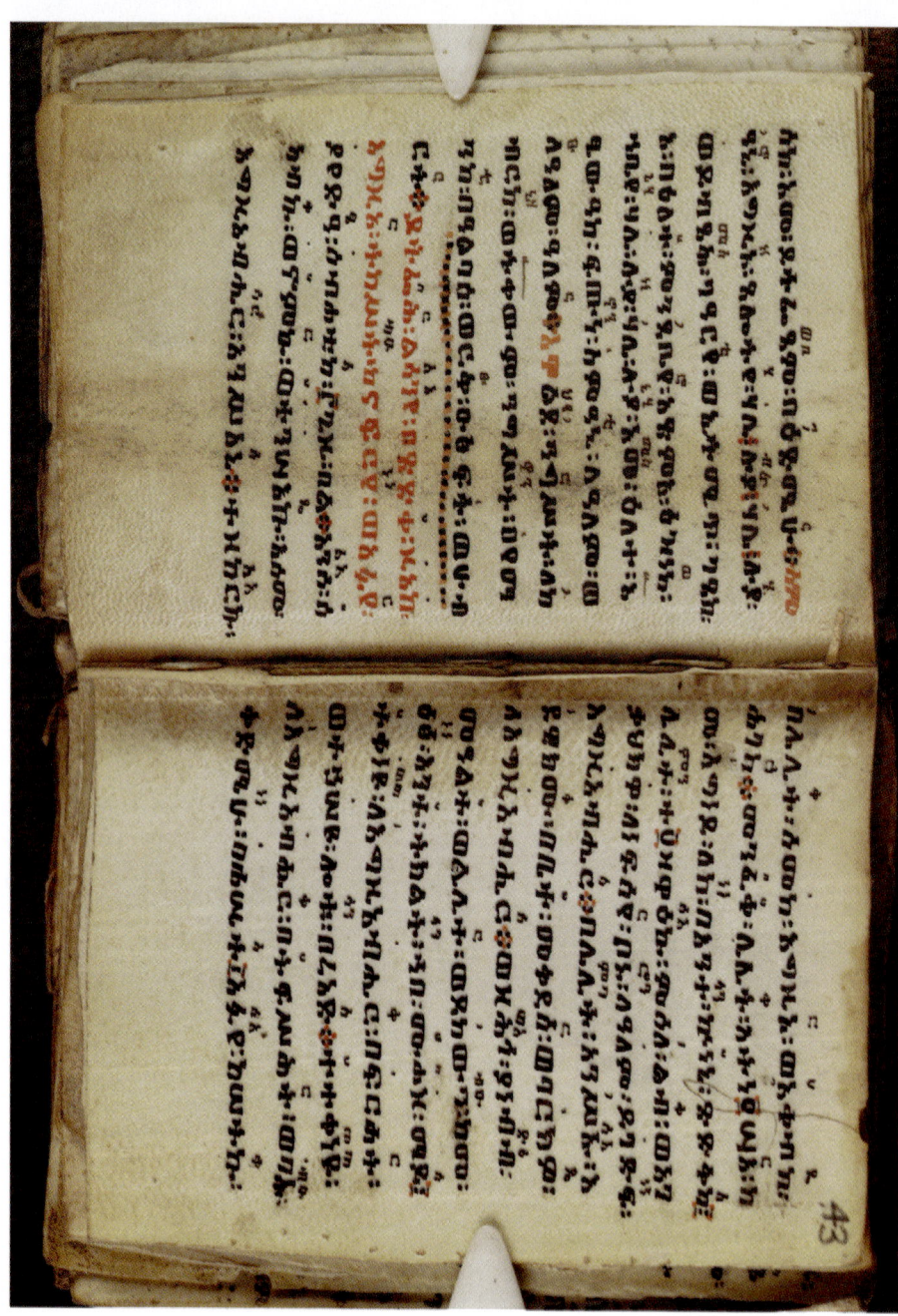

Plate 13: Bodleian MS. Aeth. g. 22, ff. 42v–43r.

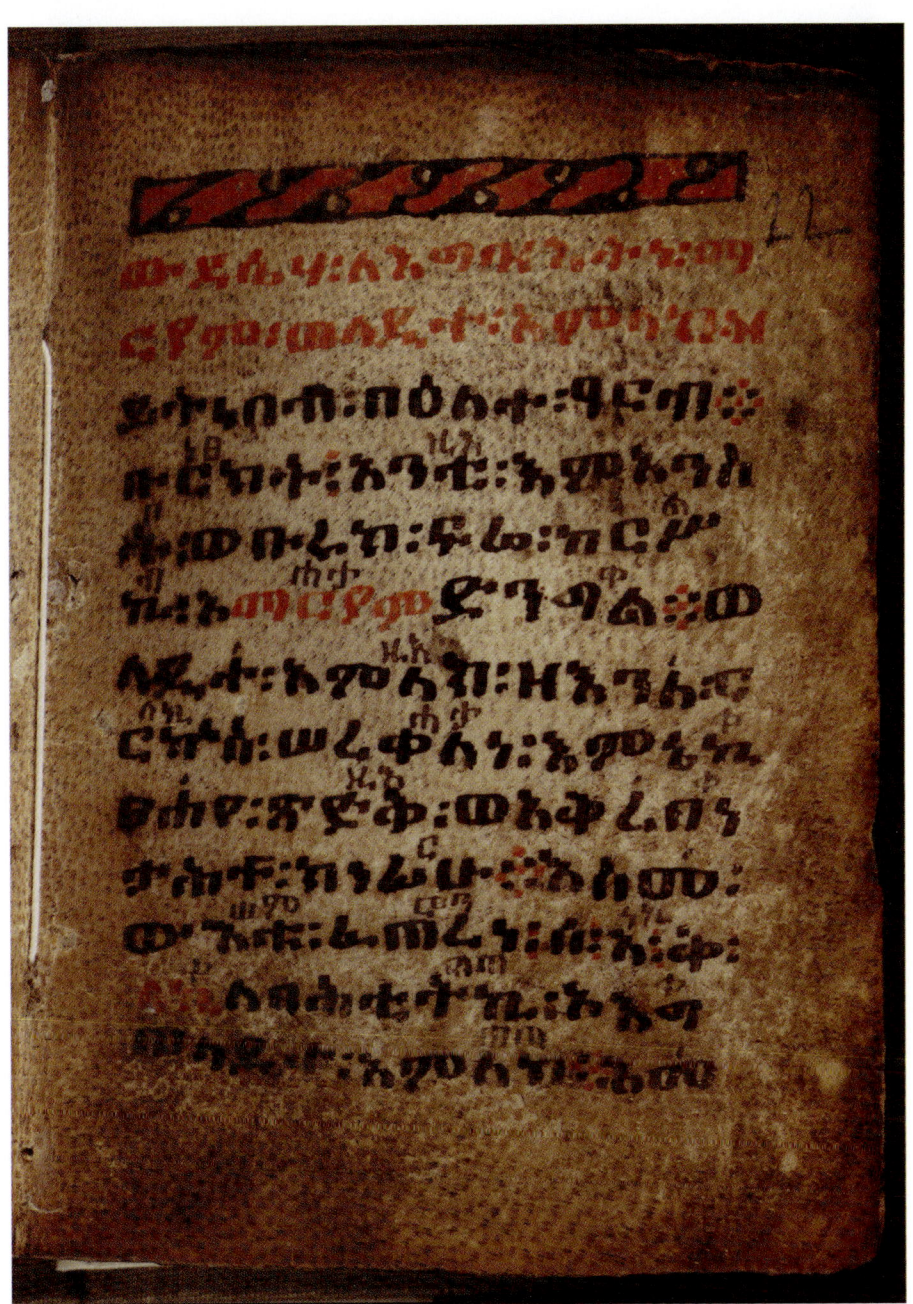

Plate 14: Bodleian MS. Aeth. g. 23, f. 22r.

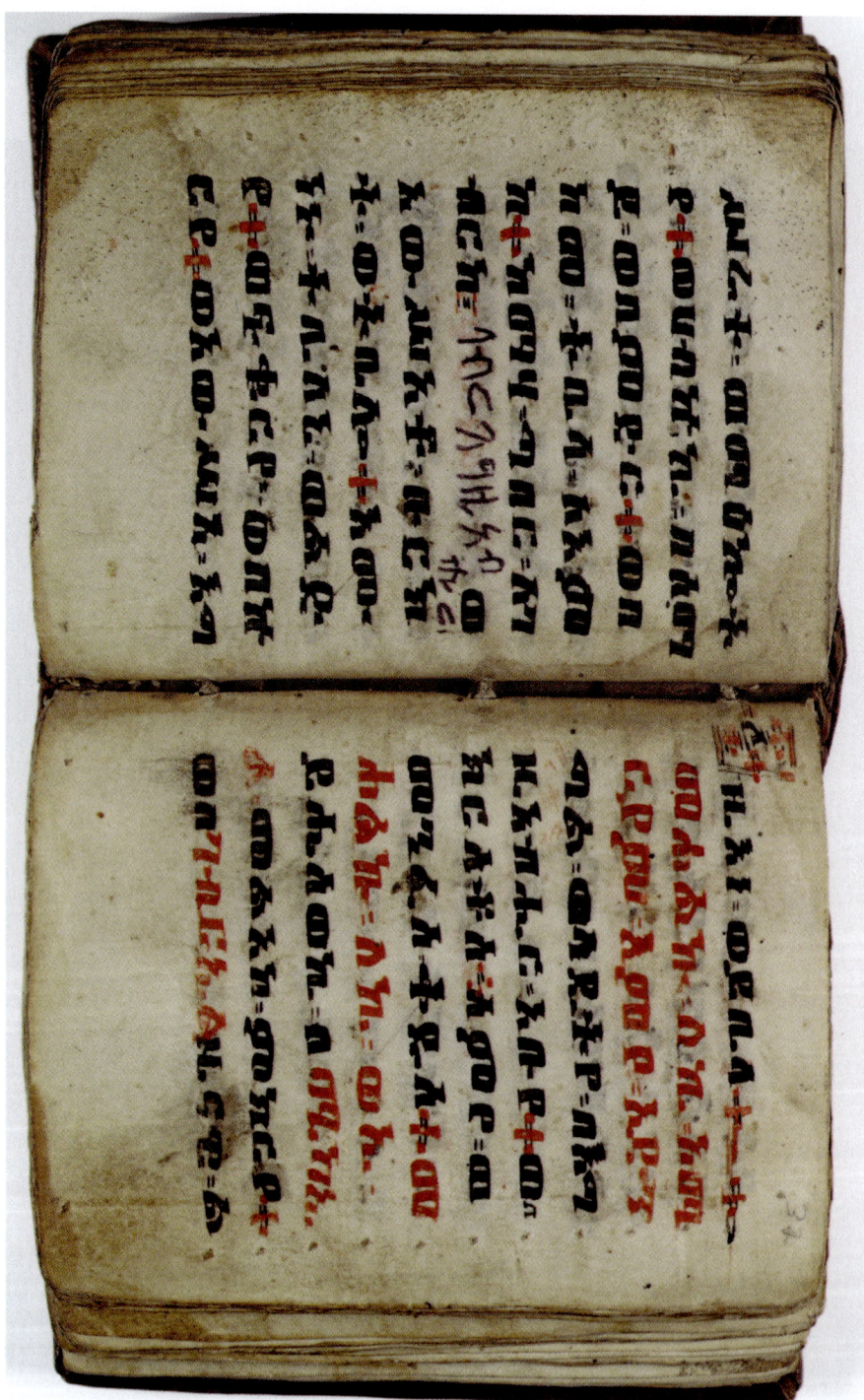

Plate 15: Cambridge University Library, Or. 2547, ff. 36v–37r.

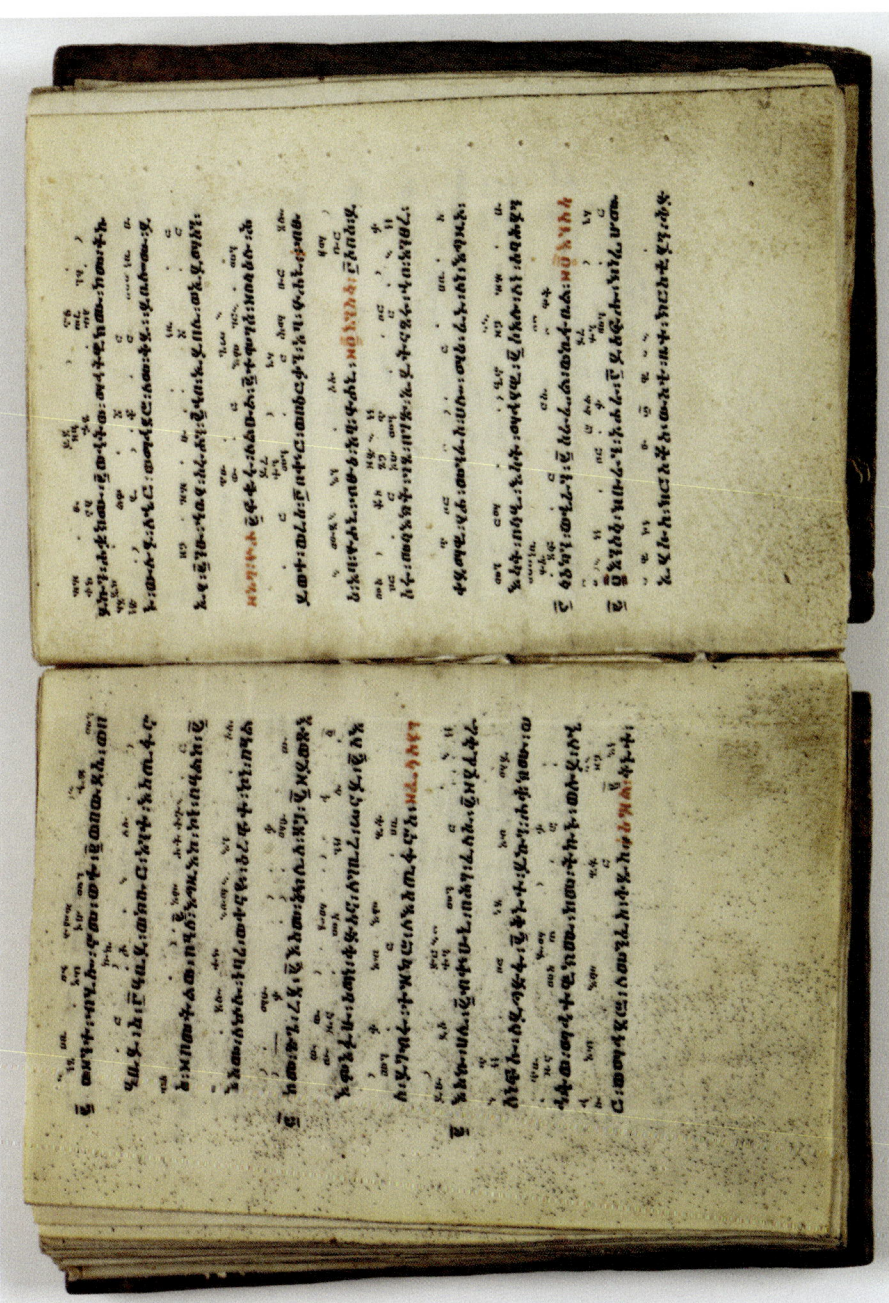

Plate 16: Cambridge University Library, Or. 2548, ff. 36v–37r.

Plate 17: Rylands Ethiopic MS 43, front cover and f. 1r.

Plate 18: Rylands Ethiopic MS 43, ff. 1v–2r.

Plate 19: Rylands Ethiopic MS 43, ff. 32v–33r.

A Catalogue of Previously Uncatalogued Ethiopic Manuscripts in England

Plate 20: Rylands Ethiopic MS 43, in case.

Plate 21: Rylands Ethiopic MS 44, spine.

Plate 22: Rylands Ethiopic MS 44, ff. 7v–8r.

Plate 23: Rylands Ethiopic MS 27 (left) and Rylands Ethiopic MS 45 (right).

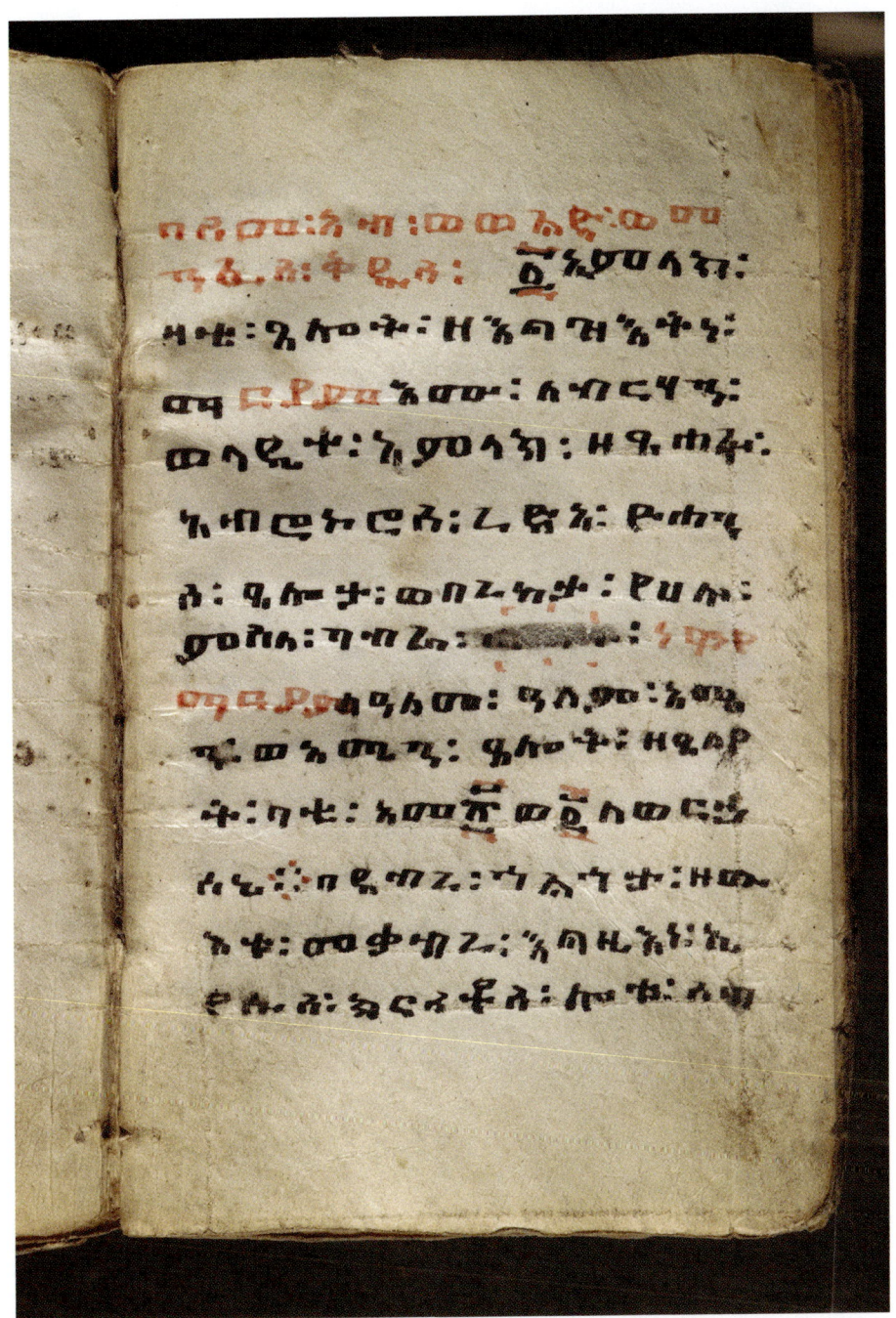

Plate 24: Rylands Ethiopic MS 45, f. 2r.

A Catalogue of Previously Uncatalogued Ethiopic Manuscripts in England

Plate 25: Mac Lennan Codex 1, with case.

Plate 26: Mac Lennan Codex 1, spine.

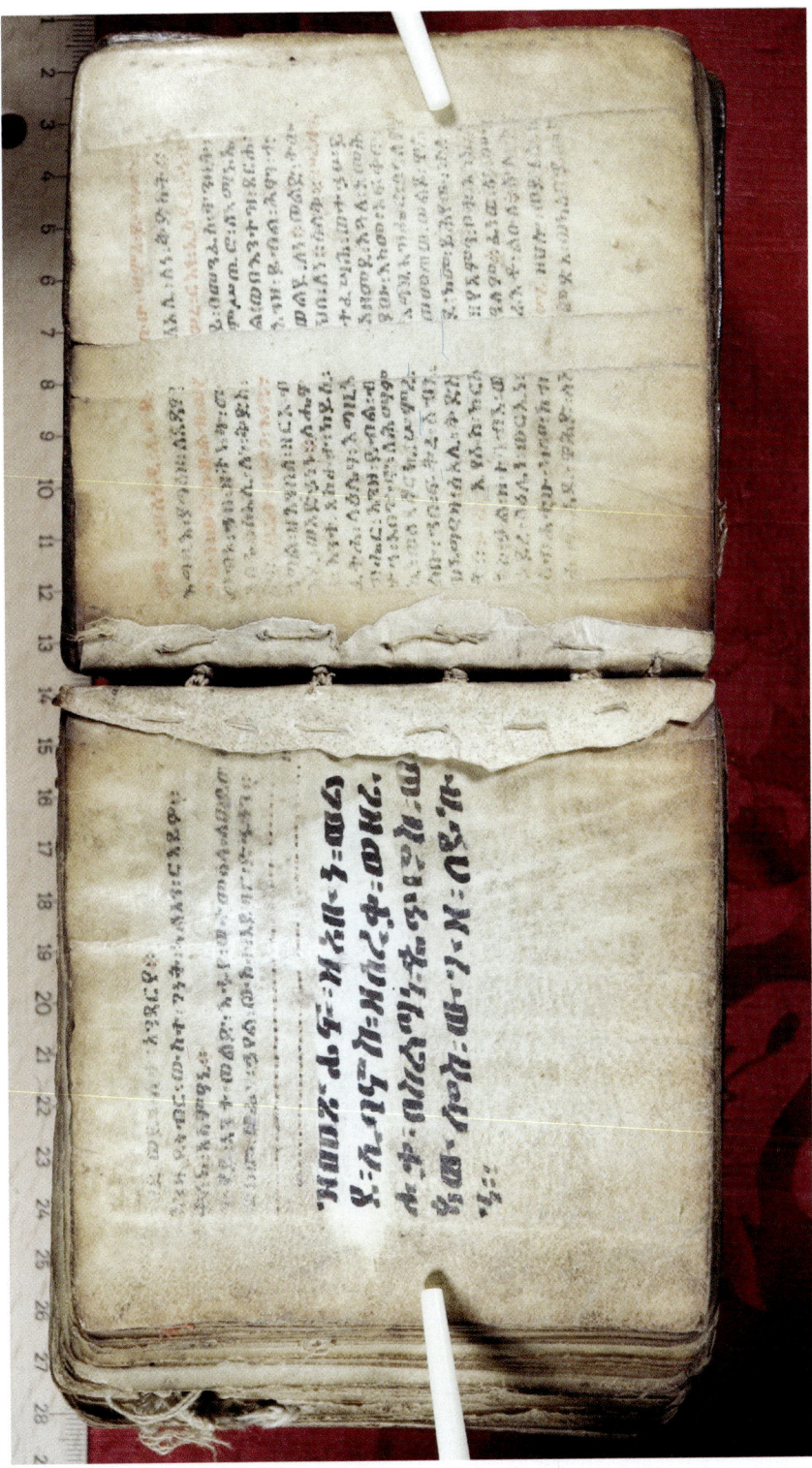

Plate 27: Mac Lennan Codex 1, ff. 152v–153r.

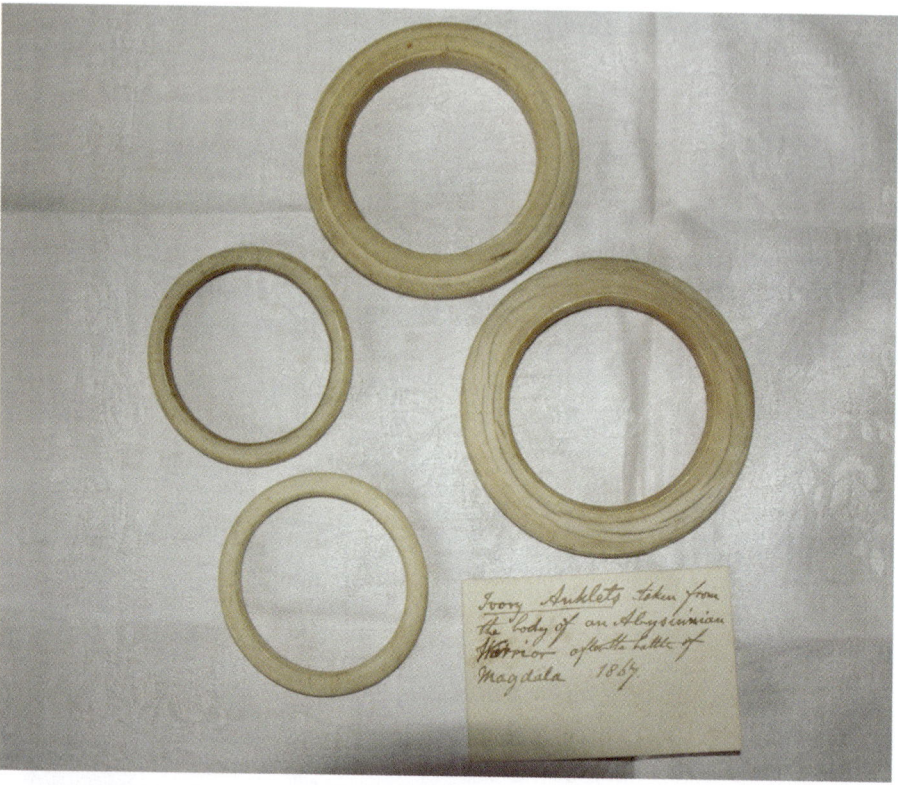

Plate 28: Anklets sharing the same provenance as Mac Lennan Codex 1.

Plate 29: Iron cross sharing the same provenance as Mac Lennan Codex 1.

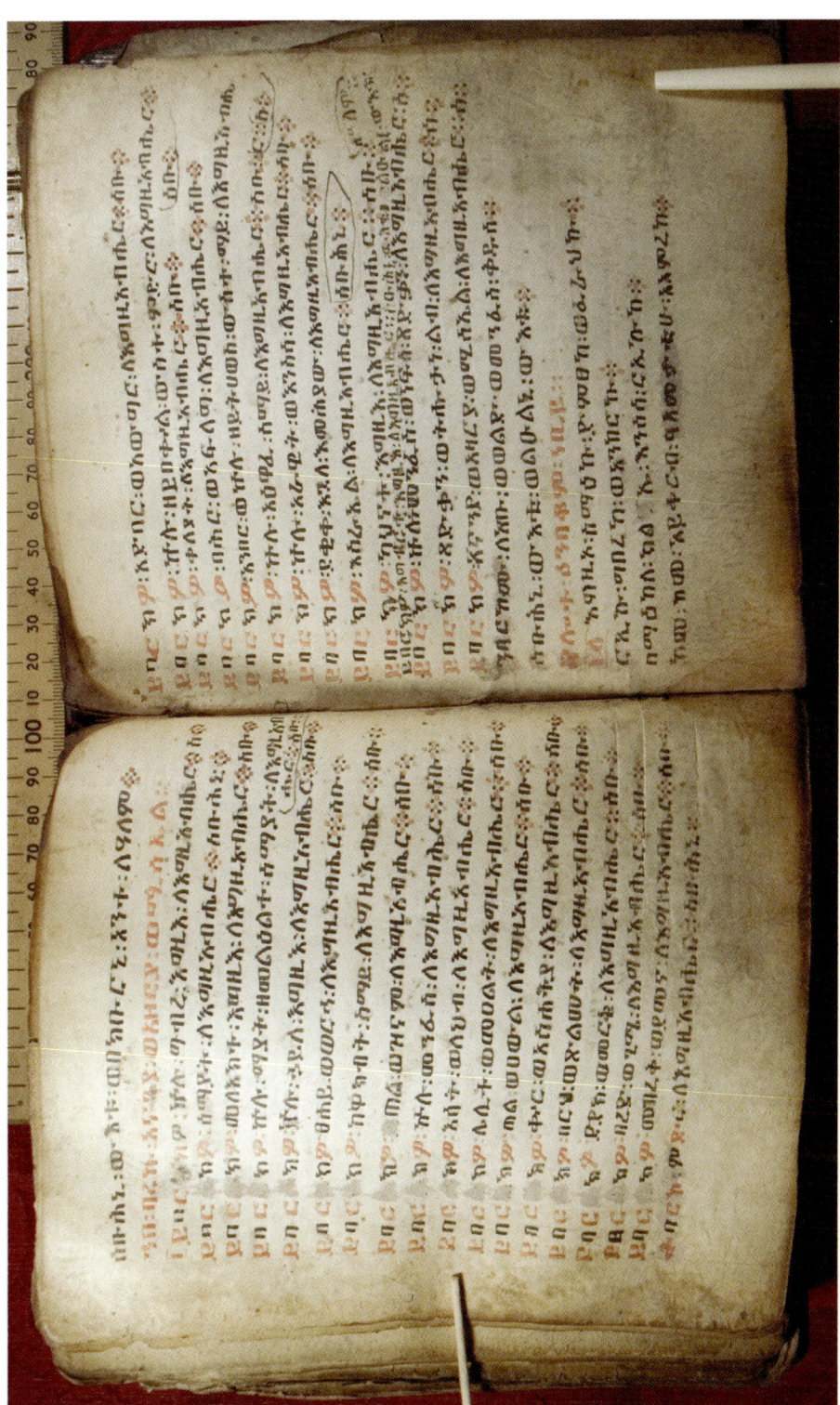

Plate 30: Mac Lennan Codex 2, ff. 137v–138r.

Plate 31: Mac Lennan Codex 3, cover and protection flap.

Plate 32: Mac Lennan Codex 3, ff. 27v–28r.

Plate 33: Mac Lennan Codex 4, cover and amulet case.

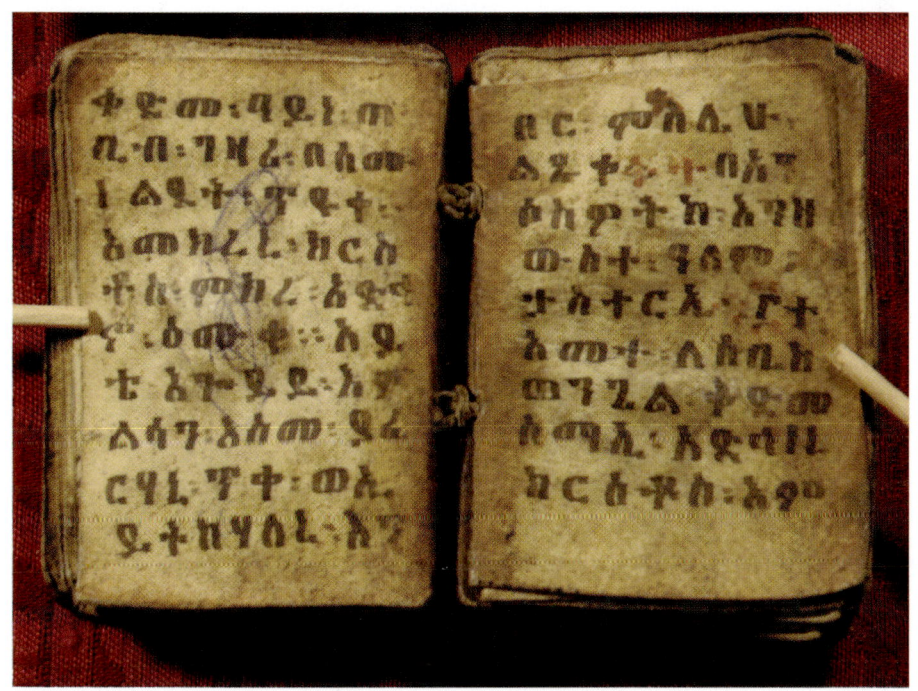

Plate 34: Mac Lennan Codex 4, ff. 8v–9r.